THE PRUDENT PEACE

THE PRUDENT PEACE

Law as Foreign Policy

JOHN A. PERKINS

THE UNIVERSITY OF CHICAGO PRESS
Chicago and London

THE UNIVERSITY OF CHICAGO PRESS, CHICAGO 60637
THE UNIVERSITY OF CHICAGO PRESS, LTD., LONDON

Printed in the United States of America
85 84 83 82 81 5 4 3 2 1

JOHN A. PERKINS is a partner in the law firm of Palmer & Dodge, Boston.

Library of Congress Cataloging in Publication Data

Perkins, John A.
The prudent peace.
Bibliography: p.
Includes index.
1. International law. 2. United States—Foreign relations—1945– I. Title.
JX3160.P43P78 341′.04 81–1200
ISBN 0–226–65873–2 AACR2

CONTENTS

Part Four THE CHOICE

PREFACE

The central perception articulated in this book, that of the role of law as prudent foreign policy, is one which I have been mulling since the closing months of World War II. The events of the intervening years, often viewed differently, have confirmed the perception, filled out its rationale and implications, and added a sense of urgency. This tentative hypothesis of 1945 became for me a matter of conviction and concern.

The idea of writing this book began to take shape a dozen or more years ago. My final commitment to it came with the adoption of a sabbatical policy by my law firm in 1975. Although most of the research and organization was completed before my departure, my six month sabbatical in 1978 provided the indispensable opportunity for writing and research, as a graduate researcher at University College, Oxford, at Harvard's International Legal Studies Library, and at our summer house in Maine.

This book owes much to the contributions others have made in a variety of ways, and I must acknowledge my indebtedness to all of them: to Francis E. Ackerman for his invaluable assistance in research and for helping in our discussions to shape the argument; to Daniel R. Coquillette for his encouragment and for leading me to University College and Oxford; to University College for making me feel a part of that fine community of scholars and opening the resources of Oxford University to me; to my law firm for recognizing through its sabbatical policy the diversity of the interests that make demands on the lives of busy lawyers; to those many friends, associates, and scholars who gave their time to read the manuscript for their encouragement and helpful suggestions; to Sonya Abbott and to my secretary, Anne Keller, for dedication beyond the call of duty in preparing, correcting, and revising the manuscript; and finally to my wife, Lydia, for encouragement, for many hours listening and reacting, and for patient indulgence of the countless evenings, weekends, and vacation days absorbed in my concentration of this task.

John A. Perkins

INTRODUCTION

The Challenge

Faith that law provides the path to peace stands badly shaken in our uneasy world. We have lived through dangerous times since 1945. The crises, the shocks, the frustrations, the continued covert maneuvering for advantage even during the official calm of détente, have all inevitably and rightly taught us to approach international affairs with a realistic intelligence, wary of wishful solutions. But we will have misread the lessons of the postwar era and failed to understand the nature and function of law, if we conclude it is the course of realism to reject law. The case for law rests no less on practical and political logic than on moral grounds, and the cogency of those considerations has become in fact even clearer during the postwar years.

This book argues that law *is* the path of realism. The prevailing attitudes about law have been focused on the wrong questions. The issue we should be considering is not the feasibility of law as a system of enforceable restraints but the necessity of law as a strategy for the resolution of conflict. The issue is not whether international law is or in the forseeable future can be enforceable but whether a foreign policy that is not based on law can be fully effective in serving the national interest. Instead of asking whether we can afford to take a chance on law we should be observing that in the real world we cannot escape it. We can make the most of it or we can reluctantly adjust to its restraints without realizing its constructive potential. It is one or the other.

The questions that need to be asked examine the potential and the prudence of law as policy. It has become imperative to ask these questions, as events increasingly make clear that power and wealth alone do not assure either respect or influence. In a world where it seems to many that to allow foreign policy to be guided by legal principle is becoming a more and more difficult choice, it is not only relevant but urgent to ask: Why in so many areas of the world does the United States seem to be unable, despite its power and wealth, to exert an effective influence even on developments that are vital to its security?

The role of law in foreign policy has been misconceived. Many have visualized that law must come to reality through conversion of the world to a belief in an ideal of law as the basis for peace or by the willingness of nations generally to submit to adjudication the disputes in which peace hangs in the balance. Many believe the path to law lies in the creation of some supranational institution with the authority to impose a rule of law. Such approaches to law miss the force of the case for law as practical and realistic foreign policy. Law that does not make sense in these terms cannot determine the actions of nations on important issues in our time. If the world is to move toward the rule of law, it is because law can provide a sound course of policy, sound for the world in which we live, a policy which can build the future out of the present. That is what this book is all about—law as foreign policy.

The lesson of our difficult times is not to reject law but rather to understand its role in our kind of world and to recognize the nature of the challenge this presents. Most of us in the Western world probably acknowledge at least the theoretical validity of law as the basis for the resolution of conflict. In this sense most of us undoubtedly believe in the rule of law. This apparent agreement hides, however, a fundamental difference of understanding. The rule of law in international relations is often conceived as an alternative to a world in which nations have to reckon with the realities of power. By this view, under a regime of law we can put concerns with the balance of power behind us. For others a balance of power of some kind is the indispensable premise for law. Unchecked power will be abused—in international affairs as in all other human affairs.

Events have instructed us. There were many in 1945 who believed that World War II had set the stage for a new era, one in which power politics could be relegated to history and a regime of law could become a reality. The Iron Curtain and the Cold War quickly shattered these dreams, just as disillusionment had earlier destroyed the high hopes of many after World War I that the world was ready to substitute law for power. The naïveté of the belief that the rule of law can simply replace the concerns of power has been made plain to everyone.

Unfortunately, the notion that we can shape our policy by law on any terms has become an innocent victim of these same events. This is perhaps understandable. The times have not encouraged us to contemplate a central role for law in foreign policy. The role of power has had to be our ever present concern. We have come to think of the strategy of peace in terms of containment, of credibiility and dominoes, of nuclear deterrence and second strike capability, of power blocs and alliances. The calculus of power is all too clearly an essential part of the strategy of peace. But we make a great mistake if we allow these concerns with power to obscure the necessary role of law in our foreign policy.

Yet this is precisely what has happened. A pervasive cynicism reigns. The world has lost confidence that any nation, including the United States, is prepared to respect law in matters it regards as vital. A profound skepticism as to the realistic role of law affects international lawyers and foreign policy leaders no less than the general public.

While the frustration is understandable, we must not let the frustration blind us to the nature of the challenge. As we shall see, the balance of power must realistically be seen, not as an alternative to law, but as a part of the structure of law, supporting law and supported by it. What the experience of the postwar years teaches is that the rule of law that we need and must seek is one that comes to terms with the realities of power and politics. It must realistically recognize the security concerns that are inherent in a world of independent nation states. The challenge to those who guide foreign policy is to chart a course to a just and secure peace under a rule of law that takes account of the realities of power and contention. This is a task for dedicated but practical-minded men and women who understand the perils of the world in which we live as well as the forces and developments that move the world toward law. This book examines the prospects of that kind of law.

The Roots of Apathy

In presenting the argument for law as policy I hope I have fairly addressed what I take to be the underlying assumptions upon which the current apathy regarding law is based. It seems useful at this point to identify these assumptions.

The first of these assumptions is that law is not addressed to the central concerns of foreign policy. International law is seen as at most imposing some kinds of peripheral restraints on foreign policy, whereas the true concerns of foreign policy are the security and vital interests of the nation. The effective result of this assumption must be that international law can govern only issues that do not really matter and the rule of law in matters of vital interest has to be reserved for some ideal world, presumably where nations no longer have to be concerned about power for their own security.

This assumption reflects the misconceptions that the postwar era has encouraged. It is time to rethink the prevailing assumptions about the role of law in foreign policy. I believe this rethinking will reveal that the fundamental errors of the prevailing assumptions are in failing to see that we cannot escape law, that law, realistically conceived, provides the only viable basis for the resolution of conflict and must, in fact, be seen not as a distant goal but as the essential basis now of an effective foreign policy for the United States.

The second assumption standing in the way of our assigning a central role to law in foreign policy is that the law is insufficiently defined on critical issues to provide a prudent basis for acceptance of law. It is widely perceived that nations twist law to their own ends. All wars are begun under a claim of self-defense. All intervention is justified under some claim of right. It is widely assumed that essential questions remain unresolved, whether, for example, self-determination and non-intervention are principles of law or merely policy goals, and if they are principles of law how and when they apply.

These are important concerns and cannot be dismissed lightly. They are, I believe, at the heart of the issue whether the United States can prudently make a full commitment to law. This book examines issues on which the substantive resolution provided by law may be vital. What emerges is that much of the current cynicism about legal developments is misplaced. While the world has seemed to many to be disintegrating into a chaos in which only power counts, it has in fact been making important progress in the evolution of legal rules appropriate for the resolution of conflict in the real world. Treaties and U.N. resolutions present a clearer and sounder basis of emerging law than is yet generally understood. Some provide more cogent and effective principles of foreign policy than those we tend to adopt in the name of realism. Even many international lawyers seem not to have absorbed the impact of the developments that have already occurred. The delegates at the United Nations working on the firing line have, as is probably often the case, been ahead of the writers and the theorists. Prudence will dictate stipulations on some doubtful points, but the scope and thrust of legal developments present no bar to a foreign policy commitment to law.

The third assumption paralyzing action toward a commitment to law is that, since most nations are not yet ready to bind themselves to law, there is nothing we can prudently and usefully do alone. The assumption that most nations are not ready to bind themselves to law should be taken as true for purposes of formulating any proposal, for any proposed commitment to be bound by law which has to be joined in by most nations to be made at all would be too fanciful to merit further consideration. But the further assumption that nothing is to be accomplished by a commitment of our foreign policy to the resolution of conflict by law reflects again the assumption that law is not itself a prudent foreign policy. If, as this book will argue, it provides a more cogent and effective foreign policy for the United States than any other, it misses the point to object that most nations are not ready to be bound by law.

When we once understand our stake in law, how law does provide a prudent foreign policy, we can see there is something to be accomplished by an explicit commitment of our policy to law, even if we proceed alone or with one or more like-minded nations. We have to rethink the role of adjudication in this perspective. The relevant question is not whether nations generally are ready to accept adjudication of disputes but whether we can prudently strengthen our own policy by declaring terms on which the United States will be willing to adjudicate disputes that cannot be settled by negotiation.

In short, the answer to the assumption that there is nothing the United States can do alone is the examination this book attempts of the potential and the prudence of law *as* policy.

Ideals and Policy

If we approach the role and the prospects of law purely on a scale of risks and benefits for the United States, we leave an important element out of the equation. One cannot take a true measure of affairs that involve the human spirit by ignoring the ideals that move us as human beings. No realistic appraisal of the prospects of law in international affairs can ignore man's moral commitment to the concept of law.

Some things we do as much because they are right as for any calculation of benefit. I think it is fair to say that this book would not be written, however much law might add to the foreign policy of the

United States from a risk/benefit analysis, without the conviction that law is right, right for us and right for mankind.

This is the source of thc power of the idea of law. The only true calculus of the pros and cons of law is a calculus that takes account of the moral power of law.

Think-tank analysis of international relations is a necessary and useful process. But nations move to the power of ideas. Foreign policy in the end has to be something a people believes in.

It is, indeed, a part of the disillusionment and frustration of our perception of international relations that we want to believe in something better. Near the end of our involvement in the Vietnam war President Kingman Brewster of Yale accurately, I think, assessed the unfulfilled spirit of America. "In addition to a renewal of a belief in what we are and might be for ourselves as a society, we—like the Athenians—also badly need to feel that we have a role in the world which is not just meanly self-serving. We yearn for some belief that our nation has a significance for mankind generally which can be measured by some scale larger than our own survival and well-being."[1] One cannot realistically consider the role and the prospects for law without such a sense of our national purpose and commitment.

This book is written to demonstrate that we can move aggressively now to implement our belief in law, that it is the best foreign policy for the United States, that it is a policy which realistic, practical-minded, responsible men and women can and must support. Part one examines how the conflict solving strategy of law is already interwoven in U.S. foreign policy and argues that an effective foreign policy for the United States has to be grounded in law. Part two tests the idea that emerging law may provide rules suitable for a realistic foreign policy and evaluates the viability of the key principles of the emerging law. Part three considers what prudent initiative toward law might be taken by the United States, unilaterally if need be, and sets forth a proposal to provide direction and momentum for the forces that can move the world toward law. Part four attempts to define the kind of choice the United States now has to face.

Part One

THE ROLE OF LAW IN FOREIGN POLICY

One

THE RELEVANCE OF LAW

Our habits of thinking about law are largely conditioned by our relationship to the internal laws of the nation. We see these as rules imposed by authority that forbid us to do certain things or require us to do certain things. Most of us do not have occasion to stop to think why these restraints and requirements take the form of laws of general application.

Most of us tend to think of international law in a similar way, although there is no comparable legislative authority enacting international law. The impact of international law is seen as imposing certain restraints to be observed in the conduct of foreign policy. We do not ordinarily think of international law as itself a foreign policy, and rarely if ever as the central core of foreign policy.

We see the rule of law as a goal and look toward some future time when the system of restraints by international law can be sufficiently developed to make the rule of law a reality. Our habits of thought condition us to see law only as a reliable system of restraints. This seems to leave relatively little place for law in foreign affairs of nations in the world as it is. For most Americans foreign policy in our time and for a long time to come has to be concerned with the national interest and national security, and law has very little to do with it.

These attitudes and assumptions miss the point of law. We cannot begin to assign a realistic role to law until we understand the relevance of law to the foreign policy enterprise.

The wonder is that law is not the first principle of foreign policy, for law is the only successful strategy man has ever evolved for the resolution of conflict. This is its chief relevance to foreign policy. The essential idea of law is not the application of force by legal authority but the concept that conflicts are resolved by rules that apply equally to all persons. The genius of law is that everyone is subject to the same rules. The application of rules of law is governed only by their terms. It is this same concept of law that makes international law relevant to the central concerns of foreign policy.

Three essential keys to law as a strategy for resolution of conflict apply to international relations in much the same way they apply to law governing individuals and groups within a nation. These three keys are:

1. That the rules of law apply equally to all according to their terms;

2. That the rules respond to and implement the felt necessities of the time;

3. That conflicts to be resolved under law can in the last resort be resolved by third party determination.

Equality of right is the essence of all law. We cannot expect others willingly to accept restraints we are not willing to accept for ourselves. Equality of right means reciprocity of application.

It is sometimes thought that the diversity of legal systems and cultural traditions may stand in the way of acceptance of international law. There is no doubt that in terms of legal theory and substantive principles legal systems differ widely. And they implement very different approaches to political organization and social and economic policy. But they all employ the first key to the strategy of law. The principle that rules must apply equally to all according to their terms is recognized in all cultures and all legal systems.[1]

It is inherent in the principle of equality that if law is to serve as a basis for resolving conflict the rules must apply to all nations, the powerful and the weak, and to all cases, not just to the ones that do not really matter. If the United States claims the right in Chile to act in disregard of the rules of law, this invites the U.S.S.R. to do likewise where it will. At the time of the Cuban missile crisis Ambassador Thompson shrewdly observed in reference to a possible Russian response in Turkey, "The Russians like parallel situations."[2] So indeed do all nations. It is the basis on which nations can justify restraint. A settlement imposed against the principle of equal application of law to all is one that festers. It sows the seeds of its own undoing.

The sense of the equality of nations that requires that rules must apply equally to all is no mere verbal analogy from the application of laws to individuals. Nations are not individuals, but they are made up of individuals. And the insight that less than equality for a nation means less than equality for the individuals who compose it is bound to be the common sense perception of all peoples.

The second key to the strategy of law is that it be responsive to what Oliver Wendell Holmes called the "felt necessities of the time." Law is not imposed from outside the real world. It is shaped by it. It is defined in the process of reconciling claims for recognition of competing interests. It must be capable of changing and growing as the world changes and as perceptions and priorities change. Law performs its function of reconciliation not merely by rules that apply reciprocally, as all law must, but by rules that are perceived in their time as fair, that adjust as necessary to respond to change,

Holmes's famous summation applies equally to international law:

> The life of the law has not been logic, it has been experience. The felt necessities of the time, the prevalent moral and political theories, intuitions of public policy, avowed or unconscious, even the prejudices which judges share with their fellowmen, have had a good deal more to do than the syllogism in determining the rules by which men should be governed. The law embodies the story of a nation's development through many centuries, and it cannot be dealt with as if it contained only the axioms and corollaries of a book of mathematics.[3]

Only law that responds to the felt necessities of the time can provide a feasible strategy for peace.

The lack of an adequate process for change has been one of the problems that has impaired the usefulness of international law. Law that simply freezes the status quo cannot succceed and should not. Whether by legislative action, when a legislative competence exists, or by a common law process of evolution, the law must be able to change and to grow.

Law that cannot change and grow will not continue to command respect. A perception that law is tied to the status quo frustrates willingness to submit disputes to legal settlement. It encourages resort to force in self-help in preference to resort to legal process.

The third key to the strategy of law is that in the last resort there is some means to resolve an issue by third party determination. With respect to the internal law we usually think of this third party action in the process of adjudication by independent judges. We recognize that in this process a man may not be the judge in his own case. A purely subjective application of the law could destroy the confidence that the law genuinely applies equally to all.

If we think about it, we can see that vesting the power to change law in a broadly representative legislature elected by all the people also serves the same function. It, of course, implements the right of the majority to rule within constiutional limitations. But it also provides some assurance that no one and no one group can destroy the impartiality of law by making it merely an instrument of that group's own interests.

Assurance that in the last resort law is formulated and applied by some process of third party determination is an essential element of international law just as it is of national law. A world of independent nation states presents some special problems for law, which this book attempts to address, but it does not change the fundamental considerations that define the strategy of law for the resolution of conflict. International law surely cannot be respected if each nation is free to insist on its own version of controverted facts and to formulate and interpret the law by its own lights to serve its own ends.

Whatever else it may be, law is a strategy for the resolution of conflict. This is the function that shapes the key components of law. These are the components that give law the moral power to command assent. It is this strategy and this power that gives international law its critical role *as* foreign policy.[4]

The relevance of law to foreign policy is nothing less than that its approach provides the strategy by which a just and stable peace must be sought. But one must still ask whether the strategy of law is compatible in our time with that hard-nosed calculation of risks and benefits by which leaders responsible for the conduct of foreign policy must weigh the nation's course. To answer that question it is necessary to examine the diplomatic pressures and political logic of foreign affairs that in actual experience are already defining the role of law in our foreign policy.

Two

THE TOUCHSTONES OF U.S. FOREIGN POLICY

Despite the cogency of law as a strategy for the resolution of conflict, we do not think of law as itself a foreign policy. The historic principles of American foreign policy were not conceived or formulated as law. But they have not stood still. And what is not fully understood is the degree to which our foreign policy as it has evolved presupposes some concept of a world order based on law. The truth is, indeed, that our policy is shaped on significant issues by our concept of the rules of that legal order.

Our policy has evolved in this way, not because someone conceived it this way but because when we act we find it necessary to present our actions on a basis that can stand up to challenge by others and by ourselves. This can be seen in the evolution of the Monroe Doctrine and in the evolution of policies based on resisting aggression.

From Monroe Doctrine to Law

President Monroe did not enunciate his doctrine in terms of law. Rather, he declared simply that the American continents "are henceforth not to be considered as subjects for future colonization by any European powers," that the United States would consider any attempt to extend the European systems to any portion of this hemisphere as "dangerous to our peace and safety" and any attempt by a European power to oppress or control the new republics in South America as "the manifestations of an unfriendly disposition toward the United States."[1] Although justified at least in part on the basis of considerations believed to be matters of principle, the doctrine was not asserted by President Monroe or for some seventy years by his successors as a matter of right under law.

What might be termed the legalization of the Monroe Doctrine began with Secretary Olney's famous instructions of July 20, 1895 to U.S. Ambassador Bayard in London for transmission to Lord Salisbury on the subject of Great Britain's refusal to arbitrate with Venezuela in full the boundary dispute between Venezuela and British Guiana.[2] Secretary Olney, noting first a right of interposition in certain circumstances under international law, invoked the Monroe Doctrine as a form of this general rule.[3] After giving background and reasons for the doctrine, he defined its limitations:

> It does not establish any general protectorate by the United States over other American states. It does not relieve any American state from its obligations as fixed by international law nor prevent any European power directly interested from enforcing such obligations or from inflicting merited punishment for the breach of them. It does not contemplate any interference in the internal affairs of any American state or in the relations between it and other American states. It does not justify any attempt on our part to change the established form of government of any American state or to prevent the people of such state from altering that form according to their own will and pleasure. The rule in question has but a single purpose and object. It is that no European power or combination of European powers shall forcibly deprive an American state of the right and power of self-government and of shaping for itself its own political fortunes and destinies.
>
> That the rule thus defined has been the accepted public law of this country since its promulgation can not fairly be denied.[4]

The secretary, after a review of the history and reasons of the doctrine, affirmed that "the safety and welfare of the United States are so concerned with the maintenance of the independence of every American state as against any European power as to justify and require the interposition of the United States whenever that independence is endangered."[5]

Lord Salisbury took exception to the assertion of the Monroe Doctrine as one under international law, asserting that "international law is founded on the general consent of nations; and no statesman, however eminent, and no nation, however powerful, are competent to insert into the code of international law a novel principle which was never recognized before, and which has not since been accepted by the Government of any other country. The United States have a right, like any other nation, to interpose in any controversy by which their own interests are affected; and they are the judge whether those interests are touched, and in what measure they should be sustained. But their rights are in no way strengthened or extended by the fact that the controversy affects some territory which is called American."[6] President Cleveland in his special message to the Congress on December 17, 1895, responding to this objection, again asserted the doctrine in terms of legal rights:

> Practically the principle for which we contend has peculiar if not exclusive relations to the United States. It may not have been admitted in so many words to the code of international law, but since in international councils every nation is entitled to rights belonging to it, if the enforcement of the Monroe doctrine is something we may justly claim it has its place in the code of international law as certainly and as securely as if it were specifically mentioned, and where the United States is a suitor before the high tribunal that administers international law the question to be determined is whether or not we present claims which the justice of that code of law can find to be right and valid.
>
> The Monroe doctrine finds its recognition in those principles of international law which are based upon the theory that every nation shall have its just claims enforced.
>
> Of course this Government is entirely confident that under the sanction of this doctrine we have clear rights and undoubted claims.[7]

We should not, I think, read Secretary Olney or President Cleveland as asserting that the Monroe Doctrine itself is a principle of international law but that, in the terms in which Secretary Olney defined it, the right of the United States to proclaim it and maintain it is a right existing under international law.

This grounding of the right of the United States was carefully stated by Elihu Root, who had formerly served as secretary of state, in an address before the American Society of International Law in 1914. "The doctrine is not international law," he said, "but it rests upon the right of self-protection and that right is recognized by international law. The right is a necessary corollary of independent sovereignty."[8]

There are, of course, implications for the limitations of the Monroe Doctrine in grounding it on a right under international law. However, more direct pressures from Central and South America caused the United States to attempt to define the doctrine in a manner to disclaim any right to trespass on the rights of other nations of the Americas. No doubt these pressures, increasing during the first decades of this century, stemmed at least in part from the interventionist actions the United States took in the area. President Theodore Roosevelt included assurances against "aggression" by the United States under conver of the Monroe Doctrine in his annual messages to the Congress in 1901, 1902, and 1905.[9] In his special message of February 15, 1905 submitting the proposed protocol for United States administration of Santo Domingo finances (the Roosevelt Corollary), President Roosevelt took pains to state that the United States will not treat the Monroe Doctrine as an excuse for "territorial aggrandizement."[10] Responding again to these pressures, the president in his annual message of 1906 denied that the Monroe Doctrine implied or carried any right "to exercise some kind of protectorate over the countries to whose territory that doctrine applies" and specifically approved the secretary of state's statement that "we neither claim nor desire any rights or privileges or powers that we do not freely concede to every American republic."[11]

Many similar assurances were given in subsequent administrations. In an address on August 30, 1923 Secretary of State Charles Evans Hughes declared:

> I utterly disclaim, as unwarranted, the observations which occasionally have been made implying a claim on our part to superintend the affairs of our sister republics, to assert an overlordship, to consider the spread of our authority beyond our own domain as the aim of our policy, and to make our power the test of right in this hemisphere. I oppose all such misconceived and unsound assertions or intimations. They do not express our national purpose; they belie our sincere friendship; they are false to the fundamental principles of our institutions and of our foreign policy which has sought to reflect with rare exceptions, the ideals of liberty; they menace us by stimu-

> lating a distrust which has no real foundation. They find no sanction whatever in the Monroe Doctrine.[12]

The assurances did not stay the concern, and Secretary Hughes himself lent the color of right to interventions as friendly assistance to promote stability in certain situations.[13]

Faced by mounting pressure in 1930 the United States repudiated the Roosevelt corollary.[14] In an address on February 7, 1931, Secretary Stimson, giving further assurance that the Monroe Doctrine involved no "assurance of suzerainty over our sister Republics," declared that in the Monroe Doctrine "our policy has coincided with the basic conception of international law, namely the equal rights of each nation in the family of nations. The law firstly regards this conception as the chief protection of weak nations against oppression. Our people led in the protection of the independence of those countries with an instinctive readiness which was based upon their sympathy with the doctrine upon which that independence rested."[15] In 1933 President Franklin D. Roosevelt completed the process of disclaimer by declaring that "the definite policy of the United States from now on is one opposed to armed intervention."[16]

Such unilateral disclaimers by the United States, even wrapped in the mantle of international law, did not satisfy the concern of other American states. The concept of converting the Monroe Doctrine into a generalized commitment had been foreseen by President Wilson in 1916 as an agreement among American states "guaranteeing to each other absolutely political independence and territorial integrity."[17] His concept of the mutual commitment contained in the Covenant of the League of Nations was as an adoption of "the doctrine of President Monroe as the doctrine of the world: that no nation should seek to extend its polity over any other nation or people, but that every people should be left free to determine its own polity, its own way of development, unhindered, unthreatened, unafraid, the little along with the great and powerful."[18] And it was on this premise that he won a specific approval of the Monroe Doctrine in Article 21 of the Covenant of the League in a category of "regional understandings . . . for securing the maintenance of peace."[19] In 1933 President Franklin D. Roosevelt again pursued the concept of a generalized commitment asserting that when the failure of orderly processes of government in one American state affects the others, "it becomes the joint concern of a whole continent in which we are all neighbors."[20]

However, the new Roosevelt administration, despite its clear declaration against intervention, does not seem to have been quite prepared to incorporate the principle in treaty form. Nevertheless, pressured by other American states it did so, consenting, with a reservation, to the inclusion as Article 8 in the Convention on the Rights and Duties of States signed at Montevideo on December 26, 1933, the unequivocal statement "No state has the right to intervene in the internal or external affairs of another."[21] The reservation to Articles 1 through 11 by the U.S. delegation protested the innocence of the United States "especially since March 4," cited the Roosevelt administration's opposition to interference with the "internal affairs" of other nations, and regretted the lack of time for uniform interpretation and definitions. It assured that the United States would follow the doctrines and policies pursued since March 4 and embodied in its public address "and in the law of nations as generally recognized and accepted." The Senate ratified, and the principle of nonintervention became a matter of multilateral treaty commitment.

The principle of nonintervention in terms derived from the Montevideo convention has been included in the subsequent conventions by which the inter-American system has evolved.[22] The same principle has been further generalized for application to all nations in Resolution 2625 adopted in 1970 by the United Nations General Assembly.

What we have seen is that a policy originally asserted without reference to law has evolved out of political necessity to a policy defined by principles having the character of law, that is, in the nature of a generalized rule applicable equally to all according to its terms.

The Monroe Doctrine by a similar process has evolved from a unilateral policy to one that is to be applied, ordinarily at least, by the collective action of the nations of the Americas. This evolution is a response to the political force of the concept of the equality of nations.

Both Root and Hughes maintained that other American states had an equal right in their own self-protection to proclaim their own Monroe Doctrines.[23] In the face of the concerns and resentments of other American states it was necessary to reconcile our policy to fundamental ideas of equality. Root and Hughes attempted to argue on the same premise that our policy cannot be transmuted into a joint or common declaration by the American states.[24] Yet this is, of course, exactly what has happened, subject to whatever residue of unilateral right may still remain.[25] The process began with the obligation to consult under the Convention for the Maintenance, Preservation and Re-establishment of Peace, signed at Buenos Aires on December 23, 1936.[26] This was followed by a declaration of common concern and solidarity in the Declaration of Lima, adopted December 24, 1938,[27] the declaration of a zone of security by collective action in the Declaration of Panama in 1939,[28] collective action in 1940 against transfer of territory to a non-American state in the Convention and Act of Habana with a declaration that "any attempt on the part of a non-American state against the integrity or inviolability of the territory, the sovereignty or the political independence of an American State shall be considered as an act of aggression against the States which sign this declaration."[29] At Chapultepec in 1945 the Latin American states called for a treaty to provide for collective measures against aggression. By the Rio Treaty of 1947[30] and the Charter of the Organization of American States in 1948, this further step in the legalization of the Monroe Doctrine was completed, vesting the decision-making function in an international organization of defined powers and defined purposes.

The Cuban missile crisis in 1962 provided a moment of truth for the legal framework into which political forces have caused us to recast the Monroe Doctrine. In an earlier day faced with the ultimate threat from a non-American power incapable of carrying it out in this hemisphere if we interposed our own force, our reaction would have been direct and unilateral. The force of the considerations which have shaped the new legal framework is attested by our cautious attention to the principles of that framework.

President Kennedy's address to the nation on October 22, 1962 made passing reference to the fact that the missile buildup occurred "in an area well known to have a special and historical relationship to the United States and the Nations of the Western Hemisphere." He referred to "the traditions of this nation and Hemisphere" and to "American and Hemisphere policy." He never referred to the Monroe Doctrine by name nor to a policy or right of the United States asserted outside of a context of regional policy. He announced unilaterally that a quarantine "is being initiated," but also that action by the Organization of American States was being sought, as well as action by the U.N. Security Council.[31] It is indicative of the importance attached to taking action under the authority of the O.A.S. that the president held off signing the actual proclamation of quarantine until the O.A.S. had acted.[32]

The missile crisis revealed also the extent to which the changing world had made it essential to be able to justify the right we claim to exercise in terms that we can equally acknowledge for others. No doubt some element of this consideration had accounted for Secretary Olney's invocation of international law in attempting to call Great Britain to account in 1895. In 1962 the imperatives of this consideration had become much greater. In a preliminary legal memorandum to the attorney general our right to act to preclude missile bases in Cuba was tested in relation to the potential claim of the U.S.S.R. to take a similar position against U.S. missiles in Hungary, Poland, or Finland.[33] But it was the actual presence of U.S. Jupiter missiles in Turkey which was drawn into the internal discussions of the U.S. strategy planners, into the public discussion by Walter Lippmann and others and into the negotiations in Krushchev's letter to Kennnedy on October 27, 1962.[34] The force of the argument of parallel between the cases was obvious and gave great concern to the president, who had ordered our missiles out of Turkey months before.[35] While keeping the question of our missiles in Turkey out of any of the public arrangements, the issue was regarded as serious enough for Robert Kennedy to advise Soviet Ambassador Dobrynin in a private conversation that the president "had ordered their removal some time ago, and it was our judgment that, within a short time, after the crisis was over, those missiles would be gone."[36] Abram Chayes, who had been legal advisor to the State Department at the time, thought it a reasonable assessment to regard the assurance given as a "deal."[37]

There is still a further way in which the Cuban missile crisis events confirm the political logic of the evolution toward law. In the letter on the basis of which the crisis was resolved, President Kennedy, picking up on Krushchev's hint that he might be prepared to remove the Soviet missiles in exchange for a pledge by the United States not to invade Cuba, included a specific commitment on that point in the proposed settlement.[38] This seemed an assurance that cost us nothing. The relevance of it, however, should not be minimized. One can speculate whether there would ever have been a Cuban missile crisis if there had not been a Bay of Pigs. Perhaps the Soviet missiles, although at a high cost in Soviet prestige, accomplished their purpose. In any event, the legal rule of nonintervention, which the United States had clearly violated in the Bay of Pigs fiasco,[39] was reinforced again by the force of events, this time by action from outside of the hemisphere posing dangers far beyond the pressures from within the hemisphere which had principally forced our acceptance of the rule of nonintervention in the first place.

There is a curious irony in the fact that probably nothing has contributed more to the evolution of the Monroe Doctrine to a system of inter-American law than our own misuses of it. U.S. interventions in Latin America agitated the feelings that prompted our repeated disclaimers of any right of interference, and created the pressures to embody the principle of nonintervention in a treaty commitment. The ultimate folly of the Bay of Pigs invasion under the preposterous notion that the United States by avoiding overt participation could disclaim any responsibility[40] only led to extending our commitment to a non-American state. Breaches by the United States may have been promoted by men who believed that they were realists not unduly inhibited by law, but they only contributed to tightening the rule of law.

Of such is the force of law in international affairs. Law is imposed by the realities of foreign policy. It responds to the inexorable logic of international relations.

From Avoiding Entanglements to Resisting Aggression

The evolution from the historic U.S. policy of avoiding entangling alliances to a policy to resisting aggression, plainly grounded in a concept of a legal order, exhibits a similar process. It is important to understand this process and the roots of the legal framework by which we applied our power to the problems presented by the Cold War and continue to apply it in a period of a guarded détente, for these are problems over which the issues between a policy based on law and a policy based on power most directly contend.

We did not emerge from our historic isolationism by theory or policy. We were forced out of it by events. Although many Americans had long argued for our entry into World War I because of our stake in the ideals for which the Allies were believed to be fighting or because of our own stake in the European balance of power, America's choice had been to stay out of the war. The resumption of unrestricted submarine warfare by Germany in January 1917 presented a new situation to those who had wished to stay out of the war, a choice between submission to violation of our rights or entering the contest. President Wilson in his war message in April 1917, declining to accept a course of submission, advised "that the Congress declare the recent course of the Imperial German Government to be in fact nothing less than war against the government and people of the United States; that it formally accept the status of belligerent which has thus been thrust upon it."[41] A deeply divided America, which in the 1930s flirted again with the course of avoiding foreign entanglements, found itself involved in World War II, again by events more than by policy. Only the attack on Pearl Harbor put an end to the national debate and united the nation in common purpose.

Our entry into both world wars, however reluctant on the part of many, demonstrated that America has a stake in some kind of world order. Only in an international order could we be free to achieve our aims, the freedom to live and grow as the kind of nation we want to be, which had been the purpose of our historic policy of avoiding foreign entanglements. It is not surprising that we should have conceived of an international order based on the rights of peoples and nations that we claimed for ourselves.

The United States had already had some part in applying these principles to the reconciling task of permitting nations to live together in peace. In the Monroe Doctrine, as seen, we had applied the shield of American power to exclude the competitive aggrandizement of European powers from the Americas. In 1900 Secretary Hay had attempted to forestall the further destruction of China through great power competition for special rights by obtaining acceptance of the policy of the "Open Door." This policy was not addressed merely to trade access for the Western powers but also "to seek a solution which may bring about permanent safety and peace to China, preserve Chinese territorial and administrative entity."[42] This policy later was expressed in the Nine-Power Treaty of 1922 in a commitment: "(1) To respect the sovereignty, the independence, and the territorial and administrative integrity of China; (2) To provide the fullest and most unembarrassed opportunity to China to develop and maintain for herself an effective and stable government."[43] America's approach to relations among nations in those areas where we had occasion to assert our interest was based on their freedom, independence, and equality.

Our historic policy of avoiding foreign entanglements was partly based on a view that European affairs operated on different principles, that Europe's wars were fought for purposes inconsistent with the principles on which America was founded. Washington's farewell address asked, "Why, by interweaving our destiny with that of any part of Europe, entangle our peace and prosperity in the toils of European ambition, rivalship, interest, humor, or caprice?"[44] The Monroe Doctrine was formulated in President Monroe's message as a reciprocal to our nonentanglement in European affairs, noting

> the political system of the allied powers is essentially different in this respect from that of America. This difference proceeds from that which exists in their respective Governments; and to the defense of our own, which has been achieved by the loss of so much blood and treasure, and matured by the wisdom of their most enlightened citizens, and under which we have enjoyed unexampled felicity, this whole nation is devoted.[45]

These statements reflected the views held by most Americans before we ourselves were forced onto the world stage in World War I.

The premise for involvement of American power in European and world affairs was necessarily that we should use it for purposes we could approve. If we were to become involved in these affairs by the actions of others, we had a stake in the peace and should aim to secure with our power the basis for a stable and just peace. When President Wilson addressed the Senate and the world in January 1917 before our entry into the war on the foundations of peace he outlined "the conditions upon which it [this government] would feel justified in asking our people to approve its formal and solemn adherence to a League for Peace."[46] These conditions included "equality of rights" for all nations and "the principle that governments derive all their just powers from the consent of the governed, and that no right anywhere exists to hand people about from sovereignty to sovereignty as if they were property."[47] He characterized the principles as "no breach in either our traditions or policy as a nation, but a fulfillment, rather, of all that we have professed or striven for," asserting: "I am proposing, as it were, that the nations should with one accord adopt the doctrine of President Monroe as the doctrine of the world."[48] In his approach President Wilson was not only asserting his own ideals, he was also reflecting the unquestionable reality that American influence and power could be asserted only in accordance with our traditions and principles.

The U.S. rejection of the League of Nations involved no rejection of these principles. As noted, we promptly made them the cornerstones of the Nine-Power Treaty of 1922 relating to China. And we entered into the Kellogg-Briand Pact of 1928 by which sixty-three nations declared that they "condemn recourse to war for the solution of international controversies, and renounce it as an instrument of national policy in their relations with one another."[49] History has revealed the fragile nature of both the Nine-Power Treaty and the Kellogg-Briand Pact, which many, perhaps most people, recognized at the time. What is relevant here is not the effectiveness of the treaties but the evolution of the legal framework by which the United States guides its assertion of power in international affairs. Whether effective or not in restraining dictatorships bent on domination, they reflect and consolidate the principles by which the United States reacts to and attempts to shape events.

The Kellogg-Briand Pact may also have provided the premise for a somewhat more active U.S. role in international affairs. Henry L. Stimson, who as secretary of state under President Hoover had to deal with the first of the crises that led to World War II, commented later that cooperation between the United States and Great Britain in 1930 and 1931 "was largely based upon the effective influence of the Kellogg-Briand Pact in promoting the recent emergence of the United States from the accentuated isolationism which had marked its attitude toward the League of Nations since the Great War."[50] The United States co-operated with the League of Nations in dealing with Japan's occupation of Manchuria. Faced with apparent disregard of the League actions by Japan, Stimson in a note of January 7, 1932 enunciated the position that the United States "does not intend to recognize any situation, treaty, or agreement which may be brought about by means contrary to the convenants and obligations of the Pact of Paris of August 27, 1928, [the Kellogg-Briand Pact] to which treaty both China and Japan, as well as the United States, are parties."[51] This nonrecognition doctrine was also adopted by the League of Nations Assembly on March 11, 1932.[52] This is the doctrine now firmly embodied in United Nations General Assembly Resolution 3314 (XXIX) adopted December 14, 1974, Definition of Aggression, which in Article 5(3) provides: "No territorial acquisition or special advantage resulting from aggression is or shall be recognized as lawful."

Thus the policy frame by which the use of force against another state would be judged by the United States was essentially determined by 1932. The view according to which Europe had previously accepted war in the pursuit of national interest as legitimate was rejected. The structure of peace upon which the Covenant of the League of Nations and the Kellogg-Briand Pact were based, the equal rights of nations and respect for their territorial integrity and political independence, was fully accepted. Aggression was to be condemned, even if not actively opposed by force. The bias of the Covenant of the League of Nations in favor of the status quo and the absence of any adequate machinery to effect needed and justifiable change was a matter of concern to many. But on the central point there was no doubt. Despite the unsuccessful struggle by the League of Nations in the 1920s and 1930s to arrive at a definition of aggression, it was the firm view of the United States government and of the American people that the use of force to deprive another nation of its freedom or independence could not be justified on any consideration of national pride or power or advantage. The American people were not divided in their condemnation of the Japanese seizure of Manchuria, or the Italian seizure of Ethiopia, or the German seizure of Czechoslovakia after Munich, or Germany's attack on Poland or the Soviet attack on Finland. Nor were they divided on the right of the world to oppose those aggressions. They were deeply divided on whether it was advisable for the United States to become involved in that task. Thus, even before World War II, the use of force in international relations had largely passed from the area of policy choice to the frame of law.

At the close of the war the process was carried still further. The United States played a leading role in establishing the International Military Tribunal to try war offenses under a charter giving it jurisdiction over crimes, including the "planning, preparation, initiation or waging of a war of aggression."[53] And the United States argued for and supported the judgment of the tribunal declaring that a war of aggression had already become a crime under international law before 1939 and that "the charter is not an arbitrary exercise of power on the part of the victorious Nations, but in the view of the Tribunal, as will be shown, it is the expression of international law existing at its creation; and to that extent is itself a contribution to international law."[54] Whatever concerns some Americans had based on their own conception that an ex post facto application of law was involved or based on concern over a procedure of enforcement that could never be applied to the victors, these doubts involved no quarrel with the condemnation of aggression.

The United States and other members of the United Nations have made an explicit, even if somewhat imprecise, commitment against the use of force in article 2(4) of the Charter, providing:

> All Members shall refrain in their international relations from the threat or use of force against the territorial integrity or political independence of any state, or in any manner inconsistent with the Purposes of the United Nations.

This commitment does not use the term "aggression," although it is used in the Charter in other provisions, and it seems clear that the commitment is even broader than a prohibition of the use of force amounting to an act of aggression.

These were the attitudes and commitment deeply rooted in our history and traditions with which the United States faced the new issues presented by the Cold War that confronted us as the close of World War II. It is not surprising that our reactions were framed within the terms of the legal principles governing the use of force that our American attitudes had done so much to shape. Contributing strongly too, were the lessons we supposed we had learned from the 1930s that "appeasing" aggression promises only a worse day of reckoning in the future.

Our reaction to the crisis in Greece in 1947 set the pattern for the future. Our intelligence indicated the collapse of the Greek government was imminent "due to mounting guerilla activity, supplied and directed from the outside, economic chaos, and Greek government inability to meet the crisis."[55] The Truman administration viewed the outside pressure on Greece as part of a larger strategic design concluding in Acheson's words that "Soviet pressure on the Straits, on Iran, and on northern Greece had brought the Balkans to the point where a highly possible Soviet breakthrough might open three continents to Soviet penetration."[56]

President Truman's message to the Congress urgin assistance to Greece and Turkey placed the recommended course within the framework of action to resist aggression:

> The United Nations is designed to make possible lasting freedom and independence for all its members. We shall not realize our objectives, however, unless we are willing to help free peoples to maintain their free institutions and their national integrity against aggressive movements that seek to impose upon them totalitarian regimes. This is no more than a frank recognition that totalitarian regimes imposed on free peoples, by direct or indirect aggression, undermine the foundations of international peace and hence the security of the United States.[57]

The policy of resisting direct or indirect aggression became a fundamental tenet of U.S. policy in the postwar years.

Under this policy we acted in Korea and in Lebanon, and under it we condemned the Israelis, British, and French in the Suez crisis and the Soviet aggressions in Hungary and Czechoslovakia. And, of course, we acted under that policy in Vietnam.

The controversy that ultimately enveloped the U.S. involvement in Vietnam should not be permitted to obscure the role of the policy of resisting aggression in our involvement. Documents published in the Pentagon Papers show that as early as November 11, 1961 Secretaries Rusk and McNamara advised President Kennedy that "we should be prepared to introduce United States combat forces if that should become necessary for success. Dependent upon the circumstances, it may also be necessary for United States forces to strike at the source of the aggression in North Vietnam."[58] President Johnson's address on April 7, 1965, before the escalation in July of that year, identifying the reasons the United States was in South Vietnam, noted that "the central lesson of our time is that the appetite of aggression is never satisfied," and after outlining the actions taken by the United States stated: "We do this in order to slow down aggression."[59] In a speech on March 15, 1967

President Johnson identified as one of the United States' basic objectives in Vietnam "a concrete demonstration that aggression across international frontiers or demarcation lines is no longer an acceptable means of political change."[60]

Many would argue that the claim of aggression from the north was without foundation and even that the policy of resisting aggression was invoked hypocritically. It is not relevant to debate those issues here. If there is merit to them, it only attests further to the perceived vitality of the U.S. attachment to the legal framework for the use of force.[61]

To understand the significance for our purposes here of our policy commitment to that legal framework it is necessary to understand what that commitment is and what it is not. First, it is not a commitment to oppose all aggression with force. We did not do so in Hungary or Czechoslovakia. One of the objections that blocked U.S. membership in the League of Nations was unwillingness to accept the open-ended commitment in Article 10 of the Covenant to "preserve as against external aggression the territorial integrity and existing political independence of all Members of the League." No such commitment was included in the Charter of the United Nations. At the time of the original aid to Greece and Turkey in 1947 the Senate Foreign Relations Committee Report made clear that the application of the Truman Doctrine to other cases would depend on the circumstances of each case.[62]

The United States clearly does not commit itself to oppose all aggressors with force. There are probably at least three limitations on our use of force to oppose aggression. (1) We will not oppose aggression with force, if it is militarily impractical to do so or for other reasons will be ineffective. Hungary and Czechoslovakia may fit this category, but even if force were feasible in those cases, the stakes for the United States might be insufficient, since these countries were already de facto on the Soviet side of any weighing of a balance of power. (2) We will not use force unless our vital interests are threatened. This usually means when the world power equilibrium is threatened. Such considerations clearly weighed heavily in aid to Greece and Turkey and in Vietnam, as they do in our commitments under the NATO treaty and others. (3) On principle, I suspect we would not use force and would qualify the concept of aggression itself in a case in which our force would only support those unwilling to accept the rightness of just demands for change, for otherwise, lacking a legal process for change, collective security could become security for an unjust status quo.

Second, our commitment to the limitation of the use of force by law is not a commitment against military assistance to a country at its request, which is to be used against another nation only if it is guilty of aggression. Aid to Greece and Turkey in 1947 was not dependent on the fact of indirect aggression against them by other nations. Aid not involving the use of force against a third state involves only questions of a rule of nonintervention.[63] This was the understanding of the Senate Committee on Foreign Relations at the time of the aid in 1947 to Greece and Turkey.[64]

Finally, and this is the essential point of argument here, it *is* a policy condemning aggression whether by friend or foe. It is a commitment that the United States will not itself use force against another country in violation of the legal restraints that we have helped to create. We opposed our friends, Israel, Britain, and France in the Suez crisis of 1956, and most Americans stand ready to condemn their own country should it be guilty.

The Change in Unifying Principle

The United States has given concrete form to a concept of a legal order in the reshaping of the Monroe Doctrine and in moving from a policy of avoiding entangling alliances to a policy of resisting aggression. However, the full implications for foreign policy of the principles of a legal order have not yet been consciously accepted. As a nation, we are in the process of rethinking the premises of foreign policy.

For many Americans the premises of foreign policy are still conceived in terms of the historic touchstones of U.S. foreign policy: our commitment to the principles of the Declaration of Independence upholding the right of oppressed peoples to choose freedom, Washington's farewell address to the nation to avoid entangling alliances, Monroe's warning to Europe to keep hands off the Americas. In their origins these policies reflected not only the interest but the ideals of the United States. At its inception Washington's advice against entangling alliances was in response to French meddling in U.S. politics. Avoidance of foreign entanglements was an affirmation of independence and national sovereignty. And looked at on its affirmative side, it was a policy of keeping ourselves free to live and grow as the kind of nation we wanted to be. Our sympathies, reflecting our own beginnings and our principles, have always run to oppressed peoples attempting to overthrow their oppressors, to independent nations trying to maintain their independence. The ideological roots of the Monroe Doctrine were in defending the independence of the newly free nations of South America.

These traditional policies expressed a coherent tradition. They could be understood and felt. They were sustained by a shared conviction. They were tied together and reinforced by unifying principle.

That sense of unifying principle has, however, been placed under serious stress since the emergence of the United States as a world power. The traditional touchstones of foreign policy did not equip us for the world in which the United States itself has to play some role in the maintenance of world order. This stress was reflected not only in the conflict between isolationist and internationalist viewpoints but also in the loss of even shared premises of policy. In 1972 Eugene V. Rostow found eight different major premises producing eight conflicting foreign policy approaches by Americans.[65] Paradoxically, premises that in our time lead to conflicting approaches and policies can trace their roots to the same historical past. Those who would award or withohold U.S. support to other governments according to whether those governments uphold democratic institutions can see themselves as standing in our historic tradition. But so also can those who would avoid taking sides and those who would oppose the aggressor who seeks to subjugate a free people. While tracing roots to a common tradition, they seem to be judging the use of American power by premises that in our time do not relate to one another.

The sense of unifying principle is broken. Actions that will be seen as resistence to aggression by some will be seen as aid to dictatorships by others. What will be seen as avoiding foreign entanglements by some will be seen by others as defaulting on our responsibilities to help maintain the peace.

We are in need of a new national sense of the premises of foreign policy. Although we have not as a nation settled our mind, the political logic of international relations is moving us to the acceptance of a new unifying principle. Thus, in reshaping the Monroe Doctrine and in shifting from a policy of avoiding entangling alliances to one of resisting aggression, our response to events has led us to policies in which our actions are guided by the principles of a legal order. Even without a new grand design we find ourselves required to shape policy by a concept of the rules of a legal order. Need we then hold back from an explicit assertion of the strategy of resolution of conflict by law?

Three

THE RELATION OF LAW TO THE BALANCE OF POWER

Law Depends on the Balance of Power

It is an unfortunate inheritance from the past that law and the balance of power are seen by many as opposite approaches to foreign policy. Today, with the lessons of the Cold War still fresh, there must be few who believe that the world can rely on law and disregard considerations of the balance of power. The 1930s taught us that the world cannot rely on a generalized commitment to use force against an aggressor. The Cold War taught us that we cannot rely on the dedication of all nations to law nor on the force of world opinion. Though there are few who would rely on law and disregard the balance of power, there are many who make the opposite mistake and argue for a policy of maintaining a balance of power as if this policy could be implemented in the contemporary world in disregard of law. In our time this is as unrealistic an approach to foreign policy as the disregard of power.

American presidents from Washington to Franklin Roosevelt have scorned the European system of the balance of power as something foreign to American ideals. They have also, however, as Professor Gordon A. Craig has documented, had an astute understanding of America's stake in the balance of power when that consideration has been relevant.[1]

The founding fathers who set us on a course of avoiding the struggles by which the European balance of power was maintained were well aware that we owed our own independence to an alliance with France which was directly attributable to that same criticized system of European balance.

American criticism was at least in part directed to the ruthless manipulation, the "power politics," by which the European system of balance was maintained rather than to the principle of balance itself. The underlying conception of the balance of power, as enshrined by the Treat of Utrecht in 1713, was "a general and fundamental law" designed "to take away all uneasiness and suspicion, concerning such conjunction [of France and Spain], out of the minds of the people, and to settle and establish the peace and tranquillity of Christendom, by an equal balance of power (which is the best and most solid foundation of a mutual friendship, and of a concord which will be lasting on all sides)."[2] The American criticism was generally aimed at pursuit of power for its own sake and, in the words of President Wilson, at the practice of achieving balance by the barter of peoples and provinces "from sovereignty to sovereignty as if they were mere chattels and pawns in a game, even the great game, now forever discredited, of the balance of power."[3] The criticism reflected principles to which we have always been deeply attached, no less today than in the past. But we have emerged into a world in which we have to distinguish between the practice of power politics by which the balance of power was frequently maintained in Europe prior to World War I and the essential concept of the balance itself.

A realistic view of the role of the balance of power in U.S. policy today has to take account of two different developments. One is the emergence of the United States to a position where its power is a principal component of the world's power balance. With our emergence as a world power and now as one of the two superpowers the preservation of a world equilibrium of power has had to become an explicit fundamental of U.S. foreign policy. The second development is that the right of self-determination, to which we have always been attached under the banner of our own Declaration of Independnece, has become an article of fighting faith world wide. We are in a world where maintaining a balance of power by the bartering or subjugation of peoples is no longer, for democracies at least, a viable instrument of foreign policy. The relation of law and the balance of power in the world today is shaped by these developments.

The fundamental fact is that in a world where power rests in independent nation states an equilibrium of world power is the indispensable underpinning for law, for such law as we now have and for the prospect of further growth toward a rule of law. This essential equilibrium of power is just that. It is not a balance to be manipulated by one nation to advance its interests. It is not a system in which maximization of power is itself the aim. It is a counterpoise of power for protection against its abuse. It is a system of checks and balances. A world balance of power is a precarious security, but it is the best there is, and it is the only road to law.

The nature of the equilibrium may vary. It may be bipolar or multipolar. It may be based on three major power centers or four or five or more. It is made up of economic and political and ideological as well as military components, and the alignments and weights of each may not correspond. Analysis in these terms performs a useful function, demonstrating, for example, the more dangerous pressures of a bipolar balance than of a balance based on a larger number of power centers,[4] but this is not the point here. The components of an equilibrium will also change as they have in the past. An equilibrium can never be frozen against economic growth, technological change, discovery, or exhaustion of resources. The essential requirement is no particular alignment or form of equilibrium, only some overall world-wide equilibrium of power in place and effective enough to provide a check against the abuse of power by a nation or combination of nations bent on domination, or bent on acquiring the power to dictate to others.

The point was well stated by Professor Nicholas J. Spykman arguing in 1942 for a U.S. policy based on the balance of power:

> An equilibrium of forces inherently unstable, always shifting, always changing, is certainly not an ideal power pattern for an international society. But while we can deplore its shortcomings, we shall do well to remember that it is an indispensable element of an international order based on independent states. It encourages co-operation, conciliation, and the growth of law and is more likely to preserve peace and maintain justice than any other type of power distribution. The founders of the United States were impressed with the value and importance of balanced power. They created for this nation a government of checks and balances in the profound conviction that only in that manner could tyranny be avoided. Our government has been criticized for being slow and cumbersome, and it has irritated many who prefer quick and efficient responses to executive

command, but it has lived up to the hopes of its founders and preserved the political and civil liberties perhaps better than any other government. A similar merit extends to balanced power in international society.[5]

Without some equilibrium of power there is little chance of law.

To understand that some kind of a power balance is not an alternative to law but the necessary precondition for law is to grasp only a part of the relationship between equilibrium and law. The condition under which law can operate and grow is not just an incidental by-product of a policy of maintaining a balance of power. It is the aim of that policy.

At the time when the Truman Doctrine, enunciated in proposing aid to Greece and Turkey, seemed to provide the framework for postwar policy for the United States, many were concerned with its formulation in legal concepts and sought to emphasize its true purpose and rationale as action aimed to preserve the balance of power. Our involvement in World War I and World War II were accounted for in similar terms. Professor Hans Morganthau in an influential book urged Americans to avoid the errors of legalism and sentimentalism and to define our policy in terms of the national interest identified in that instance as "the traditional American interest in the maintenance of the European balance of power."[6] In point of fact the formulation in legal terms was appropriate. Our national interest in the balance of power is in providing the basis for a legal order in which the freedom and independence of nations can be respected.

The security of the United States is at stake in the maintenance of the balance of power, and that security is defended indirectly by protecting the independence of other states. Through the balance of power we seek to protect our security, not through dominating half the world, not through reliance solely on our own military capability, though that is a component of the balance of power, but through the counterpoise assured by the power of other free and independent sovereign states who can be expected to insist upon and defend their own rights under the same legal order in which we claim our rights.

We also have special security interests in the independence of some states, involving considerations beyond their potential weight in the world's power equilibrium. The independence of Greece and Turkey was vital to us in 1947 because domination of those countries by the U.S.S.R. or its satellites would open the way for domination of nations of the Middle East and even ultimate control of our access to Arab oil.

It was vital also because their domination could create increasing pressures on Italy and France, by means of which the unity of western Europe, upon which its defense depends, might be broken. Considerations of national security give certain areas a unique importance in the maintenance of a balance of power. These considerations provide special reasons for supporting the independence of certain states, and the balance of power serves as a shield for those special security interests as well as our general security interests.

The true significance, thus, is that in such critical areas we have a double stake in the balance of power and the regime of legal order that such a balance is intended to promote. We have a direct concrete stake based on specific national security considerations. We also have the larger stake in a world order that will allow us and other nations to live and grow in peace.

There could be no greater fallacy than the notion that we have to make a choice of either a policy of preserving the balance of power or of a foreign policy grounded in law. A balance of power serves its ends by affording a chance for law, and there is no other way to law. In the words of Professor Eugene V. Rostow, "if one's goal is not simply the absence of war but a condition of peace compatible with the independence of nations, then the course of prudence is that power be organized so that no state likely to succumb to hegemonial ambition be in a position to achieve hegemonial power. Achieving and preserving a balance of power is the indispensable first step."[7]

The Balance of Power Depends on Law

The concern which I think many have that law and the balance of power may present opposite choices derives from an uneasy sense that in some circumstances the necessity of preserving the balance of power may require actions that law would not permit. This unease is reflected, for example, in Secretary Kissinger's dissatisfaction with the proposition that we must resist aggression anywhere it occurs since peace is indivisible. "A corollary," he says, "is the argument that we do not oppose the fact of particular changes but the method by which they are brought about. We find it hard to articulate a truly vital interest which we would defend however 'legal' the challenge."[8] Professor Hedley Bull, while reluctant to argue that considerations of the balance of power should override international law or vice versa, nevertheless maintains that "international law, or some particular interpretation of international law, is sometimes found actually to hinder measures to maintain international order. A classic case is the clash between international law and measures deemed necessary to maintain a balance of power."[9] There is an ambivalence to such views, for in any specific case the writer seems to recognize that flouting the law is not a practical option.

Kaplan and Katzenbach in 1961 posed what may be the ultimate test, a Communist victory in a free election in France, but shrank from the supposed logic of the balance of power. They comment: "The extent to which committed states will be permitted to change political orientation is doubtful. Hungary is a case in point, and we may be dubious whether, faced with a Communist revolution in France or Italy, the United States (probably acting *qua* NATO) would not react in the same way. Communist victory in a free election in France or Italy, or a shift in Poland's international position, would pose more difficult problems; moderation, however, may be met with moderation, if the break with past political orientation is not too decisive."[10]

In October 1975 the question was answered more directly by Secretary Kissinger in a *Time Magazine* interview. Asked, "Could we tolerate Communists in the government of Italy or in France?" he replied: "If you deal with a modern complicated democratic state, like Italy or France, it is not directly in our power to prevent it. It must be the responsibility of the governments concerned to prevent it. The alienation from government cannot be remedied primarily by the United States."[11]

It is not surprising that in the war in Vietnam, fought under the banner of upholding the right of self-determination of the people of South Vietnam, the United States made clear we would abide by their choice, even if that choice was for a Communist government. Stated in general terms on many occasions, President Johnson on April 3, 1967 said: "We do not seek to impose our political beliefs upon South Viet-Nam. Our Republic rests upon a brisk commerce in ideas. We will be happy to see free competition in the intellectual marketplace whenever North Viet-Nam is willing to shift the conflict from the battlefield to the ballot box."[12] President Nixon in his third annual foreign policy report to Congress said:

> The only serious barrier to a settlement which remains is the enemy's insistence that we cooperate with him to force on our ally at the negotiating table a solution which the enemy cannot force upon him in the field, and is unwilling to entrust to a political process. That we are not willing to do. We are ready to reach an agreement which allows the South Vietnamese to determine their own future without outside interference.[13]

The unease that leads many to fear that the balance of power may be compromised by an acceptance of law comes, I think, from a failure to face up to the fact that the diplomacy of balance of power in the modern world is something quite different from the old power politics. It is not realistic to suppose that in defense of the balance of power we could deny peoples their freedom or independence or the right to determine their own destiny, even if we were of a mind to do so. The political consequences of the attempt would keep us from trying. It is a symptom of the political power of the right of self-determination that we have found it impractical even to try to hold on to the Panama Canal under a treaty we already had.

The unease ignores not only the political force of the world's attachment to the right of self-determination but our own history and traditions as well. The process by which our foreign policy has evolved into a framework determined by a conception of a legal order was traced in chapter 2. It is with us, and it is part of us. Can any one seriously imagine an American president asking the American people to support a policy by which we undertook by force to unseat the freely elected government of another state under the banner of preserving the balance of power?

None of this is contradicted by the revelations of the United States undercover machinations in Chile through the C.I.A. The C.I.A. activities in Chile seem clearly to involve an illegitimate intervention in Chilean affairs and should be condemned.[14] The fact that revelation of this undercover intervention, not involving any use or threat of force by the United States, has raised a storm of protest in the United States confirms rather than denies that the use or threat of force to block peaceful change by a legitimate exercise of a nation's right of self-determination is not an instrument the United States can practically use to maintain the balance of power.

The modern principle of the balance of power has to be seen realistically as one of preserving the balance of power against attempts to alter it unilaterally by an illegitimate use or threat of force or coercion direct or indirect. The balance is to be created and maintained by the free actions of the peoples involved. It is to be protected againt the illegitimate acts of others by acts that are legitimate for such response.

In acting to protect the balance of power since World War II the United States has made clear that it was acting within such limitations. President Truman himself in his 1947 message on Greece and Turkey explicitly stated:

> The world is not static and the status quo is not sacred. But we cannot allow changes in the status quo in violation of the Charter of the United Nations by such methods as coercion, or by such subterfuges as political infiltration.[15]

As noted above President Johnson defined our aims in Vietnam not in terms of blocking change but in providing "a concrete demonstration that aggression across international frontiers or demarcation lines is no longer an acceptable means of political change."[16] Professor Eugene V. Rostow attempted to define the modern balance of power policy represented in the Truman Doctrine in these terms:

> I should put it this way: equilibrium, and therefore the possibility of détente, requires mutual understanding that neither side should attempt to change the frontiers of the system by force or by the threat of force. For such attempts, unlike certain other forms of change, threaten the general world equilibrium, and therefore risk a confrontation between great powers and world war.[17]

Although stated on an assumption of a bipolar balance of power, which does not reflect the condition of the world today, the essential point is correct. A policy of maintaining the balance of power is one of preserving it against change by force or the threat of force, or, I would add, any other illegitimate interference with the right of self-determination. Such a policy cannot conflict with law. It can only support it.

Some may still see a risk that the balance of power can shift against us even by peaceful means, and that in some cases we might have to act against law to survive. Conceding that it is impossible to foresee all eventualities, the risks to American interests of some presently unforeseen future embarrassment from a commitment to law must be preferred over the clear and present damage to our standing and political influence from a refusal to accept in our own conduct the principles of law by which the balance of power is now supported.

Other considerations support the same result. There is surely a difference between a threat to the balance of power by force and a shift of political attachment by free choice. Allowing force to succeed whets the appetite of the aggressor and undermines the credibility of our own commitment to order. Permitting freely chosen, peaceful changes to happen, where subversion or intervention in the process by the other side has not contributed, does neither. If it poses a threat, it is a future and speculative thing.[18]

Finally, there is reason for faith in the common sense of law to permit a nation to take action that it reasonably must take for its own survival. As Professor Louis Henkin has well said:

> For my part, I cannot agree that there can be behavior that "has to be done" but which violates the law. No legal system accepts as law that which "has to be" violated. No view of international law, no interpretation of any norm or agreement, could concede that a nation may be legally required to do that which would lead to its destruction, or jeopardize its independence or security. Nations, surely, would not accept such law for themselves or impose it on others.[19]

Law is continually changing to define rules of general application to reconcile the felt necessities of the time. Where national survival is at stake there should be no reason to doubt that articulable grounds deserving recognition in law can be found and respected for what "has to be done."

It is time for Americans who understand the nation's stake in the balance of power to understand that it is a policy that depends upon and is reinforced by law. It is not an alternative to law but the way to law. And, realistically, the only actions by which the balance of power can be maintained in our time, the only supportive actions we can take and still be true to ourselves, are those that conform to law.

Four
HOW RIGHT MAKES MIGHT

The Contribution of Law to Effective Action

Individuals bearing responsibility for the conduct of foreign plicy need to recognize that the issue a nation must address is not whether international law is enforceable but whether a foreign policy not rooted in law can be fully effective.

Foreign policy leaders are rightly wary of relying on the power of world opinion to enforce law. And although law, as traced in chapter 2, represents a necessary political response to international realities, international law lacks the kind of enforcement authority that exists to enforce domestic law. It would be thoroughly irresponsible to rely on law as a substitute for adequate defense and a prudent concern for the balance of power and protection of other vital interests. The "faith that right makes might"[1] has a role to play, but the constructive power of law need not be taken on faith. It works in concrete ways, and the lessons of history are there to be read.

The need for an effective foreign policy to be founded in law can be seen in contrasting the Bay of Pigs fiasco of 1960 and the Cuban missile crisis in 1962. U.S. assistance to would-be Cuban insurgents in the Bay of Pigs invasion was in direct violation of inter-American treaty commitments against intervention. It was no less so because it was covert or because carried out under a C.I.A. "ground rule" to protect the ability of the United States to disown the project. Because it was illegal, President Kennedy had to answer rumors of an impending invasion with the assurance that "there will not be, under any conditions, an intervention in Cuba by the United States Armed Forces."[2] Thus the illegality of the affair precluded the U.S. support required for its success. When the invasion force ran into trouble effective steps could not be taken to rescue it.

The planning for the Bay of Pigs invasion failed to evaluate the viability of the enterprise as one which had to proceed without the benefit of even the claim or color of legal right. Schlesinger makes clear there were persistent confusions and misunderstandings as to the support that could be expected from the United States. The costs even to U.S. international relations that were bound to follow from evidence that the United States had been prepared to commit a clear, though as initially planned, covert, violation of our treaty commitments, were apparently not directly addressed. The consequences of acting illegally became apparent, except to a very few dissenters, including Senator Fulbright, only in retrospect.

From time to time a variety of conclusions has been drawn from the Bay of Pigs fiasco. President Kennedy seems to have read the lesson as teaching him not to rely too much on the experts, those who thought the enterprise was militarily sound and could succeed without overt U.S. military support.[3] Schlesinger himself concluded principally that it is a mistake to undertake a covert action whose cover cannot be sustained.[4] Most Americans, I believe, have concluded that an action that flouts international law is likely to be a foreign policy disaster. For purposes of the argument here, that conclusion, right as it is, obscures a more precise and more relevant lesson, namely, that an action not firmly grounded in law procedes under the handicap that it cannot be effectively defended or supported. In the most realistic terms there is a power in law, and for lack of that power an action may fail. It may fail, as the Bay of Pigs invasion did in fact fail, to attain even its immediate objectives.

The Cuban missile crisis in contrast demonstrates how law can be power and how it may even provide the critical margin for success. In its response to the Soviet missile threat the United States took pains to limit its action to a "defensive quarantine"[5] and to proceed on the legal basis of action by the Organization of American States under Article 52 of the United Nations Charter with a report to the Security Council in compliance with that article. The reasonableness and restraint of the U.S response, its reliance on established regional procedures arising out of a long history, its support by a cogent, if not universally accepted, legal position, the dramatic presentation of the U.S. position in open Security Council debate were all important elements of the U.S. response. The remarkable fact that no widespread opposition to the U.S. position developed is testimony to the power of an effective appeal to the sense of law in the world community.

Happily, the successful conclusion under the steps taken keeps us from knowing what course events might have taken if our action had not presented a reasonable justification under law. Under a different course would the O.A.S. have acted favorably? Without O.A.S. support, would active opposition have been asserted from nonaligned nations or others? Without O.A.S. action or with encouragement from other nations would Russia have agreed to remove its missiles before the United States felt compelled to implement its back-up course of air strikes to destroy the missile sites?[6] If not, what would Russia's response to those air strikes have been? Whatever the answers, it seems clear that during the Cuban missile crisis grounding our response in law was a vital element of an effective course of action.

The lessons of the Cuban missile crisis in demonstrating the power of law to contribute to effective action rest on more than the manner in which the United States implemented its action in that crisis. The foundations had been laid before. The premises for action by the United States and the American nations owed their acceptability to the nations of this hemisphere and of the world to the evolution of policy from the Monroe Doctrine to principles of law supported by the collective responsibility of the members of the O.A.S. By that evolution the exclusion from this hemisphere of security threats by non-American nations were placed on a footing of principle, which the nations of this hemisphere could support and other nations of the world could respect.

Other cases also make clear the contribution law can make to effective foreing policy action. Professor John N. Moore has made the point well:

> International law, particularly on issues of war and peace, does not always manifestly control the behavior of states. But is is not widely perceived that even when international law does not control behavior, there are international norms—community expectations about the authority of national action which may in a variety of ways translate into power realities. For example, an action such as the Korean War, in which perceptions as to law-

> fulness are high, is likely to produce more allies than actions which are controversial such as the Indo-China War or widely regarded as unlawful such as the British and French invasion of Suez.[7]

One should add that a reasonable legal justification that other nations can understand and accept can not only win friends but can deter enemies as well and avoid providing easy targets around which hostile coalitions can form.

President Carter urged the importance of the new treaty for permanent neutrality of the Panama Canal as providing the "legitimacy" for action, if necessary, to defend the Canal, a legitimacy he sees as equivalent to the Security Council action that provided the United States a legitimate position in Korea, a legitimacy that can avoid problems encountered by United States action in Vietnam where "we were looked on as being an illegal entity."[8]

The contribution that law can make to effective foreign policy action may depend on the perception of the action as grounded in law as well as on its actually being legally justifiable. Few Americans will ever forget the crisis generated by President Nixon's announcement of the invasion of Cambodia on April 30, 1970. The action was perhaps bound to receive a hostile reaction from many however presented, but there was a reasonable legal basis for acting, a rationale and justification that could have had weight and provided some framework for a more moderate public dialogue. Yet the president presented the actions without any attempt at legal justification. The country was torn apart, and the administration was embarrassed into making commitments limiting its action. Kissinger has written that "the panicky decision to set a June 30 deadline for the removal of our forces from Cambodia was one concrete result of public pressures."[9] If the action was worth taking, it was worth taking with full advantage of the available legal justification.

Reluctance to ground foreign policy explicitly in law simply ignores the power of law to contribute to effective action. This is a power that responsible leaders cannot afford to throw away.

The Folly of Holding Back

History also teaches that to use law effectively a nation has to accept law. This simple truth will strike many as an unduly moralistic principle for the hard-nosed business of foreign policy. However, the point being made here is not one of morality but of understanding how a nation effectively uses the power of law in the real world. Holding back from the full acceptance of law denies us the full power of law. It can mean that we lose on both ends. We are denied the benefit of the full potential of law on one end and eventually have to accept the constraints of the principles we assert anyway.

These generalizations are demonstrated by our experience on the two issues that have most agitated the American people in recent years: Panama and Vietnam.

Panama

Our holding back in relation to the application of emerging principles of international law to U.S. rights in the Panama Canal occurred in the crisis over Egypt's nationalization of the Suez Canal Company in July 1956. Egypt's action, while charged with political fire, was taken on a careful legal position. Egypt asserted its rights of sovereignty and in particular its right to nationalize a domestic company, assuring compensation for the shareholders, and asserted its full commitment to its international obligations under the Convention of 1888. The United States and other user nations saw the guarantees of freedom of passage through the Canal being put in jeopardy, since the Suez Canal Company would no longer stand as a buffer against violation and Egypt's guarantees under the Convention of 1888 would rest only on its good faith. But a legal position insisting on international rights to the continued operation of the Suez Canal Company as a buffer could not find a firm basis in the treaties themselves, since under the concession to the Company its rights were to terminate in any event in 1968. If the user nations were to claim a right for some buffer entity to operate the Canal or otherwise assure Egypt's compliance with its treaty guarantees for free passage through the canal, they would have to look beyond the language of the treaties themselves.

A respectable case might have been made for some measure of international operation or supervision on the basis that the Canal, having been permanently dedicated to the use of the world and having been used and relied upon by other nations, had become affected with an international interest and was subject to regulation as an international public utility. Although writers are divided as to the existence of any international right of regulation,[10] it was clear at least that an international interest entitled to protection under international law did exist. In 1923 the Permanent Court of International Justice in *The S. S. "Wimbledon"*, affirming international rights in the Kiel Canal, referred to precedents concerning the Suez and Panama Canals and recognized each of them as an artificial waterway connecting two open seas which "has been permanently dedicated to the use of the whole world."[11] Although the argument for protection of acknowledged international rights through some kind of international agency was not established in law, it was open to be made and Suez presented the case to make it. Indeed, if it was not made, the careful legal position upon which Egypt relied strongly to resist the pressures brought to bear upon it was probably irrefutable.

Nevertheless, the United States held back. Professor Robert R. Bowie, who had been an assistant secretary of state at the time of the crisis, explains:

> Another obvious approach was to claim user dependence on the Canal made it an international public utility which the world community was entitled to regulate. The United States was deterred from adopting this theory by its interests in the Panama Canal. For the U.S. that Canal had a strategic importance rather different from the Suez Canal's importance for Egypt. Since the U.S. was not prepared to accept international operation or control of Panama, it could not rely on a general claim of global interest in Suez. Hence the U.S. had to base the Suez case on the treaties specific to Suez, taking the tenuous line that the treaty status of Panama was wholly different.[12]

The attempt to support international arrangements for Suez while protecting U.S. rights in Panama became an explicit position of the United States. In a news conference on August 8, 1956 President Eisenhower called Suez "completely unlike the Panama Canal."[13] On August 28, 1956 Secretary Dulles, relying on alleged treaty and factual distinctions called the situations "totally dissimilar."[14]

Despite the handicap of having in effect waived the essential argument to confront Egypt's position, Secretary Dulles provided imaginative leadership first to devise an Eighteen Power Proposal for an international operating agency, which Egypt rejected, and then arranged the formation of a Suez Canal Users Association, which became the subject of negotiations among Egypt, Britain, and France in the consideration of the Suez Canal issue in the United Nations Security Council. On October 13, the Security Council, with the approval of Egypt, voted six principles to be embodied in a settlement, including the principle that "the operation of the Canal should be insulated from the politics of any country." This might seem to provide the basis for some form of international participation in Suez Canal affairs, but Egypt apparently thought the requirement would be satisfied by a renewal or reaffirmation of the 1888 Convention.[15] The Secretary-General by letter on October

24 outlined what he understood the representatives of Egypt, Britain, and France had contemplated, including provision for joint meetings between an Egyptian operating authority and an organized representation of the users with provision for adjudication of disputes,[16] and on these points the Egyptian representative on November 2 confirmed by letter the Secretary-General's understanding.[17] However, the scene was dramatically changed by the concerted resort to force by Israel, Britain, and France, begun by the Israeli attack on Egypt of October 29, 1956. No arrangements for international participation in Suez Canal affairs were consummated.

Of course, no one can say that some international participation for the protection of international rights in the Suez Canal would have been achieved in 1956 even if the United States had been willing to press for such a regime as a matter of international law, accepting the consequences for U.S. rights in the Panama Canal. Nor, recognizing the sensitivity of the Panama Canal issue in the United States, is it my purpose to criticize the Eisenhower administration for failing to take a position on Suez that would, in effect, have committed the United States to give up its right to control and operate the Panama Canal in favor of an international agency, without the benefit of full consideration and negotiation and an opportunity for public discussion. But we can all look back now. Pressures in support of the ideas of self-determination and nonintervention, which the United States helped to shape, have forced us to negotiate new treaties by which we agree to yield control of the Panama Canal, and we yield it not to an international agency, but to Panama itself. In retrospect it is clear that our holding back on Suez in 1956 for the sake of Panama was in vain. And what is worse, it may have cost us and other nations dependent on the Canal the protection of international participation in *both* canals.

The folly was inherent in our position in 1956. Was it not clear in 1956 that if Egypt were sustained in its claim to exercise sovereignty over the Suez Canal without any international buffer, that victory would make it more difficult for the United States to retain control over the Panama Canal? In August 1956 the government of Panama identified its interests with those of Egypt and served notice that it would never allow the Panama Canal to be placed under international control.[18] By deliberately distinguishing Panama from the grounds on which the case for international participation in Suez was asserted, we not only weakened the case on Suez but also in effect foreclosed any opportunity to make that case for the Panama Canal in negotiations with Panama. In the eyes of the world, and, candidly, in our own, Suez and Panama were parallel. We could not have it both ways. In the end we have not. We have certainly gained nothing by the attempt, and we may have lost something in both situations.

Vietnam

Our experience in Vietnam makes the same point in a somewhat different way. For those who believed we were fighting to support South Vietnam against an aggression by North Vietnam (aided and abetted by China and Russia) and to enable the people of South Vietnam to determine freely their own future, it was a painful frustration that others could so successfully portray our action in an entirely different light. Our policies had taken root from the bitter experience of the 1930s and our involvement in two world wars. These policies sprang from the lesson learned at enormous cost that appeasing the aggressor leads to disaster, that the essentials of order sometimes have to be defended even at great sacrifice, and far away from our shores. And yet opponents of the war often saw the efforts of the United States as intervention in a civil war, as blocking compliance with the 1954 Geneva agreements and even as thwarting self-determination for the Vietnamese people.

There are, of course, many reasons contributing to the agony of the American people over the war in Vietnam, including some of the U.S. actions in the conduct of the war, disagreement as to the feasibility of U.S. involvement in a land war in Asia, recrimination between those who tried to end the war by opposing it and those who believed the opposition itself was prolonging the war, draft inequities, war weariness, and a widely felt suspicion that our government was acting hypocritically. Certainly, among the important contributing causes was the confusion and disagreement of the American people about the underlying premises of the war. The tragic division of the country as to what the war was all about is an ineradicable part of our memory.

At the root of the problem, I suggest, was the attempt by the U.S. government to use one answer to an underlying legal issue without resolving the issue itself. The public does not ordinarily think of its attitudes as being based on legal grounds. Yet I think one can see that an unresolved legal issue lay at the bottom of much of the argument about what our war effort was all about.

Our peace aim in Vietnam as it came to be clearly stated, was to secure an opportunity for the people of South Vietnam to choose freely their own future, to defend the right of South Vietnam to self-determination. In defining this aim, while hitching our action to a great principle of the emerging international law, we were at the same time bypassing a legal resolution of still-contested issues at the core of the conflict.

To recall familiar ground, in the 1954 Geneva Accords[19] the division between South and North Vietnam was fixed under an agreement between the commanders of French and Democratic Republic of Viet Nam (North Viet Nam) forces by a line that was described in Article 1 as a "provisional military demarcation line," on either side of which the forces of the two parties were to be regrouped after withdrawal, the forces of the People's Army of Viet Nam to the north of the line and the forces of the French Union to the south. The cease-fire agreement provided in Article 2 for the withdrawals to each "regrouping zone" to be completed within 300 days, and it referred in passing in Article 14 (a) to "the general elections which will bring about the unification of Viet Nam." The Final Declaration of the Geneva Conference stated in paragraph 6 that "the esential purpose of the agreement relating to Viet Nam is to settle military questions with a view to ending hostilities and that the military demarcation line is provisional and should not in any way be interpreted as constituting a political or territorial boundary." It expressed the conviction that the declaration and agreement created the necessary basis for the achievement in the near future of "a political settlement in Viet Nam." The declaration further stated in paragraph 7 that the settlement of political problems "effected on the basis of respect for the principles of independence, unity and territorial integrity, shall permit the Vietnamese people to enjoy the fundamental freedoms, guaranteed by democratic institutions established as a result of free elections by secret ballot" and stated that to ensure that "all necessary conditions obtain for a free expression of the national will, general elections shall be held in July 1956," and further provided that consultations would be held on this subject between "the competent representative authorities of the two zones from July 20, 1955, onwards."

Although these provisions clearly contemplated a unified Vietnam, the relationship between the provision for elections in July 1956 and the provisions for reciprocal withdrawals and other matters could easily be seen differently by different groups. Nor did the agreements clearly provide what determinations as to the terms of voting were to be vested in the "competent representative authorities" of each zone. Some writers have argued that in fact some of the parties, despite the provisions of the accords, contemplated and intended a more or less indefinite partition.[20]

The principal complications, however, arose from the fact that neither the government in South Vietnam nor the United States was a party to the cease-fire agreement or the Final Declaration. Each in fact made its own statement.[21] The Bao Dai government in South Vietnam, acting as the State of Viet Nam, specifically declared its objection to the date set for general elections, although insisting no less than the government in North Vietnam on the aim of a unified Vietnam, and it disputed the right of the French authorities to act in behalf of the State of Viet Nam.

The objections of the Bao Dai government foreshadowed the course of events. In 1955, when the time came to commence consultation for the elections, the government in South Vietnam refused to consult on the grounds that under current conditions free elections could not be held in North Vietnam, nor would the government in North Vietnam permit truly democratic institutions to exist there.[22] Whatever merit there was in this position,[23] the refusal to proceed with general elections under the terms of the Geneva Accords meant that the government in South Vietnam, with United States support, was opting for a de facto partition in Vietnam for the foreseeable future.

Many, of course, believed that a de facto partition of Vietnam was not only the practical result of refusing to participate in the consultations provided under the Accords but also and in fact the intended aim of the refusal. Although at the Geneva conference the Bao Dai government had proposed general elections under United Nations auspices,[24] many suspected that it did not want general elections at all. Some felt that the record of the government in South Vietnam after the accords gave reason to doubt that its refusal to participate in general elections on the grounds of the impossibility of free elections and democratic institutions in North Vietnam reflected any genuine attachment to democratic ideals. In the controversy that later developed in the United States after 1965 the suspicion that the government in South Vietnam was in fact trying to duck any general elections was nurtured by the widely quoted comment by President Eisenhower in his memoirs appearing in 1963 that "I have never talked or corresponded with a person knowledgeable in Indo-china affairs who did not agree that had elections been held as of the time of the fighting [referring, presumably, to 1954], possibly eighty percent of the population would have voted for the Communist Ho Chi Minh as their leader rather than Chief of State Bao Dai."[25]

Against this background many saw South Vietnam as, in effect, blocking the unity of the Vietnamese people and argued that the United States by aiding South Vietnam in this was interfering in a Vietnamese civil war. These issues became involved in the war controversy in the United States and abroad.

The issue that underlay this controversy was how the right of self-determination should be implemented in Vietnam. Under the United Nations Charter the right of self-determination belongs to a "people," a concept that presents some issues considered further in chapter 8. For Vietnam the issue in 1965 at the time of the major U.S. escalation and thereafter was whether the "people" entitled to exercise a right of self-determination was the entire population of Vietnam considered as one people, or, given the history that had clouded the relations between the North and South, the people of each part acting separately

Although the governments in both North and South Vietnam based their positions in 1954 on the idea of one Vietnam, they had not agreed on the provisions of the Geneva Accords. The resulting impasse and subsequent events presented a number of issues. Did the Geneva Accords by their terms provide for a one-Vietnam solution—that only the people of Vietnam as a whole were entitled to exercise a right to self-determination? If the Accords by their terms purported to do so, did either the government designated as the Democratic Republic of North Vietnam or the French authorities have the right to bind the people of South Vietnam? Did the de facto partition of Vietnam after 1954 or the alleged violation of the Accords and aggression by North Vietnam provide reason to entitle the people of South Vietnam to make their choice for themselves?

The principle of self-determination could not be appropriately implemented in Vietnam without a resolution of these issues. The United States, in stating as its peace aim the right of self-determination for the people of South Vietnam, was relying on a position that had not been established and, indeed, depended on the answers to some very controversial questions.

The problem in the U.S. position was not that it was necessarily wrong. I take it to be true that, if neither the 1954 Geneva Accords nor other history dictated a one-Vietnam solution, the principle of self-determination would itself require a result in which the people in North and South Vietnam would decide for themselves whether they should act as one people or two.

Nor does this analysis impugn the legitimacy of our use of force to resist aggression by North Vietnam.[26] Although others have so argued, my point is not the any problem existed in the declared basis of our military action, the asserted right of collective self-defense against an aggression by North Vietnam constituting an "armed attack" under Article 51 of the United Nations Charter.[27] We had a right with South Vietnam to block North Vietnam's attempt to impose its claimed right to a one-Vietnam solution by force, but that did not give South Vietnam or the United States the right to try to impose a two-Vietnam solution by force. The irony is that our insistence on a right of self-determination for South Vietnam without resolution of the underlying issue made it possible for even our action in resisting aggression to be made to appear as intervention in a civil war, as blocking compliance with the 1954 Accords, as indeed thwarting self-determination for the Vietnamese people.

In failing to face up to the issue directly the U.S government permitted the impression to be made that we were not really committed to law but to using it for our own purposes. This is part of the tragedy, because our stake in Vietnam was in the rule of law. Nothing could have served our purposes better than to have the issues involved in Vietnam resolved by law rather than by aggression.

But a full commitment to law in Vietnam required something more than resisting aggression. And it required something different from an attempt to force a solution reflecting U.S or South Vietnamese answers to unresolved and highly controversial issues. It required, in short, something more than a contest of force. A determination was needed as to what right or rights of self-determination were applicable. Without that determination our position was controversial and vulnerable. Holding back from this full commitment to law weakened us and put our whole effort in jeopardy.

Just as the U.S. effort was weakened by our holding back, so I think it can be seen, although a consideration of might-have-beens is necessarily speculative, that it would have been strengthened by a full commitment to law. Recourse to some international process was called for. This process could, for example, have been an offer to adjudicate the issue (on terms such as are proposed in part three below).

An offer to adjudicate the issues would have fortified our position, whether or not the offer was accepted and no matter how the issue was ultimately decided if an adjudication did take place. If an offer to adjudicate had been made and was turned down by North Vietnam, it would have left us with a clear course to insist on self-determination by the people of South Vietnam. North Vietnam, by declining to pursue a legal determination of the legal issue it pressed against us with such success, would have unmasked its own hypocrisy. We would have cleared the air and fortified our moral and legal position.

If the offer to adjudicate had been accepted by North Vietnam, we would have benefited even more clearly. This is obviously true if the resulting adjudication had affirmed the right of South Vietnam to make its separate choice. If North Vietnam, after losing the adjudication, still persisted in trying to force a one-Vietnam solution, it would have had to contend with a unified South Vietnam and a unified United States, strengthened by enhanced support in the rest of the world. But it is equally true that we would have benefited even if the adjudication determined that only Vietnam as a whole could choose. We would have blocked an attempt by North Vietnam to impose its solution by force. We would have required it to rely not on force but on right. The challenge of China and Russia attempting to shift the balance of power thorugh force in the form of so-called wars of national liberation would have been met. The credibility of our commitments would have been reinforced. And we would have advanced the rule of law.

A solution through adjudication even with a one-Vietnam determination would have been a U.S. victory, for we had no other essential stake in Vietnam than to preserve the international order. Interests such as keeping open access to rubber or other resources would also have been served by a result that buttressed Vietnam's ability to choose its course for itself and checked the ability of China and Russia to use Vietnam for their own purposes. Indeed, in relying on the principle of self-determination we were already committed to risking the kind of government that might constrict such other interests. We were explicitly committed to the risk of honoring a free choice in supporting self-determination for the people of South Vietnam. In one sense specific interests are always put at some risk by the principle of self-determination. But in a larger sense that principle provides better assurance of access to resources than a tightly compartmentalized world.

South Vietnam might have feared the oppression which could follow after the years of bitter struggle if an adjudication affirmed a one-Vietnam solution. This fear also undoubtedly influenced our support of self-determination for South Vietnam. This concern could, of course, have been pressed in an adjudication, and coupled with the aggression by North Vietnam it would probably have provided one of the most compelling arguments in favor of a separate right of self-determination for South Vietnam. The better answer to such fears, however, is to consider them in context. It is difficult in this matter not to be influenced by subsequent events. In view of the evident weakness of the South Vietnamese government, one can wonder whether the South Vietnamese really had more to fear from the acceptance by North Vietnam of a course of adjudication than from ultimately having to stand against North Vietnam after a military stalemate, a paper peace, and withdrawal of U.S. forces.

On principle, some kind of international process had to be involved in any event. The principle of self-determination could not be implemented even in South Vietnam without such a process.[28] The 1954 demarcation line between North and South Vietnam would not on principle necessarily provide the delineation of the areas by which choice should be made. And, if full effect is to be given to the principle of self-determination, not only must appropriate areas be fixed, but provision must also be made for exercise of choice by plebiscite or other appropriate means. The U.S. insistence on self-determination for South Vietnam, however sincere and dedicated, bypassed issues and steps that in the context of the contest between North and South Vietnam could not be avoided, if our position was to reflect a full commitment to law.

An adjudication approach to resolution of an issue vital enough to be the cause of armed conflict is not in the tradition of statecraft as it has been practiced. Leaders of foreign policy might even be reluctant to appear to be so "idealistic." They might be troubled by a possible imprudence in risking the outcome of a genuine adjudication. But if intractable issues requiring such a resolution are involved, it can hardly any longer be thought to be prudent or realistic to rely on trying to wish them away. The experience of Vietnam makes quite clear that a course that isolates us from much of the rest of the world and through internal controversy destroys our capacity to act effectively as a nation is not a sensible way to win wars or sustain policy.

In Vietnam we laid our case on law but followed it only part way. The issue left unresolved exposed us to upheaval at home and isolation abroad. It severely embarrassed the effectiveness of action taken, I believe, in a genuine commitment to a policy of resisting aggression. The point here is not to criticize but to understand how holding back from law can prove to be a folly.

The Power of National Commitment

The earlier sections of this chapter have shown concrete ways in which the commitment to law brings strength to foreign policy and how attempting to use the law while holding back from a full commitment can result in losing the power of law without avoiding the constraints of a genuine commitment. The events discussed suggest also a broader truth.

The reality that must shape all foreign policy for open societies such as the United States is that a foreign policy not firmly grounded in law will not command the energy and sacrifice of the people. This may be the real lesson of Vietnam. A free people has to believe in what it is doing. Even a foreign policy that is sound may fail if it does not command the belief of an essentially united people. The necessity is all the greater for a policy which, if challenged, may demand great sacrifice. It must be believed with a conviction that justifies that sacrifice.

The significance of law is not that the general citizenry thinks about foreign policy matters in legal terms, for certainly it does not. Its significance is derived from the principles by which the strategy of law is defined. Rules that, conforming to that strategy, apply equally to all according to their terms and successfully reconcile the felt necessities of the time are rules that people can believe in as fair and right. Just as such rules provide the only basis for a peaceful resolution of conflict between nations, so they also provide the basis for national unity in their support.

The process by which the Monroe Doctrine evolved toward law and by which the assertion of U.S. power in foreign affairs came to be shaped as a policy of resisting aggression attests to this. These policies evolved in response to our own ideals as well as in response to the political logic that reinforces the strategy of law between nations.

The broader truth here is not just the self-evident proposition that strong foreign policy action requires basic support by the people. The broader truth is that to command the commitment of the people, to sustain the unity of the people, foreign policy must be grounded in law. An effective foreign policy has to be more than just a policy people support as a prudent calculation. It has to be one they can believe is based on a simple sense of right and justice.

Too often, I am afraid, the realization that the people need to believe in what they are asked to support has resulted in a lack of candor with the public, springing perhaps from the notion that considerations of foreign policy are too sophisticated for public consumption. In an effort to assure public support, policy is sometimes framed in what are not its true colors. Policy based on considerations of the balance of power has been wrapped in the banner of simplistic and improvident anticommunism. A long-considered escalation in Vietnam was presented as if in response to the attack in the Tonkin Gulf. These tactical manipulations of the truth can be dangerous. In the end, as in Vietnam, they can be counterproductive, damaging the public's confidence in the credibility of their government.

More to the point, such manipulations of public opinion midjudge the problem. The public can understand the kind of right on which law is based. The problem is the failure to ground foreign policy explicitly in the people's sense of law. Sustained commitment to the nation's foreign policy does not come from manipulating public understanding or stirring dangerous passions to serve some current end but from making explicit our commitment to law. That is something people can believe in. In our open society it has to be the premise for the national commitment required for an effective foreign policy.

Five
THE ROLE OF EMERGING LAW

The Problem of Change

The appropriate role of law in foreign policy cannot adequately be identified without dealing with the special problem of change in international law. As noted in chapter 1, it is one of the keys to the success of law as a strategy for resolving conflict that it must respond to and implement the felt necessities of the time. Law that does not respond loses touch with reality. Such a static law cannot provide the basis of a realistic and effective foreign policy.

For the conduct of foreign policy the need for law to change and grow is not just a theory. Without this capacity a commitment to law would be a fatal mistake. The problem of change in international law has, indeed, led some to perceive international law as law for the defense of the status quo, as law for the haves against the have-nots, for the developed nations against the developing nations. If a commitment to law would give or even seem to give the foreign policy of the United States such a bias, the commitment would be counterproductive.

If law is to serve our foreign policy interest in promoting a just and stable peace, if it is to enhance the influence and effectiveness of the United States in world affairs, it must implement the three keys on which the strategy of law is based.

The underlying problem of change in international law derives from the lack of any international legislature. Neither the Covenant of the League of Nations nor the Charter of the United Nations provides for any true legislative competence (other than in the organization's internal affairs). Technically, it can be argued that a true legislative competence is provided through amendment of the United Nations Charter under Articles 108 and 109. However, those provisions, requiring ratification by two-thirds of the members of the United Nations including all the permanent members of the Security Council, do not provide practical legislative machinery. Furthermore, it was apparently contemplated by the San Francisco Conference, which prepared the Charter, that any member nation that does not concur in an amendment and "finds itself unable to accept" it, would be free to withdraw from the United Nations.[1] In some circumstances a sort of legislative authority may also be vested in the Security Council of the United Nations. In threats to the peace, breaches of the peace, and acts of aggression, the Security Council has the power under chapter VII of the Charter, if it can muster seven votes and avoid a veto by any of the permanent members, to take binding action, which may accomplish the substantive effect of legislation. That power, however, like the power to amend, was not intended to be and cannot in practice in a divided world be used as a feasible process for substantive legislation.

Although the nations have not been prepared to vest any true legislative power in any international legislature, the necessity of change has been recognized. Article 18 of the Covenant of the League of Nations authorized the Assembly to "advise the reconsideration . . . of treaties which have become inapplicable." Articles 10, 11, and 39 of the Charter of the United Nations provide powers of recommendation to the General Assembly and the Security Council.

International law itself recognizes that, even without any international legislature, law is nevertheless subject to a process of change by which new principles emerge to become law. The Vienna Convention on the Law of Treaties adopted in 1969[2] recognizes that treaties may not only be vitiated by fraud or coercion or (under strict limitations) by a fundamental change in circumstances, but also under Article 64 by the emergence of "a new peremptory norm of general international law" in conflict with the treaty. Although the Convention by its terms applies only to treaties made after it became effective among the parties, the United Nations International Law Commission's commentary on its own corresponding draft articles (Articles 50 and 61) makes clear that the concept of emerging peremptory norms was seen as declaratory of existing law.[3]

The Vienna Convention, even if declaratory of existing law, is significant in that it addressed the problem of change and has firmly laid to rest the notion that the lack of an international legislature must result in a static law. John R. Stevenson, who as legal adviser to the Department of State was deeply involved in the codification of the law on treaties, has commented:

> But the larger significance of the convention, it seems to me, is the fair balance it strikes between the forces of change and stability. By codifying the doctrines of *jus cogens* [peremptory norms] and *rebus sic stantibus* [change of circumstances] it provides a framework for dealing with change. By reasserting the principle of *pacta sunt servanda* [treaties must be kept] and by incorporating impartial procedures for settlement of disputes it provides a safeguard which will go far in helping to maintain the stability of treaty relations.[4]

The possibility of change is now firmly established in international law.

Foreign policy, however, must also be concerned with the process of change. It is the deficiency of this process that makes it necessary for foreign policy to develop a concept of emerging law.

The Concept of Emerging Law

The problem in implementing change in international law is that emerging principles can acquire a cogency and reality that foreign policy must respect long before they become absorbed into international law under currently prevailing views by which binding law is defined. Under current formulations, if actually applied, by the time a new reality is absorbed into international law the old law has, to put it bluntly, already become antediluvian.

The point may be seen in considering the principle of self-determination. As late as 1974 a scholar of international law could write an article on the subject "Has Self-Determination Become A Principle of International Law Today?" and conclude that it had not.[5] Respected scholars have taken differing positions.[6] And yet under General Assembly Resolution 1514 (XV) adopted on December 14, 1960, solemnly declaring the right of all peoples to self-determination and calling for an end to colonialism in all its forms, the colonial era had already been essentially brought to an end within ten years. Even reluctant colonial powers in this relatively short period of time accorded to Resolution 1514 something like the force of law. For purposes of the real world of foreign policy the principle of self-determination has been a principle of law for a long time, whether or not it has even yet become a principle of binding international law.

A nation that proclaimed its commitment to law and denied the principle of self-determination would be loudly and justly accused of hypocrisy or at least of playing some kind of game with words. In the foreign policy context the distinction made by R. A. Falk that "the characterization of a norm as *formally binding* is not very significantly connected with its *functional operation* as law"[7] is fundamental. The United Nations Charter itself called for "respect for the principle of equal rights and self-determination of peoples."[8] Even when the principle remained in that inchoate form, with many unarticulated and unresolved problems, a member of the United Nations committed to law could hardly fail to regard that commitment as including a commitment to give effect to the principle of self-determination and to cooperate in delineating and resolving the issues that arise under it.

The dichotomy between binding law and operational law reflects limitations that have been felt to be necessary on the lawmaking function of the International Court. Article 38 of the Statute of the International Court of Justice declares it is the function of the Court to decide disputes submitted to it "in accordance with international law" and then directs it to apply law from designated sources. The list of sources is similar to the corresponding provisions that governed its predecessor, the Permanent Court of International Justice. Most emerging principles will have to become recognized as law if and when they qualify as such under the category of "international custom, as evidence of a general practice accepted as law." Despite the debate on the subject, it seems to be generally accepted that, since the General Assembly lacks legislative authority generally, its resolutions are not recognizable by their own force as custom. Rather, in the words of the Office of Legal Affairs of the United Nations as to the effect of even a resolution purporting to be adopted as a "declaration":

> However, in view of the greater solemnity and significance of a "declaration," it may be considered to impart, on behalf of the organ adopting it, a strong expectation that Members of the international community will abide by it. Consequently, in so far as the expectation is gradually justified by State practice, a declaration may by custom become recognized as laying down rules binding upon States.[9]

The relationship is as provided in Article 38 of the Statute itself. Law is established by the "general practice" of states and is evidenced as "custom."

The term "general practice" is not defined in the Statute, but the International Court of Justice and its predecessor have taken a position that makes absorption of emerging principles into law very difficult. Even leaving aside a sweeping statement in an early case to which perhaps should not be attributed too much significance,[10] the decisions of the International Court of Justice hold that state practice does not establish law unless the practice is "constant and uniform" nor in any event unless it "is established in such a way that it has become binding on the other Party," basing this conclusion on the language of Article 38 of the Statute of the Court.[11] Clearly, these requirements make it very difficult to demonstrate a general state practice, at least against a challenge to its existence. They put it into the hands of even a few states to block the absorption of emerging principles into law, that is, into law which the International Court believes it is permitted to apply under the terms of its Statute.

This standard is not appropriate in the context of foreign policy to measure or implement a nation's commitment to law. It may or may not be appropriate as a limitation on the lawmaking jurisdiction of the International Court of Justice. Some fairly restrictive standard may be appropriate for that purpose out of concern to preserve the court's acceptability to nations that display varying degrees of commitment to the process of adjudication in international affairs. It may even be an absolutely essential basis for conferring compulsory jurisdiction on the court. For purposes of foreign policy, however, commitment to law has to involve a commitment to law that is not distorted by the standard of Article 38 of the Statute of the court as the court has interpreted it.

Even the Vienna Convention on the Law of Treaties giving effect to the emergence of new peremptory norms binding on nations, permitting "no derogation," provides that they become such only when "accepted and recognized by the international community of States as a whole" (Article 53). The words "as a whole" contemplate something less than unanimity.[12] Such a requirement would make a farce of the concept of peremptory norms that are binding on all nations. But even under the concept of acceptance by the international community of states "as a whole," there may be a dichotomy between emerging principles entitled to be respected by nations committed to law and those that have won the degree of universality of acceptance required for them to be given effect under the Convention.

A commitment to law as an act of foreign policy must include a commitment to what may for convenience be called the principles of the emerging law. The realities of foreign policy require that the concept of emerging law include principles, which, even if not received as binding law, still command the respect of the international community, and which, in Falk's terms, functionally operate as law. The aim of law as foreign policy requires that the concept of emerging law include also those principles that serve to promote a just and stable peace, based on the resolution of conflicts by law. The principles of the emerging law, in short, are those principles commanding international respect, although not yet established as binding law, that are consistent with the charter of the United Nations and are of a character, merit, and acceptability that make them appropriate for recognition as law. (This concept of emerging law is considered further in chapters 6, 13, and 14.)

What are some of these principles? Are they consistent with the realities of power in a divided world? Do they allow for a reasonable recognition of the interests of the United States? Do they provide rules on which a just and stable peace can be based? In the foregoing pages the cogency and necessity of a foreign policy based on law has, I hope, been demonstrated. The case for law still requires an examination of the principles of the emerging law. This is the task of part two.

Part Two

THE PRINCIPLES OF EMERGING LAW

Six

MYTHS AND MUDDLES

Myths about Emerging Principles

Any attempt to examine and evaluate the principles of emerging law as rules by which the conflicts between nations can be resolved in the real world must take account of a widespread skepticism as to whether these principles are seriously intended as rules of behavior at all. This skepticism is reflected in many ways. Some see the emerging principles only as political goals, which have not been thought through as rules and are in fact incapable of generalized application as rules. Some see in them only the aspirations of the Third World or the developing nations not adapted to the realities of power or economics with which the major powers or advanced economies have to live. To some they represent only pretenses for the powerful nations behind which they seek their own aims.

A judgment has to be made in the end, of course, on the terms of the principles themselves as they have developed and are developing. But it is useful to identify some fallacies about the emerging principles which I suspect have provided much of the intellectual underpinnings for the skeptical views so widely held. To say that these are the myths by which the popular skepticism of law is sustained should in no way suggest that these fallacies are the mark of ignorance. Quite to the contrary, they have been held by many well-informed persons and have been seen as evidence of the sophistication of their views. They are, however, I suggest, fallacies, which the developing law should have rendered obsolete.

For many years discussion of the principle of self-determination struggled with the problem of secession. In World War I the concept of self-determination had originaly been applied in situations where the principle allowed the areas of a nation occupied by an ethnic minority to become independent. If the right of self-determination in this manner extends to a people within a nation, however, does it conflict with the right of a nation to its territorial integrity? How can a generalized right of self-determination exist unless a right of secession is recognized? This apparent dilemma had led countless editorial writers, columnists, speech-writers, and even writers on international law, to reject the principle of self-determination as giving rise to anything that a coherent legal system can recognize as a legal right. The possibility for reconciling the principles of self-determination and territorial integrity was, however, always at hand, and in General Assembly Resolution 2625 (XXV), adopted on October 24, 1970, the reconciliation was attempted. Thus the adviser on legal affairs to the United States Mission to the United Nations wrote:

> The Committee also came forthrightly to grips with the application of the principle [of self-determination] to people within an existing independent state. To have failed to deal with this problem would have been to diminish the universality of the principle. The Committee faced these problems and produced a reasonably satisfactory statement. Although paragraph 7 is drafted in a somewhat remote manner in the form of a saving clause, a close examination of its text will reward the reader with an affirmation of the applicability of the principle to peoples within existing states and the necessity for governments to represent the governed.[1]

What Resolution 2625 did was simply to make clear that the right of self-determination does not authorize or encourage the dismemberment of a nation which by respecting the equal rights of all the people of the nation is "thus possessed of a government representing the whole people belonging to the territory without distinction as to race, creed or colour." It never was, after all, necessary to the principle of self-determination that a portion of the integral area of a nation whose inhabitants are accorded full political rights should have a right to secede by international law (this issue is considered further in chapter 8). The point here is simply to note how a resolvable issue, now substantially resolved, has served to create skepticism about the enterprise of the developing law itself. And it continues to do so, as indicated, for example, by the repetition of the old doubts even in a paper delivered in 1974, which concluded that "any attempt to convert self-determination into a legally recognized right amounts to an attempt to legitimize revolution and to absorb it into the existing legal system."[2]

Another kind of fallacy has stalked the principle of nonintervention. This is the notion that a rule of nonintervention could never realistically be a rule of law, because the realities of power require intervention by great powers when vital power relationships are at stake. Even such a noninterventionist as R. A. Falk[3] has argued that "in areas of competitive interaction, there is no political basis for a comprehensive prohibition of intervention in civil-war situations."[4] Basing this point in part on the experience of the Spanish Civil War, Falk commented that "to refuse intervention on one side, out of deference to the earlier ethos [neutrality] was to influence the outcome in a perverse way by clearing the way for intervention on the other side."[5] This comment reveals the fallacy. It is not a rule against intervention that is wrong. Respect for such a rule by both competing power blocs may be the only realistic alternative to escalating conflict. Falk's point should be that if the rule of nonintervention is violated by one side, some appropriate right of counterintervention must be recognized for the other. This is the adjustment to the realities of power that makes a rule of nonintervention viable.[6] Surely there is a fallacy in identifying the rule as the problem, when the point is rather to permit measures to counter its breach. This is much more than a matter of semantics or logic, for by disparaging a rule against intervention the conduct that the rule is aimed to prevent is encouraged. Fortunately, the General Assembly of the United Nations has not fallen prey to this self-fulfilling act of supposed realism (see further discussion in chapter 9).

A third fallacy is also related to the nonintervention issue. It is the idea that a rule of nonintervention cannot be a rule for the real world where peace rests on reciprocal respect by the United States and the U.S.S.R. for what are seen as our respective spheres of influence.[7] The fallacy is demonstrated in our own experience. As has already been shown in chapters 2 and 4, the premise of effective action in this hemisphere has become a principle of nonintervention and of collective action. Our effectiveness does not depend on intervention but on the absence of it. The real world still requires action by the United States for inter-American security, but as further discussed in chapter 10, our action depends on a principle of regional responsibility. Those who disparage the principle of nonintervention and characterize inter-American relations as a United States sphere of influence only encourage the U.S.S.R. to assert over its neighbors an hegemony we disclaim for ourselves.

These myths have tended to distract people for the task of practical judgment. The emerging law deals with practical issues and must be weighed with the same kinds of practical insights one would bring to the examination of legislation on the national level.

The crucial questions are not those involved in the myths that divert us from a realistic evaluation. The crucial tests are whether there is any action the United States and other nations legitimately must be able to take that the emerging principles would prohibit or any asserted right we legitimately must be free to deny that they would require us to respect. For those tests we will need to consider the emerging principles with a sharpened understanding of their practical impacts taken in their entirety.

The myths, however, are not the only hurdles to a realistic appraisal of the emerging law. There are some conceptual problems that tend to muddle thinking about law at the international level. These too need to be sorted out, if the real substantive issues involved in the emerging principles are to be approached with sound sense.

The Mystery of Law without Legislation

We are accustomed in the area of national law to think of changes in law being accomplished by legislation enacted by a legislature. Even though we know the courts also revise or overrule the law that the courts themselves have laid down in prior cases, we tend to think even such judge-made law is made by the nation in the exercise of its sovereignty. It is true, of course, as noted in chapter 5, that there is no international legislature, and it is also true that at the international level there is no sovereign as we conceive sovereignty. Yet there is international law.

This apparent anomaly is one that has given rise to extended philosophical controversy as to the nature of law and even as to whether international law is truly law at all. However, this philosophical controversy is not the problem that is relevant here. Foreign policy has to deal with the realtiy of international law and of what was identified in chapter 5 as emerging law.

The relevant concern arising from the lack of an international legislature is a sense that there are no necessary directions or bounds to law. A legislature reflects the will of the people. What can be behind emerging international law other than the opinion of those who purport to declare it? On what grounds, by what right, do some rules get to be respected as law? There are several answers to these questions.

Those who are familiar with the process by which the common law has grown do not find the concept of international law evolving without a legislature a very strange one. The courts whose decisions in particular cases provide the legislative process by which the common law evolved and continues to change and grow do not act in a vacuum. As Oliver Wendell Holmes observed (in the passage quoted above at p. 5), the principles by which courts act tend to reflect the felt necessities of the times. International law can develop in a similar fashion. Professor H. Lauterpacht, later a judge on the International Court of Justice, outlined (perhaps overoptimistically) the process in these terms:

> In what manner do international tribunals proceed when confronted with novel situations in the course of their judicial activity? There is a variety of ways in which they accomplish their task when confronted with an emergency of this nature:
>
> (a) They may proceed by analogy with specific rules of international law or by recourse to general principles of international law.
>
> (b) They may apply general principles of law, notably of private law.
>
> (c) They bridge the gap by an even more conspicuous recourse to creative judicial activity aiming at solving the controversy by shaping a legal rule through the process of judicial reconciliation of conflicting legal claims entitled to protection by law.
>
> (d) They may accomplish the same task by a consideration of the larger needs of the internatinal community and, in particular, by the necessity of rendering the contractual relations between States effective rather than ineffective.[8]

There does not have to be any fundamental problem in the process of growth of international law reflecting community perceptions without legislation enacted by a legislature.

A second answer is that the process by which emerging law grows contains its own restraints. These restraints arise not simply from a sense of the appropriate limitations of the judicial process that may be exepcted of individuals serving on an adjudicatory tribunal given the right to take account of the emerging law. There are also restraints in the process by which the emerging law itself is generated. A tribunal in acting upon and delineating the principle of self-determination, for example, would, as we shall see, be acting upon a grist of United Nations resolutions which in being adopted succeeded in commanding widespread support. These resolutions may also be supported by implementing action by nations affected. Often community attitudes will be reflected in positions asserted by some states and acquiesced in or contested by others. Richard A. Falk points out that "much international law develops through the assertion by principal governments of unilateral claims in an effective form, supported by a world-order rationale and fully or partly acquiesced in by other governments. The interaction of claims and counterclaims provides the legislative energy within international society."[9] A tribunal applying the emerging law does not invent the law it applies. It sifts and tests and adapts the products of the political and diplomatic process to identify and define law.

Finally, the emerging law is ultimately determined by the strategy of law itself. To qualify as law a rule must provide a basis on which nations disposed to act according to law are prepared to permit disputes in which they are involved to be resolved, a rule that can govern all nations equally according to its terms, that can provide an acceptable reconciliation of conflicting claims and interests. For our purposes law is a strategy for the resolution of conflict, a strategy that demands an objectivity of law. The criteria that define law are the principles that enable that strategy to work.

National Sovereignty

The political sensitivity toward anything seen as encroaching on the nation's sovereignty is all too clear. On any specific issue there may be many considerations that can be advanced for and against the limitation of the power of national action by international law. But there is nothing in the idea of a nation's sovereignty to require it.

There is, indeed, a curious illogic to arguing that the sovereignty of a nation provides *any* reason limiting the scope of international law. If the term sovereignty is intended merely to describe the fact of the nation's power to act, it carries no connotation of right. If, however, the idea of sovereignty is used to argue that it is illegitimate to limit the sovereign right of a nation, it invokes a concept of sovereignty which itself rests on another level of law or right. The law or principle from which sovereignty derives its legitimacy must also define its limitation.

The United States has always held to the view that its sovereignty exists under and is defined by international law. In the Declaration of Independence we declared that as independent states the colonies have power "to levy War, conclude Peace, contract Alliances, establish Commerce, and to do all other Acts and Things which Independent States may of right do." The United States Supreme Court, taking the same view, has held that the "right and power" of the United States in external affairs is based on its sovereignty under "the law of nations."[10]

The idea of any absolute national sovereignty never had any place in U.S. doctrine, and history has now passed beyond any such notion for all nations. The judgment of the International Military Tribunal in Nuremberg in 1946 declared: "He who violates the laws of war cannot obtain immunity while acting in pursuance of the authority of the state if the state in authorizing action moves outside its competence under international law."[11] Any remaining doubt is finally put at rest by the provisions of the Vienna Convention on the Law of Treaties, discussed in chapter 5, recognizing that there are peremptory norms of general international law that are binding on nations and permit of no derogation. No one, I suggest, would seriously contend today that, for example, sovereignty confers on any nation a right to exterminate any ethnic group of its population, whether or not that nation has limited its own sovereignty in this regard by accepting the genocide convention.[12]

There could be no meaningful regime of international law at all if national sovereignty were an absolute. It is rather a concept respected, but defined and limited, by international law. It is a concept to be shaped and reshaped in the changing accommodation of national and international interests.

Part of the sensitivity toward what may be regarded as an encroachment on national sovereignty is expressly protected under the international law doctrine of the "domestic jurisdiction" of a nation. This refers to "matters which, though they may very closely concern the interests of more than one State, are not, in principle, regulated by international law. As regards such matters, each State is sole judge. The question whether a certain matter is or is not solely within the jurisdiction of a State is an essentially relative question; it depends upon the development of international relations."[13]

Any principle of emerging law has to be approached directly in terms of the substantive policy issues involved. Its limitations on the power of the nation to act unilaterally is a very material consideration, which is a part but only a part of the issue. National sovereignty presents no immovable rock around which the growth of law must flow.

The Role of National Security and Vital Interests

It is necessary, finally, to assign national security considerations their appropriate place in the shaping of emerging law. The view that international law is for less important issues and must yield where national security concerns or other vital interests are involved is probably still widely held. It in effect once obtained official sanction in the Hague Conventions of 1899 and 1907. Both conventions called for resort to international commissions of inquiry for factual issues in disputes of an international nature but only for those "involving neither honor nor vital interests."[14] The conventions also called for arbitration of questions "of a legal nature," a term apparently intended to reflect the same limitation.[15] The arbitration treaties inspired by the conventions expressly excluded arbitration of differences affecting "the vital interests, the independence, or the honor" of the parties.[16] Although the specific exclusions were eliminated in the reformulation of matters subject to arbitration as included in the later unratified U.S. arbitration treaties of 1911 and eventually in most arbitration treaties, the notion that law cannot be permitted to control the action a nation takes to protect its vital interests has persisted in various forms.[17]

The problem with this view is not that it overstates the importance of national security concerns, but that it envisages international law as taking less account of such concerns that it clearly must. It is difficult to imagine on what premise law could evolve that would require a nation, in the words of Louis Henkin (see p. 32) "to do that which would lead to its destruction, or jeopardize its independence or security."

The challenge of emerging law is to provide a rule of law that takes due account of the realities of power. It must, indeed, provide, within a legal framework, for those policies and actions essential to national security. As will be seen in chapters 8 through 12, security concerns play an important part in the shaping of the principles of emerging law.

The notion that national security is to be protected by reserving certain grounds upon which actions do not have to conform to law is the very reverse of law. Rules of law that nations accept only when they do not really matter are a mockery of law. They deny the heart of law, for such rules apply neither equally to all nations nor to all cases to which by their terms they would be applicable. That is not the strategy of law by which man has learned to resolve conflict. It is, rather, the strategy of big power hypocrisy. It is a route that leads neither to peace nor to justice.

Seven

FILLING OUT THE LAW OF THE CHARTER

The Special Place of Resolution 2625

Any attempt to understand the emerging law must take account of the special significance of General Assembly Resolution 2625 (XXV) adopted October 24, 1970, approving a text entitled "Declaration on Principles of International Law Concerning Friendly Relations and Co-operation Among States in Accordance With the Charter of the United Nations." The full text of the resolution is set forth in appendix 1. Even though it must be recognized that under the Charter the General Assembly is given neither authority to enact law governing relations between nations nor any authority to enact even binding interpretations of the Charter itself, a very high order of authoritativeness attaches to the 1970 Declaration on Principles of International Law. Any notion that General Assembly resolutions may be looked upon as only political declarations made for political purposes would be completely irresponsible if applied to Resolution 2625. Like any legislation, in its development and adoption it was subjected to the conflicts and compromises of the political process. The result in this instance probably adds to the authority of the final declaration.

The authoritativeness of the Declaration on Principles of International Law results from four factors. First, the principles it attempts to define are stated in or were believed to derive from the terms of the Charter of the United Nations. The principles, therefore, were already binding on the members of the United Nations. This does not automatically make their elaboration in the 1970 Declaration binding. But the Declaration purports to be an elaboration of what is already binding, and if the elaboration in the Declaration represents a correct interpretation or implementation, that elaboration is something to which the member nations are bound by their previous adherence to the Charter itself.

Second, the 1970 Declaration was developed and adopted on the basis of consensus. The primary task was assigned to a Special Committee, which agreed at the outset to work on the basis of consensus. This process forced the Committee to seek agreement that went beyond any majority political purposes and to produce a text that all nations could accept on every point. In some instances the committee had to settle for generality, but on the whole it proceeded successfully on the basis that the text had to resolve differences if the Declaration was the serve any purpose. The Declaration was endorsed unanimously by the Sixth Committee (Legal Questions) of the General Assembly, Ecuador indicating that in the event of a vote it would abstain, and it was adopted without vote by the General Assembly itself. In the process of reaching consensus many nations, including the United States, altered positions taken at an early stage, as formulations were refined to accommodate points pressed in argument.

Third, the Declaration was developed to provide a statement, not of policy or goals but of law. This is reflected in the title and in section 3, which provides that "the principles of the Charter which are embodied in the Declaration constitute basic principles of international law." More concretely, the intention that the elaboration of the Charter principles should be declaratory of binding law is demonstrated in the wording of the individual paragraphs. With only one exception, the paragraphs were phrased in terms used to state legally operative provisions, declaring existing right or duty or using a mandatory "shall." The use of a contrasting "should" in paragraph D3 to state what was only desirable reinforces the intent to state binding legal rules in other paragraphs.[1]

Fourth, in formulating the 1970 Declaration prior resolutions dealing with the same matters were reviewed. An effort was made to include in the Declaration everything that belonged there to the extent that consensus could be achieved in the formulation. Thus, paragraphs from prior resolutions that appear in the Declaration can be viewed as having survived a process of reexamination and reevaluation as law. Where they appear in somewht modified or more precise terms the Declaration can be viewed as the authoritative text.

The statements made by various governments in the Special Committee and in the General Assembly's Sixth Committee indicate that several governments regard the resulting Declaration as binding international law, qualifying as such under Article 38 of the Statute of the International Court of Justice. This is not on the theory that the General Assembly has any authority to legislate or to enact binding interpretations of the Charter, but on the theory that the unanimity of acceptance gives it authority as law, either as "general principles of law recognized by civilized nations" under Article 38 (1) c or as a binding agreement on the interpretation or applicatin of a convention, the United Nations Charter, made between the parties to the Convention (see Article 31 of the Vienna Convention on the Law of Treaties).

It is not necessary for the purposes of this study to resolve the issue. The significance of the 1970 Declaration here is as an authoritative statement of rules that the United States and other United Nations members have accepted, so far as they go, as a correct implementation of the principles of the Charter and by which they declare themselves to be bound.

To view the Declaration in a realistic perspective, however, some problems with the argument that the Declaration has become a part of international law fully recognizable by the International Court should be mentioned. There is some equivocation in the Declaration itself. Paragraphs A13, B6, and C5 preserve the priority of the Charter in the event of conflict with the provisions of those parts of the Declaration, and section 2 provides generally that "nothing in this Declaration shall be construed as prejudicing in any manner the provisions of the Charter or the rights and duties of Member States under the Charter or the rights of peoples under the Charter taking into account the elaboration of these rights in this Declaration." Furthermore, a reading of the statements made by governments in the Special Committee and the Sixth Committee makes clear that significant points of disagreement between the member nations remain. One would have to be very careful to be sure that the disagreements relate only to matters left open expressly or by deliberate generality and do not constitute disagreements as to the effect of the operative language itself before giving full effect to the Declaration as law on the basis of the unanimity accorded the Declaration.

It is important to recognize the limitations of the 1970 Declaration. Nevertheless, on many previously contested issues it provides an authoritative text for the implementation of the law of the Charter, which all the members of the United Nations have accepted and committed themselves to respect.

The Seven Charter Principles of Law

The extent to which the 1970 Declaration provides a viable basis for resolution of conflict situations can be briefly indicated, reserving for further consideration in subsequent chapters issues that bear most significantly on considerations of balance of power and national security.

Section 1 of the 1970 Declaration identifies seven principles of law stated in or derived from the Charter and elaborates a number of points under each. An extended preamble contains provisions that bear on the construction of the principles. (See especially the Preamble, paragraphs 7, 9, 13, 14, and 15.) The seven principles complement one another. Thus the corollary of the prohibition of the use of force is the duty to settle disputes by peaceful means. The corollary of equal rights and self-determination of peoples is the duty not to intervene. The corollary of sovereign equality of states is the duty to cooperate as members of the international community.

In very practical terms, the principles and their elaborating paragraphs are integral parts of one bargain. The premise for the abstention from the use of force is that the rights that provide an acceptable basis for life as members of an international community are respected.

This is reflected in the Declaration itself. Section 2 declares that "in their interpretation and application the above principles are interrelated and each principle should be construed in the context of the other principles." It is not surprising to find that there is considerable overlapping of points under the different principles. Thus, for example, the use of force to deprive a people of its right of self-determination is prohibited in paragraph A7 as well as in paragraphs C3 and E5.

The seven principles derived from the Charter are the following:

1. That States shall refrain in their international relations from the threat or use of force against the territorial integrity of any State, or in any other manner inconsistent with the purposes of the United Nations. (See Charter Article 2 [4].)

2. That States shall settle their international disputes by peaceful means in such a manner that international peace and security and justice are not endangered. (See Charter Article 2 [3].)

3. The duty not to intervene in matters within the domestic jurisdiction of any State, in accordance with the Charter. (See Charter Article 2 [7] applying to intervention by the United Nations itself.)

4. The duty of States to cooperate with one another in accordance with the Charter. (See Charter Articles 1 [3], 13 and 56.)

5. Equal rights and self-determination of peoples. (See Charter, Articles 1 [2] and 55.)

6. Sovereign equality of States. (See Charter Article 2 [1].)

7. That States shall fulfill in good faith the obligations assumed by them in accordance with the Charter. (See Charter Article 2 [2].)

Some of these principles are discussed in detail in later chapters, and this is not the place to try to define them or consider their implications and qualifications. What is important here is to recognize that the implementing paragraphs of the Declaration apply the general principles to most of the controverted issues of the postwar years. Thus, the implementing paragraphs contain, in part, the following provisions:

—The threat or use of force in violation of principle A constitutes a violation of international law (A1).

—The prohibition applies to the threat or use of force "to violate international lines of demarcation, such as armistice lines, established by or pursuant to an international agreement to which [the offending state] is a party or which it is otherwise bound to respect" (A5).

—The prohibition bars acts of reprisal involving the use of force (A6).

—It bars "organizing or encouraging the organization of irregular forces or armed bands, including mercenaries, for incursion into the territory of another State," as well as "organizing, instigating, assisting or participating in acts of civil strife or terrorist acts in another State or acquiescing in organized activities in its territory directed towards the commission of such acts, when the acts referred to . . . involve a threat or use of force" (A8, A9, see also C2).

—"No territorial acquisition resulting from the threat or use of force shall be recognized as legal" (A10).

—The principle of nonintervention is identified as a principle of law and bars "the right to intervene, directly or indirectly, for any reason whatever, in the internal or external affairs of any other State" (C1).

—The rule of nonintervention bars any type of measures "to coerce another State in order to obtain from it the subordination of the exercise of its sovereign rights and to secure from it advantages of any kind" (C2, see also Preamble 9).

—Under it no State shall "organize, assist, foment, finance, incite or tolerate subversive, terrorist or armed activities directed toward the violent overthrow of the regime of another State, or interfere in civil strife in another State" (C2).

—The duty to cooperate is identified as a legal duty (D1; see further in relation to access to resources in chapter 11 below).

—The right of self-determination applies to all "peoples" (E1).

—It may be satisfied by independence, free association, or integration with an independent State or "the emergence into any other political status freely determined by a people" (E4).

—"Forcible action" to deprive a people of their right to self-determination and freedom and independence is prohibited (A7, C3, E5).

—In resistance to "such forcible action" peoples are entitled to seek and to receive "support in accordance with the purposes and principles of the Charter of the United Nations" (E5).

—The right of self-determination is satisfied where a State observes human rights and fundamental freedoms in accordance with the Charter and is "thus possessed of a government representing the whole people belonging to the territory without distinction as to race, creed or colour" (E7).

—"Every State shall refrain from any action aimed at the partial or total disruption of the national unity and territorial integrity of any other State or country" (E8, see also Preamble 15).

—The obligation to fulfill obligations in good faith extends to "its obligations under the generally recognized principles and rules of international law" (G2).

The principal issue unresolved in the Declaration concerned the scope allowed for the lawful use of force under Article 2 (4) of the Charter, prohibiting the threat or use of force against the territorial integrity or political independence of any state "or in any other manner inconsistent with the Purposes of the United Nations." The provision plainly implies that the use of force that is not against the territorial integrity or political independence of any state is lawful if consistent with the purposes of the United Nations.[2] But, obviously, a test of lawfulness as broad as consistency with the purposes of the United Nations presents the danger of great abuse. Some cases are generally accepted, such as exercise of "the inherent right of individual and collective self-defense if an armed attack occurs," specifically provided for in Article 51. In 1970 the member nations were unable to come to agreement on cases in which use of force might be lawful under Article

2 (4). The Declaration therefore in paragraph A13 merely reserved the issue, stating that "nothing in the foregoing paragraphs shall be construed as enlarging or diminishing in any way the scope of the provisions of the Charter concerning cases in which the use of force is lawful." The issue is also reserved in paragraph C5.

In paragraph E5 the issue was reserved in a context that was expecially significant because of its broader implications. That paragraph allows peoples resisting forcible action that deprives them of their right of self-determination to seek and receive "support in accordance with the purposes and principles of the Charter of the United Nations." The statements of governments before the Special Committee and the Sixth Committee in some cases asserted and in some cases denied the right to assist by military means peoples resisting forcible action that deprived them of their right to self-determination. The anticolonialist claim of a right to seek and receive suitable force to resist a violation of a right of self-determination accomplished by force was denied by the United States[3] and other Western nations. The U.S. position seems both shortsighted and wrong on principle. Depriving a people of its right of self-determination by "forcible action" is itself a violation of paragraph E5. The elements necessary to establish the right of self-determination are considered in the next chapter, but assuming there is in truth a violation by forcible action, which is the only case to which the second sentence of paragraph E5 applies, to deny that it may be met with force denies what must be fundamental. If the principles of the Charter and the Declaration are to have any force, the legality of resisting their violation by commensurate and necessary means must be recognized. It is the principle upon which a right of counterintervention must rest, a right which, as argued in chapter 9, is an essential premise for a full commitment to law.

However this may be, Rosenstock seems historically correct in his summary:

> The final paragraph [A13] is a general formulation which avoids the existing disagreements among the Member states. The text thus accommodates those who support and those who oppose the residual peacekeeping role of the General Assembly in cases in which the Security Council is unable to act, those who regard regional organizations as able to authorize the use of force under certain circumstances and those who do not, those who subscribe to the notion of an inherent right of self-defense against colonialism and those who do not, those who read Article 51 restrictively and place their emphasis on the phrase "if an

> armed attack occurs," and those who do not. It cannot be gainsaid that the generality of this paragraph diminishes the utility of the text as a whole, since it leaves unanswered so many important questions relating to the use of force.[4]

Despite this serious deficiency, the 1970 Declaration resolved a number of very controversial issues concerning the application of the Charter principles and provides a framework within which those principles can be given effect.

The Definition of Aggression: Resolution 3314

The achievement of the General Assembly in 1974 in finally developing and adopting a consensus definition of aggression in Resolution 3314 (XXIX)[5] (see full text in appendix 2) must also be seen as part of the process of filling out the law of the Charter. However, the relevance of the definition of aggression to the argument of this book is indirect.

Although the term "aggression" is used in Articles 1(1) and 39 of the Charter, the concept of aggression is not the heart of the Charter scheme for regulating relations between nations. Preamble paragraph 5 of the Definition of Aggression makes clear that the concept of aggression does not define the limitations on the lawful use of force. Aggression is only "the most serious and dangerous form of the illegal use of force." Aggression may be a basis of Security Council jurisdiction under Article 39, but it is not the only basis or even the most likely to be invoked. The consequence that an act is not only illegal but of that kind of illegality that constitutes aggression is stated in Article 5(2) of the Definition providing that "aggression gives rise to international responsibility" and that "a war of aggression is a crime against international peace." (See also paragraph A2 of the 1970 Declaration.)

Our concern is different. It is how law purports to limit the conduct of the United States and other nations, or, in other words, what a commitment to law entails. Some of the criticism of the definition of aggression adopted in Resolution 3314 seems to assume that the concept of aggression measures the lawful use of force and that what is not aggression is therefore permitted. We have already seen that this is not the case as appears from the terms of Resolution 3314 itself. A commitment to law is measured by the limits on the lawful use of force, not by the limits according to which that egregious kind of breach called aggression is defined.

There are, however, four respects in which the definition of aggression bears indirectly on our concerns. First, under Article 1 of the

Definition, it is only the use of armed force in a manner "inconsistent with the Charter of the United Nations" that is aggression, and under Article 2 it is only the first use of armed force "in contravention of the Charter" that constitutes prima facie evidence of an act of aggression. In line with these provisions, allowance is expressly made in Article 6 for the lawful use of force.

Second, among the enumerated acts held to qualify as aggression in Article 3 are "the sending by or on behalf of a State of armed bands, groups, irregulars or mercenaries, which carry out acts of armed force against another State of such gravity as to amount to the acts listed above, or its substantial involvement therein" (Article 3[g]) and "the action of a State in allowing its territory, which it has placed at the disposal of another State, to be used by that other state for perpetrating an act of aggression against a third State" (Article 3[f]). Since aggression, in the words of the preamble, is "the most serious and dangerous form of the illegal use of force," any of these acts can presumably qualify as an "armed attack" under Article 51 of the Charter. While "armed attack" may be broader than "aggression," at least any aggression ought to qualify as an armed attack. This provision does therefore bear on the permissible use of force, for in the event of an "armed attack" Article 51 specifically provides that the inherent right of individual and collective self-defense is applicable.

Third, Article 7 makes provision in the case of a people "forcibly deprived" of its right of self-determination parallel to the provision in paragraph E5 of the 1970 Declaration, which was discussed in the preceding section of this chapter.

Fourth, Article 5(3) provides that "no territorial acquisition or special advantage resulting from aggression is or shall be recognized as lawful," paralleling the provisions in paragraph A10 of the 1970 Declaration.

Thus the definition of aggression in Resolution 3314, although dealing with an issue that is not directly relevant to the argument of this book, does reinforce and confirm the 1970 Declaration in several respects. A commitment to resolve disputes according to the principles of emerging law is a commitment to a regime of law whose framework has been established and in which, despite its deficiencies, many of the controversial issues of the postwar era as to what principles the law of the Charter requires have now been resolved.

Eight
SELF-DETERMINATION

If there is any principle that surely is a part of emerging law, it is the right of self-determination. The Charter of the United Nations in Articles 1(2) and 55 calls for respect for "the principle of equal rights and self-determination of peoples." The United Nations, under its Declaration on the granting of independence to colonial countries and peoples (General Assembly Res. 1514 [XV] adopted in 1960), has transformed the political geography of the world. And in its 1970 Declaration on Principles of International Law (G.A. Res. 2625 [XXV]) the principle is declared to be a basic principle of international law.

One might suppose that this principle could be comfortably embraced as law in the foreign policy of the United States, for there is no principle to which the United States is by its own history more committed. There is indeed no principle that has had a greater influence on our foreign policy throughout our history. Yet this history, even our own genuine belief in the principle, has not prevented some disquieting concerns as to where the principle may take us.

If the principle of self-determination is a legal right that governs in all cases, do we simply encourage division and fragmentation without limit? Do we risk creating a Balkanized world? Is the principle consistent with some check on those who may act irresponsibly in support of their own interested claims of right? What is to prevent controversies over self-determination from escalating into dangerous conflict? Can the principle be reconciled with the needs of stability? Can a structure of base arrangements necessary for a balance of power be maintained in the face of the lure of self-determination?

To approach these questions requires a closer look at the principle of self-determination. The concept is not as simple as its appeal to sense and our ideals would suggest. Nor, in spite of the important hurdles overcome in the development of the 1970 Declaration, have all the issues been resolved. This is not the place for a treatise on the right of self-determination, but we must address those concerns against which the adequacy and prudence of a commitment to law as the core of U.S. foreign policy is to be judged. Not the least of these concerns must be any implication of a right of secession from the United States itself.

The Problem of Secession

Full acceptance of a right of self-determination has long been impeded by a nagging concern that such a right would imply a right of secession by any part of a nation that wished to secede. Such a right has, of course, never been acknowledged. The concern is not that such a right is contemplated but that a satisfactory distinction between a right of self-determination and a right of secession can be maintained. And this concern has given rise to doubts that the principle of self-determination is indeed a principle that can be accepted in international law. As noted in chapter 6, the notion that a right of self-determination may imply a right of secession for any self-defined group is one of the fallacies that has created skepticism about the seriousness of international law as a scheme to govern the conduct of nations.

The problem, however, was only to delineate a valid basis of a universally recognized distinction. Even in the Charter of the United Nations the distinction was implicit. The Charter, which affirmed the principle of self-determination, also recognized the legitimacy of the "territorial integrity" of nations (Article 2[4]).

When the proposal was made at the San Francisco conference at which the Charter was drafted to include a clause calling for respect for the principle of equal rights and self-determination, the committee considering the proposal noted that it "conformed to the purposes of the Charter only insofar as it implied the right of self-government of peoples and not the right of secession."[1] In 1960 when the General Assembly adopted its landmark Resolution 1514, under which the dismantling of the colonial era has proceeded, it included in paragraph 6 of the resolution provision that "any attempt aimed at the partial or total disruption of the national unity and the territorial integrity of a country is incompatible with the purposes and principles of the Charter of the United Nations."

Rejection of the notion that a right of self-determination includes a right of secession is not confined to the older nations. It has been a cardinal principle of the Organization of African Unity, which supported the position of the Nigerian federal government against the Biafran rebels. In relation to that controversy, U.N. Secretary General U Thant stated on January 4, 1970: "So, as far as the question of secession of a particular section of a Member State is concerned, the United Nations' attitude is unequivocable. As an international organization, the United Nations has never accepted and does not accept and I do not believe it will ever accept the principle of secession of a part of its Member State."[2]

In its 1970 Declaration on Principles of International Law the General Assembly attempted to resolve any apparent conflict between a right of self-determination and the right of nations to their territorial integrity. What was attempted was not the formulation of a new limitation on the principle of self-determination. The exclusion of a right of secession had always been recognized. What the 1970 Declaration did was to define and to limit that exclusion. The attempt was to formulate the distinction between a right of self-determination and a right of secession in terms that appropriately reflected the proper grounds of the distinction.

The formulation in the form of a saving clause is awkward, but the gist is clear enough. In paragraph E7 the 1970 Declaration provides:

> Nothing in the foregoing paragraphs shall be construed as authorizing or encouraging any action which would dismember or impair, totally or in part, the territorial integrity and independent status of states conducting themselves in accordance with the principle of equal rights and self-determination of peoples as described above and thus possessed of a government representing the whole people belonging to the territory without distinction as to race, creed or colour.

Clearly, the language contemplates that in some circumstances a part of an existing state may have a right by international law of self-determination under the principle stated in other paragraphs elaborating the principle of equal rights and self-determination. This possibility dictates a closer examination of the substantive effect of paragraph E7.

The first point to be made is that under the terms of the 1970 Declaration the right of self-determination is a right to which a "people" is entitled. It is a right to determine "political status," which may include "establishment of a sovereign and independent State, the free association or integration with an independent State, or the emergence into any other political status freely determined," but this right belongs only to "a people" (pars. E1, 4). The term "people" is not defined in the 1970 Declaration. It is derived from the U.N. Charter itself.[3]

The second point to be made is that where some part of a nation would otherwise qualify as a people having a separate right of self-determination, the exercise of that right by an act of secession is not excluded merely by their integration into the area of the nation itself instead of being held as a colony or other nonself-governing territory. Thus Switzerland, though composed of somewhat separate linguistic communities, is one people; Portugal, however, was not permitted to frustrate rights of self-determination of its territories around the world by the subterfuge of designating them as parts of metropolitan Portugal. In essence, a nation that governs itself as one people is one people. In such a nation, although there may be many cultural, linguistic, or racial communities, although parts may be geographically separated from other parts, none of these components can qualify as a separate people possessing a right of self-determination entitling it to secede.

The 1970 Declaration attempts to limit the conclusiveness of the fact that an area is organized as part of the integral area of a nation. This is accomplished in two paragraphs. Paragraph E6 deals with the case, like that of Portugal, where a nation attempts to block a separate right of self-determination by incorporating a previously nonself-governing territory into the nation without the consent of the people of the territory. Paragraph E7 deals with the harder case where the single state structure does not arise by such a subterfuge. In effect, it attempts to protect the integrity of a nation that governs itself as one people without foreclosing a right of separate self-determination in situations where that is not the fact.

Thus, under paragraph E7, no right of separate self-determination for a part of a nation can exist if (a) the nation conducts itself "in compliance with the principle of equal rights and self-determination of peoples as described above," which principle includes "respect for and observance of human rights and fundamental freedoms in accordance with the Charter," and (b) the nation is "thus possessed of a government representing the whole people belonging to the territory without distinction as to race, creed or colour." This seems to be a correct rule and should be acceptable on principle, even though determinations as to (a) or (b) leave a lot to be desired in the way of precision. Even if the conditions are not met, there is still the question, as pointed out above, whether the part of the state claiming a right to act qualifies as a people.

The third point to be made about the rule of the 1970 Declaration is that there may be a right of secession by international law, even if one does not exist under paragraph E7. The 1970 Declaration has to be read as a whole. One of its principles frequently stated is that forcible action that deprives peoples of their rights to self-determination is illegal, and that no territorial acquistion resulting from the threat or use of force shall be recognized as legal. Presumably, a past unlawful annexation may have ceased to be voidable under international law by reason of acquiescence,[4] but if the annexation continues to be voidable, the annexed people have in substance a legal right to secede.[5] Certainly, the clearest case of all must be that a nation cannot extinguish another people's right of self-determination by annexation accomplished through its own unlawful forcible action.

Finally, the 1970 Declaration does nothing to impair a right of secession, if such a right exists under national law. It only denies it, if and when it does deny it, as an exercise of a right of self-determination under international law.

What concerns, if any, does the right of self-determination as formulated present to the principle confirmed by the blood of our nation in the Civil War that no part of the United States has a right to secede? The right of self-determination is always a right against some nation, and rightly or wrongly it can be claimed against the United States. For it is a right under international law. It is a right no nation can be conceded the conclusive power to grant or deny by its own fiat. It is an international right or it is nothing. It is not and cannot be designed to avoid embarrassment to all nations. If it could not provide embarrassment to the U.S.S.R. in relation to its annexation of Latvia, Lithuania, and Estonia, that itself would be a reproach to the doctrine.

The 1970 Declaration would not give to any part of the United States a right of secession by its own choosing. The formulation allows for secession not by choice but by justification. The right exists where the nation against which a right of self-detrmination is asserted has forfeited the premises upon which the exclusion of any separate right of self-determination is based.[6] It is no accident that the secession formulation in the 1970 Declaration reflects the principles upon which our unity as a nation is based.

The specter of secession under the 1970 Declaration should not be exaggerated even where it would be allowed. Secession by a part of the integral area of a nation is probably in realistic terms the least likely remedy even where the conditions to exclude it under paragraph E7 are not met. The more realistic result of the formulation is likely to be pressure to assure that the conditions are met, that is, that the would-be separatists are accorded the full political rights accorded other citizens and that human rights and fundamental freedoms are respected in accordance with the Charter.

The circumstances in which under the 1970 Declaration the right of self-determination may give rise to a right of secession cannot in realistic terms be seen as a threat to the territorial integrity of the United States. It is true that as a principle of international law, the principle of self-determination, and specifically the formulation of the secession distinction in the 1970 Declaration, may subject the dealings of the United States with its citizens to international scrutiny. This is a necessary consequence of any secession formulation that reflects the principles we believe in. The 1970 Declaration supports the foreign policy position we have long maintained. It is consistent with our ideals and our interests.

It is actually the nations that deny freedoms to their citizens that have reason to be concerned about the secession formulation in the 1970 Declaration. That formulation provides a principle that protects the unity of free nations. Dictatorships, to be sure, may insulate themselves from the impact of the 1970 Declaration, as with other threatening developments, by taking the law into their own hands. But the 1970 formulation bears, wherever its weight is felt, on the side of free institutions. Although it may result in our being scrutinized at some point, it actually supports our own principles. It provides a sastisfactory basis for our traditional support of a right of self-detrmination and for full acceptance of that right under international law.

The Necessity of International Process

Concern that the right of self-determination may give a free rein to the forces of fragmentation in the world misconceives the logic of the principle and the directions to which its development seems to point. Its role in inspiring and supporting peoples asserting their right of national independence is apparent to everyone. But its potential role in providing order to the forces at work also needs to be understood. It is a principle not of anarchy but of legitimacy.

To some extent this side of the operation of the principle has been obscured by the attention focused on the process of decolonization. Even the 1970 Declaration does little to spell out how the principle of self-determination is to be implemented in noncolonial situations. This no doubt reflects the fact that the efforts of the General Assembly have largely concentrated on ending colonialism. But most colonial situations, although difficult and troublesome, are conceptually relatively simple. The conceptual issues inherent in the implementation of the principle of self-determination rarely come into sharp focus in colonial situations.

The threshold question in any issue of self-determination is necessarily to determine the "people" to which the right belongs. In colonial situations, this rarely presents enough of a problem to be seen as a preliminary question. The inhabitants of the colonial territory have generally been ethnically different from the inhabitants of the controlling power and are geographically completely separated from it. There is no question of the colonial inhabitants and the citizens of the controlling power being considered as one people or of being divided on any territorial basis other than the natural geographical separation of the dependent terrritory itself. A right of self-determination belongs to the people of the territory. It is their wishes that are to be determined and given effect.

Questions of self-determination have often first arisen in determining whether a particular territory is a nonself-governing territory under Article 73 of the Charter, which imposes obligations on the administering power. By Res. 1541 (XV) of December 15, 1960 the General Assembly adopted a set of principles for determining the application of Article 73, which included as one principle that "*prima facie* there is an obligation to transmit information in respect of a territory which is geographically separate and is distinct ethnically and/or culturally from the country administering it." The principles provide that the prima facie determination is further supported if other elements "affect the relationship between the metropolitan State and the territory concerned in a manner which arbitrarily places the latter in a position or status of subordination." In effect, the determination that the inhabitants of the territory were a "people" possessed of a right of self-determination was thus made indirectly at an early stage and in a different context, that is, in determining whether the territory was a nonself-governing territory to which Article 73 was applicable.

Implementation of the principle of self-determination in noncolonial situations and even in a few colonial situations requires a more explicit approach to the issues inherent in the principle of self-determination. Professor H. S. Johnson put the matter succinctly in 1967:

> There is no mystery that before a unit can be self-determining it must be distinguishable from other units. A right of self-determination means that some "self" is henceforth to determine its own destiny, but until that "self" is identified there can be no right.[7]

Julius Stone makes the point with an appropriate warning:

> If, indeed, the references to "self-determination" in the Charter and in the General Assembly declaration [definition of aggression] have some legal (as distinguished from political) principle, the legal critieria for identifying a "people" having this entitlement—the "self" entitled to "determine" itself—remain at best speculative. Those who do not recognize this as a problem will do well to recall the continuing stream of violence arising from it, of which the conflict in Katanga, Biafra, Cyprus, Angola, Lebanon, Bougainville and Zaire are contemporary warnings.[8]

Except in situations where identification of a people possessed of a right of self-determination is beyond dispute, that identification presents a question to be determined before a right of self-determination can legitimately be recognized as belonging to any group.

A group does not necessarily constitute a "people" by its own definition. The issue is not the kind of issue that the group claiming the right can be recognized as being entitled to make conclusively for itself, because the rights of others are also involved. The issue is not one of implementing an established right, but of determining whether the claimed right exists.

There are, in fact, several interrelated determinations that may be preliminary to a legitimate exercise of a right of self-determination. These include:

1. A determination whether the group asserting a right of self-determination qualifies as a people.

2. A determination of the territorial unit or units by which the choice is to be made.

3. A determination of the procedure (by plebiscite or otherwise, voting eligibility and administration, alternatives to be voted on, etc.)

and of the conditions necessary to assure that the choice is freely determined by the people.

4. Any special rights (e.g., equality of language) to be assured to the minority. A minority must in any event have a right to remain and enjoy full rights. See Universal Declaration of Human Rights, especially Arts. 13 and 15, adopted by G.A. Res. 217 (III) Dec. 10, 1948.

These issues are inherent in any claim of a right to self-determination, even one that is simple and in which the answers are not in dispute. When they are not simple and the answers are in dispute, the issues are preliminary to the recognition of the right and of its exercise. When there is a dispute, they can be legitimately determined only by some form of international process.

Consideration of the nature of the issues demonstrates the necessity of an international process. For the principle of self-determination does not itself provide the answers. It defines the issues, but implementation involves matters of policy judgment. If a population within an area is closely divided in its choice, is it appropriate to find that the population constitutes a people, where the result may be to give fifty-one percent of the population in question the right to decide the issue for all? In an area of mixed populations how far should maximization of choice be compromised to avoid creating politically or economically nonviable entities (e.g., the creation of a state composed of a gerrymandered area made up of noncontiguous parts)? How far should the determination of a "people" be influenced by a policy of seeking units large enough to be viable?[9]

In cases of mixed populations, where independence for each is not viable, the protection of minority rights may present a special problem. In the Aaland Islands controversy the League of Nations Council in 1921 affirmed Finland's sovereignty only on the basis of a regime assuring the Swedish population (actually a majority) protection of its cultural identity.[10] In the still vexed case of Cyprus, where the Greek majority sought union of Cyprus with Greece, the negotiated solution in the 1960 Zurich-London Accords was based on an independent Cyprus, under arrangements that prohibited either union with any other state or partition, and provided for a government in which participation by Greek and Turkish elements in fixed proportions and with fixed powers was frozen against change and under which the settlement was guaranteed by Greece, Turkey, and the United Kingdom.[11]

Here a distinction should be noted, which becomes important in the argument in part three. Cyprus presented the dilemma that if the people of Cyprus as a whole, Greeks and Turks together, were identified as one people entitled to self-determination, the Turkish Cypriots would themselves be deprived of self-determination. If Greek and Turkish Cypriots were recognized as separate peoples, no viable units could be determined, and indeed partition itself would probably not be viable. The United Nations General Assembly recognized the special problems and refrained from directing any solution, merely urging the parties to negotiate.[12]

The case of Cyprus points to a limitation inherent in the application of any international process to resolve issues of self-determination. The international process required for the determination of the preliminary issues is in substance a process of adjudication. Although policy issues are involved, they are policy issues whose answers will be shaped by the policies underlying the principle of self-determination. The first three issues—whether the group qualifies as a people, the units by which choice is to be made, and the procedure for exercise of choice—present the kinds of problems the National Labor Relations Board and the courts have had to deal with under the National Labor Relations Act. They are not beyond the capacity of an adjudicative process. But the fourth issue, assurance of minority rights, may present special problems. Some principles for the protection of minorities can certainly be determined within the limits of an adjudicative process. But the case of Cyprus suggests that in some situations an adjudicatory process may have to stop short of dictating solutions. An adjudicatory process can determine the necessity of a special regime to protect all parties. It may even lay down principles by which it is to be tested. But it can only direct the parties to negotiate in good faith to work out the implementing terms and provisions. This, indeed, was the course taken in the vote of the Council of the League of Nations in the Aaland Islands controversy in 1921.[13]

The principle of self-determination clearly does not provide a right which automatically attaches to whoever claims it. Without implementation through some international process it would, indeed, become a prescription for violence and chaos.

The U.N. General Assembly has not explicitly declared the necessity of an international process to resolve issues preliminary to recognizing or implementing a right of self-determination, but it has recognized the necessity of an international process by assuming to act itself. The General Assembly in countless resolutions (see appendix 3), and its Special Committee concerning implementation of Res. 1514 as well, have involved themselves in decisions that are in substance the issues identified above, affirming the right in a particular people, and deciding upon units and voting procedures in certain cases.[14]

One of the most perplexing problems (one that again points out the necessity of an international process) is the extent to which identification of a "people" entitled to a right of self-determination is to be dictated by past history rather than determined by the considerations that would apply if the decision were not circumscribed by past events. The discussion of the issues of self-determination in Vietnam in chapter 4 recalled the controversy as to the effect of the 1954 Geneva Accords. Had the implementation of the principle of self-determination in Vietnam been addressed on principle in some international process, the issues concerning the Geneva Accords would clearly have had to be addressed. The same is true of many of the other trouble spots of the world, including application of the principle of self-determination to Taiwan, or the two Germanys,[15] or the West Bank of the Jordan River. One can, indeed, consider the secession case discussed in the first section of this chapter as a case where the historic unification of a people overrides possible separatist choices that might currently be preferred.

U.N. practice illustrates the potential controlling effect of history. The United Nations has rejected the choice of the current inhabitants of Gibraltar, determining instead on reunification of Gibraltar with Spain under arrangements to be negotiated between the United Kingdom and Spain. The General Assembly has based this decision on the principle that "any colonial situation which partially or completely destroys the national unity and territorial integrity of a country is incompatible" with the Charter and paragraph 6 of Res. 1514.[16] In effect, this looks back to a territorial integrity that antedates the British occupation of Gibraltar and subsequent treaties affirming the British holding. M. S. Esfandiary, reporter for the Special Committee, further explains:

> Part of the answer may be found in the fact that the U.N. has taken into account that the people of Gibraltar have been beneficiaries of colonialism rather than victims of it. The present inhabitants of the Rock have been brought into this territory in order to serve the needs of the administering power. The present population, having through the years gradually replaced the original Spanish population of the territory and having completely changed the cultural and social makeup of the society of Gibraltar to serve their own particular needs, is not much interested in the idea of decolonization.[17]

If this kind of history is to have a role in deciding the issues inherent in the principle of self-determination, as it should, there can be no way in many cases for a claim of a right of self-determination to be recognized without the benefit of determinations made in some kind of international process.

Thus the necessity of an international process in implementing the principle of self-determination stands on many grounds. Its significance from the viewpoint of foreign policy is that the principle of self-determination works for the resolution of some of the explosive issues of the world by an international process focused on considerations that can be understood and respected. If it actually leads to resolution of such disputes in this manner, it will serve the foreign policy of the United States very well indeed. It is not necessary, however, to be unduly optimistic to recognize the constructive direction of its impact. The divisive, fragmenting possibilities some see in the principle of self-determination are a part of the world scene to be dealt with in one way or another. The principle of self-determination, which we are committed to uphold in any case under the U.N. Charter and by our support of the 1970 Declaration, provides a framework by which those unharnessed forces may be guided toward constructive peaceful solutions.

Foreign Bases

The most direct foreign policy concern with the principle of self-determination may be its impact on the maintenance of military bases. The principle clearly does have an impact on this part of our national security structure, and this impact has to be examined.

It is first necessary to make clear that the right of self-determination does not preclude a lease or other agreement allowing an area of a nation to be used by another nation for a military base. There may be other grounds in particular situations that preclude the grant of such rights (see chapters 10 and 11). The right of self-determination of a people is an affirmation of its sovereignty, not a limitation on its right to take action it deems advisable in its own interest. Such agreements represent no more an impairment of sovereignty than any other agreement by which a nation binds itself. As the Permanent Court of International Justice observed, "the right of entering into engagements is an attribute of sovereignty."[18]

Agreements for the establishment of foreign bases and for joint defense arrangements are not uncommon. Since World War II the United States has established foreign base agreements with a number of countries. The 1940 Lend-Lease agreement with the United Kingdom by which the United States acquired bases in Bermuda and other areas took the form of ninety-nine-year leases.[19] Postwar agreements have generally not been leases but some form of agreement in which a designated area is made available for use by the United States for the purposes and period specified in the agreement.[20]

As with other agreements between nations, the validity of a foreign base agreement is vitiated under the Vienna Convention on the Law of Treaties, if it is obtained by fraud or by the threat or use of force. Resolutions by the United Nations General Assembly go beyond this in provisions which may reflect emerging law. Thus Res. 2105 (XX) adopted December 20, 1965 and similar resolutions in subsequent years call upon colonial powers "to dismantle military bases installed in colonial territories and to refrain from establishing new ones."[21] One unstated rationale of this provision is presumably that a colonial people is not in a position to give a freely determined consent to the establishment of a base. Practical concerns clearly also played a part, for instance, the belief reflected in the Special Committee reports that the desired continuance of a military base will often inhibit the diligence of the controlling power in implementing the right of the people of the territory to make a free determination of their political status.[22]

There is no reason to conclude that rules to protect peoples from duress or to assure a free determination by colonial peoples place any cloud on the validity of a foreign base agreement freely made by an independent nation. However, we should, I think, anticipate one limitation. Grotius was ahead of his time in declaring that "in the alienation of a part of a people there is the additional requirement that the part whose alienation is under consideration also give consent."[23] The principle is probably too broadly stated by Grotius even for an era that recognizes rights of self-determination. But where a grant of a base includes an area occupied by an indigenous population, rights of self-determination become involved if the grant is a cession of sovereignty or a grant in perpetuity of rights affecting the people of the base area. A grant in perpetuity is not consistent with a retention of sovereignty and will be perceived as a violation of the people's right of self-determination. We have seen this in Panama and found it necessary to place a termination date on our rights over the Canal Zone.

The second point that needs to be made is that while the right of self-determination has to accommodate to international rights in strategic areas (see chapter 11), strategic considerations do not give one nation a right to maintain control over a dependent people either in its own interest or as the self-appointed guardian of international rights.

If some special arrangements are essential to assure international rights, this is a limitation on the right of self-determination, but it is not for one nation to impose on another by its own unilateral action. Under the U.N. Charter and Resolution 2625 the governing principle is one of "equal rights and self-determination."

Gibraltar again provides an instructive precedent. There can surely be no more strategically important site in the world, for the power that controls Gibraltar can threaten transit through the Straits. The whole world has a stake in freedom of transit through the Straits. Yet Britain in dealing with U.N. pressure to return Gibraltar to Spain argued only for a separate right of self-determination for the people of Gibraltar. It did not assert any right to control the Rock for the protection of its own strategic interests or for the protection of international rights of transit through the Straits.[24] If international rights are not to be assured by some international regime for Gibraltar, the strategic significance of the area provides no more right for Britain to hold it than for Spain.

What is the impact of these limitations? It is certainly not that strategic considerations have become irrelevant nor that foreign bases have been outlawed. All that has happened is that the era in which foreign base arrangements could be imposed by one nation on another has ended. Military planning must proceed on the premise of freely negotiated foreign base rights, which must expire or become revocable after a period according to their terms. The fact is that most of the bases around the world on which U.S. military planning relies already depend on such negotiated and limited rights.[25]

Nine
NONINTERVENTION

The New Rule of Reciprocal Neutrality

There is perhaps no area in which the insights of emerging law have more to contribute to a wise foreign policy than in the principle of nonintervention. The temptation for great powers to check the risk of unfavorable political developments in other countries by intervening openly or covertly to control those developments is very great indeed, and objections to this course are often disparaged as stemming from a lack of realism and practicality. But emerging law provides the wiser, more realistic and practical policy.

The rule of nonintervention in emerging law applies on a world scale the principle of nonintervention as it earlier evolved in the Americas. The new rule of emerging law can be vital to the prospects of peace. It also provides a principle whose support by the United States can, if we will use it, strengthen our hand in checking the Soviet involvement in the nations of Africa and Asia.

The doctrine of nonintervention is something more than merely a restriction of the use and threat of force in international relations mandated by Article 2(4) of the U.N. Charter. That restriction undoubtedly limits some kinds of intervention involving the use of force that in a prior era might have been held admissible. Thus, in the *Corfu Channel Case,* the International Court of Justice said with respect to the use of the British navy to assert rights in the Corfu Channel as an international strait:

> The Court can only regard the alleged right of intervention as the manifestation of a policy of force, such as has in the past, given rise to most serious abuses and such as cannot, whatever be the present defects in international organization, find a place in international law. Intervention is perhaps still less admissible in the particular form it would take here; for from the nature of things, it would be reserved for the most powerful States, and might easily lead to perverting the administration of international justice itself.[1]

But the rule against intervention is not limited to the restriction on the use of physical force.

Intervention, as we shall see, involves the attempt by any means to coerce another nation in the free exercise of its own sovereignty. In an era of Cold War or détente the battle lines of the world's power struggles have often been laid in the contest for power within another nation. In Hungary and Czechoslovakia, and some would say in Vietnam, intervention involved the direct use of military force. Many see Cuba's employment of her forces in African struggles as a form of military intervention by the U.S.S.R. by proxy. But in most of the world the struggle to control the power structure of other nations is conducted by less blatant forms of intervention, forms often covert, such as training and assisting local cadres, terrorism, guerilla activity, strikes, disruption, puppet regimes, and coups d'état. Contests for local authority have become battlegrounds in a larger struggle waged by a variety of means.

At stake ultimately is the ability to preserve a balance of power against attempts to shift it to the advantage of any power by interventionary actions. But a rule of law to deal with such actions has to reckon with the fact that even actions designed to advance the interests and power position of the intervening nation are rarely, if ever, undertaken except under some claim of right based on an appeal for help from the local government or from some group contesting the legitimacy of that government. A rule to govern interventions has to be based on some decision as to the right of other nations to support one side or the other in situations of civil strife.

On this threshold issue there are only four choices: (1) to allow aid (whether in limited or in all categories) to either side; (2) to allow aid to the government only; (3) to allow aid to the government or to the opposition according to which has legitimate right on its side; (4) to allow aid to neither side. Under traditional law, until a condition of belligerency was reached, aid to the government was permitted, and aid to the insurgents was not. The effect was succinctly stated by Rosalyn Higgins:

> Traditional international law is fairly clear in indicating that in relation with third states a lawful government is in a privileged position compared with insurgents, at least until there has been recognition of belligerency.[2]

This traditional doctrine has been widely criticized on a variety of grounds.[3] The older doctrine has been rejected under the principle of nonintervention as declared in United Nations resolutions, including the landmark Declaration on Principles of International Law adopted by Res. 2625 in 1970 (see appendix 4).

The older doctrine is unsound for at least five reasons. First, it is in direct conflict with the principle of self-determination of peoples. The choice of the form of government or economic or foreign policy a nation shall pursue is a choice, within the limitations of international law, for that nation to make. The right to make that choice for itself is a part of the right of the people of that nation to self-determination. If there is contention within that nation over the authority or legitimacy or policy of its government, such matters are for that nation and not for others to decide. A rule that allows other nations to intervene in behalf of the established government and forbids intervention on behalf of those contesting the government is a rule that allows foreign nations to attempt to control the exercise of the right of self-determination. The right of self-determination requires a rule of nonintervention. It is, indeed, the other side of the same coin. The older rule developed in an era before the principle of self-determination achieved the status that the U.N. Charter and General Assembly resolutions give it. In an era in which the right of self-determination is one of the cardinal principles of the international order, a rule forbidding actions that would control another people in the exercise of its right is an inescapable corollary.

Second, in situations of civil strife, the right of the existing government to act for the people is in doubt. It is probably true that the established government elected by democratic procedures may truly reflect the self-determination of a people, and the efforts directed against the government may represent an attempt to thwart that freely made exercise of self-determination. But the argument made in 1924 in the eighth edition of Hall's *International Law* against a right to intervene upon invitation still speaks with telling cogency:

> As interventions, in so far as they purport to be made in compliance with an invitation, are independent of the reasons or pretexts which have already been discussed against illegal acts etc., it must be assumed that they are based either on simple friendship or upon a sentiment of justice. If intervention on the ground of mere friendship were allowed, it would be idle to speak seriously of the rights of independence. Supposing the intervention to be directed against the existing government, independence is violated by an attempt to prevent the regular organ of the state from managing the state affairs in its own way. Supposing it on the other hand to be directed against rebels, the fact that it has been necessary to call in foreign help is enough to show that the issue of the conflict would without it be uncertain, and consequently that there is a doubt as to which side would ultimately establish itself as the legal representative of the state. If again, intervention is based on an opinion as to the merits of the question at issue, the intervening state takes upon itself to pass judgment in a matter which, having nothing to do with the relations of states, must be regarded as being for legal purposes beyond the range of its vision.[4]

The problem with intervention in behalf of an established government believed to represent the people's truly expressed wishes is that either it is not necessary or, if it is, then the conclusion as to the government's legitimacy must be in doubt. That doubt is likely to involve precisely the kinds of thorny and vexatious internal political and constitutional issues that it is the right of the people of that nation to resolve for themselves. If foreign nations are to intervene on one side or another on the basis of their own determinations of legitimacy, foreign powers will be tempted to be drawn in for their own interests, and an internal matter becomes another arena of foreign contention.

Third, in our divided world the first requirement if a principle of nonintervention is to provide any prospect of resolving conflict is the assured neutrality of the principle. Every internal contest for power presents a potential for some impact on the balance of power. The older rule would permit manipulation aimed at accomplishing some shift in the world's power scales. It would permit aid to a government that came to power by illegitimate means but not to the ousted legitimate government that seeks to regain power. Where local conflict reflects genuine indigenous popular protest against an undemocratic, corrupt, or unresponsive government, it loads the scales on the side of government. It encourages major powers to establish and maintain puppet regimes to provide a basis for armed action against insurgents whose international alignment is viewed as unfavorable. It rewards misconduct as long as it is successful. Such an easily manipulated rule cannot command respect. If it allows manipulation one way, it is inevitable that the opponents in a world poised in a tentative détente will feel free to provide aid on the other side to protect their own power position against damage accomplished through the sanctuary of a rule that favors one side in the contest. If there is to be a rule by which nations in a divided world may be willing to resolve intervention issues by rules of law, it has to be a rule that is and is perceived to be neutral.

Fourth, a rule that calls for reciprocal abstention from interference in the affairs of other states is the only means by which the escalation of local conflicts into contests of power between major powers can be avoided. One hopes that the world will always have sense enough to hold back from holocaust, but if every Angola has to be determined by one side or the other throwing in enough more outside help than the other to provide the decisive margin of superior force, every local contest will have the potential for exploding into a dangerous confrontation between the major powers. A principle of reciprocal abstention can provide the neutralizing rationale necessary to confine local contests to their local contestants.

Fifth, the old rule does not provide a sound and effective basis for the occasions when intervention is justified. As will be discussed in the next section, a right to intervene in order to offset the ilegal intervention of another foreign nation has to be recognized. This is the clear and simple basis of the legitimacy of such intervention. Attempts to ground intervention in such cases as assistance to an established government only leads to confusion and recrimination about motives and denies to the necessary counterintervention its deserved moral standing and political force.

The logic of these reasons is followed in the rule of nonintervention adopted by the United Nations, which rejects the older rule in favor of a rule against intervention in behalf of either side in a local contest. This significance of the U.N. actions is not universally understood or accepted. Some of the discussion of the problem of the old rule proceeds without apparently recognizing the import of the U.N. Declaration on Principles of International Law in Res. 2625. E. V. Rostow, who served in the Johnson and Nixon administrations, has, indeed flatly stated "I do not read the recent declaration adopted by the General Assembly as altering in any way, except conceivably for colonial regimes, the preexisting international law under which it is perfectly legitimate to assist a state which is widely recognized and not legitimate at all to assist revolutionary forces within that state. Indeed, the declaration makes that point over and over again."[5] I find it impossible to square Rostow's view with the language of the Declaration.

The 1970 Declaration provides that "no state or group of states has the right to intervene, directly or indirectly, for any reason whatever, in the internal or external affairs of any other State" and that "every State has an inalienable right to choose its political, economic, social and cultural systems, without interference in any form by another State." It prohibits armed intervention and other forms of interference or attempted threats not only "against the personality of the State" but also "against its political, economic and cultural elements." It provides not only that no State shall organize, assist, foment, finance, incite, or tolerate subversive, terrorist, or armed activities "directed toward the violent overthrow of the regime of another State" but also that it shall not "interfere in civil strife in another State." The rule of neutrality and reciprocal abstention from interference in local contests seems clear.[6]

For foreign policy this is the vital point about the U.N. rule of nonintervention. It is more than a rule of respect for the rights of weaker nations. It is a rule to avoid making every local contest a contest between the great powers with the risk of military confrontation. It is a course of foreign policy common sense and prudence.

But to understand fully and evaluate this rule as foreign policy, it is necessary to examine and clarify three other points. First, the U.N. rule does not condemn all kinds of influence upon the conduct of other states. The Declaration itself attempts to indicate the substance of the general rule by explaining that: "Consequently, armed intervention and all other forms of interference or attempted threats" against the state or its elements are in violation of law. All specifically prohibited activities have an element of force or coercion in them. Thus paragraph C2 prohibits measures of any type to "coerce" another state to obtain a subordination of the exercise of its sovereign rights or to secure an advantage. Paragraph C3 condemns the "use of force" to deprive peoples of their national identity. The U.N. rule of nonintervention discloses no purpose to restrict a nation's efforts to influence another nation to take action in the free exercise of its own sovereignty.

Second, the U.N. rule does not bar military assistance to an ally for individual or collective self-defense. The condemnation in paragraph C1 is not of military assistance, but of "armed intervention," which is characterized as "against the personality of the State or against its political, economic and cultural elements." Military assistance to a widely recognized government facing no substantial internal threat to its authority involves no kind of interference or coercion. It involves no "intervention" at all.

It is undoubtedly true that the distinction between such military assistance and prohibited interference in civil strife, although clear-cut in most siuations, becomes troublesome in cases where civil strife, even though not a serious threat, is significant enough to require some deployment of military forces to deal with it. The mandate of the U.N. rule, it seems to me, is that after a condition of civil strife exists it is incumbent on the nation providing the assistance either to insist on adequate measures to assure that assistance thereafter furnished will not be used in the internal civil strife or to terminate the aid. Clearly, a realistic nonintervention rule cannot permit the mere fact of civil strife to require a termination of military assistance to an existing government if the assistance is insulated from the local conflict. If the outbreak of civil strife automatically required termination of all military assistance, or even limited the assistance to a preinsurgency level,[7] the rule would be an invitation to covert encouragement of civil strife by major powers in the furtherance of their own strategic aims to trigger a block on military assistance by others.

There are many who in the name of realism would oppose any limitation on the uses to which military assistance to an established government may be put. Defending our allies against internal upheaval will be seen as essential to defending the balance of power itself. But the point made above, that in a case of civil strife either aid to the established government is not necessary, or if it is, then the government's legitimacy must be in doubt, is more than an argument of legal principle. It bears on the realistic limits of policy as well. If shrewdly organized and orchestrated popular unrest can force the exile of the shah of Iran despite his overwhelming military power, one has to recognize how vulnerable and unreliable for the balance of power is a government that can be sustained only by foreign intervention.[8] A government that has to be propped up against its own people by foreign military assistance is a dubious component of any strategic balance.

Third, the 1970 Declaration in effect provides one exception to the principle of nonintervention: "support in accordance with the purposes and principles of the Charter of the United Nations" for a people resisting "forcible action" that deprives them of their right to self-determination. Such support is in the nature of action to remedy a violation by the controlling power. This position has a long history in U.N. resolutions dealing with decolonization from at least Res. 2105 (XX) in 1965 (see resolutions collected in appendix 4). The point that measures to pressure another government into desisting from violations of international law are not prohibited intervention is further considered in chapter 12 in the discussion of economic coercion.

If the principle of self-determination is loosely understood, this sanction for support for a people deprived by forcible action of its right of self-determination can prove an instrument for disorder. If, however, the inherent preliminary issues as explained in chapter 8 are fully understood and the necessity of some preliminary international process in doubtful cases is recognized, then the exception of support for a people denied this right by "forcible action" can provide an appropriate remedy for the violation by the controlling power.

As noted in chapter 7, the 1970 Declaration did not succeed in resolving the controversy whether such support may include force. I argued there that on principle such support may include force. Much of the concern at the prospect of military support stems from a fear that military force would be used in support of what is really only a claimed right, or in impatience at the slow realization of a right through appropriate process. This concern that nations may shoot from the hip in improper cases should not deny the use of necessary proportionate force against a forcible denial in a proper case. The United States should not lightly reject the only principle under which we could have received the indispensable aid of France in the American Revolution.

Counterintervention

Much of the confusion on the subject of intervention would be eliminated, if the distinction between intervention and counterintervention were kept in mind. Allusion has earlier (chapter 6) been made to the fallacy that intervention must be permitted because, if it is not, those who are not prepared to play by the rules will have the advantage. That is only an argument for a right of counterinvention. If we treat it as an argument to permit invervention generally, we lose any opportunity to press a principle of nonintervention to prevent the escalation of local conflicts.

The concept of counterintervention is not new. It was stated by John Stuart Mill in 1850 as follows:

> The doctrine of non-intervention, to be a legitimate principle of morality, must be accepted by all governments. The despots

> must consent to be bound by it as well as free States. Unless they do, the profession of it by free countries comes but to this miserable issue, that the wrong side may help the wrong, but the right may not help the right. Intervention to enforce non-intervention is always rightful, always moral, if not always prudent.[9]

Hall's *International Law,* eighth edition, in 1924 recognized the principle in these terms:

> It is incontestable that a grave infraction is committed when the independence of a state is improperly interfered with; and it is consequently evident that another state is at liberty to intervene in order to undo the effects of illegal intervention, and to restore the state subject to it to freedom of action.[10]

The 1970 Declaration does not state any right of counterintervention. Possibly it was considered one of those matters covered by the saving clause in paragraph C5 that "nothing in the foregoing paragraphs [principle of non-intervention] shall be construed as affecting the relevant provisions of the Charter relating to the maintenance of international peace and security."

Where intervention involves some use of force, counterintervention may have to involve some use of counterforce. The Charter in Article 2(4) provided new limitations on the use of force, and, as noted before (pages 70–72), some controversy surrounds the effect of this provision, some persons contending that apart from action by the United Nations a nation may use force only in the exercise of the inherent right of individual or collective self-defense "if an armed attack occurs" as provided under Article 51. Of course, cases of intervention by force will often amount to an armed attack. We have seen that under the definition of aggression in Res. 3314 even some kinds of indirect use of force may constitute aggression. Where the offending intervention amounts to an armed attack the Charter presents no problem to the use of proportionate force in counterintervention. It is an exercise of the individual or collective right of self-defense. And in that case the counterinterventionary action can be carried even to the territory of the offending nation.

But even if by reason of a narrower interpretation of the words "armed attack" some intervention by force does not amount to such an attack, the language of the limitation on the use of force in Article 2(4) would have to be strained far away from its common meaning to deny a right of proportionate use of force in counterintervention. Such use of force in counterintervention cannot in common sense be regarded as "against the territorial integrity or political independence of any state." Such force is in defense of these principles. Nor can it sensibly be regarded as "inconsistent with the purposes of the United Nations." It is in support of them.[11]

If the United States is to declare its commitment to the resolution of conflict by law, the right of counterintervention must be clearly established and carefully preserved. It is not only a right that is essential to prevent the rule of nonintervention becoming a mockery of law; it is essential to the preservation of the balance of power. For the power to manipulate local contests over authority is a power to manipulate the world's power balance.

We should, however, claim and recognize a right of counterintervention in terms that will help to avoid its abuse. We should assert the right in terms limiting it to preserving or restoring the status quo pending U.N. action or action by a voluntary tribunal, as will be proposed in part three. Counterintervention is a necessary means of preserving the subject of controversy for determination by adjudication or other appropriate international process. It is not a tool to be abused in schemes to advance national interests under the color of law.[12] We need to return to a precedent we have forgotten. In a time of greater belief in law and in the United Nations, the Congress included in the U.S. Greek-Turkish Aid Act of 1947 a provision for termination of U.S. assistance "if the Security Council finds (with respect to which finding the United States waives the exercise of any veto) or the General Assembly finds that action taken or assistance furnished by the United Nations makes the continuance of such assistance unnecessary or undesirable."

The world gives little evidence that it is ready to live by the U.N. rule of nonintervention. But candor requires us to confess that the United States has on a number of occasions given little reason to suppose that we are deeply attached to it ourselves. It must be clear that the rule of nonintervention cannot serve to neutralize local conflict and block escalation if we do not abide by it and aggressively press it.

The great virtue of the simple and right U.N. rule is that it can be understood.[13] It makes sense on principle and as policy. If we press it aggressively, we will strengthen our hand in the Third World. And if others proceed to violate it anyway, we can, where we believe we must, act to check the violation under a principle that gives a readily understandable legitimacy to our action, the right of counterintervention. We can hardly lose, because counterintervention will permit us to act when we have to. And we just might find that law offers a better way, a better way to contain conflict, a better way to check the spreading involvement of the U.S.S.R. and its proxies or of any other power bent on domination, a better way to serve the interests of the United States, a better way to construct a safer, freer world.

Ten
REGIONAL SECURITY ZONES

The Concept

The term "regional security zone" cannot be found in the U.N. Charter or in U.N. resolutions. Nor is the application of Charter provisions concerning "regional arrangements" to what is here terms a regional security zone spelled out in the Charter. Nevertheless, the regional security zone is a fundamental part of the regional security system for which the Charter provisions were intended to provide a legal framework. The issues were squarely confronted and the principle vindicated in the Cuban missile crisis of 1962.

The principle involved is the collective right of the nations of the region directly affected to exclude any armed involvement in the region by an outside power that endangers the peace or security of the region. It applies whether such involvement is or is not at the invitation of a nation of the region. It is subject to any overriding action that may be taken by the Security Council of the United Nations. There may have been other grounds available to support the action taken by the United States and the Organization of American States in the Cuban missile crisis, but we put forward a specific legal argument based on collective regional action. One can generalize from that experience to assert a collective right of regional nations to establish such regional security zones, without the delay of Security Council action or the possibility of frustration by veto. This right is an essential component of the regime of law in a world where power rests in the hands of separate nations. It is an indispensible premise for a full commitment of U.S. foreign policy to resolution of conflict by law.

The principle is defined and limited by five areas of concern. First, obviously, are the security concerns of the nations within the region. These formed the original basis of the unilateral formulation of the Monroe Doctrine by the United States. We have seen in chapter 2 the evolution from a doctrine of unilateral action to one of collective action. The focus on security concerns, however, has continued, becoming an hemispheric concern as manifested in the Declaration of Lima (1938),[1] the Declaration of Panama (1939),[2] the Declaration of Habana (1940),[3] the Act of Chapultepec (1945),[4] and finally the Rio Pact and the O.A.S. Charter.[5]

The second area of concern is protection of the self-determination and sovereignty of the nations within the region and their right to be free from domination or intervention under the guise of regional security. We have seen in chapter 2 the evolution of the American principle of nonintervention as the premise of the Monroe Doctrine and the inter-American system. Article 52(1) of the U.N. Charter affirms these requirements in the provision that regional arrangements and agencies and their activities must be "consistent with the Purposes and Principles of the United Nations."

A third area of concern is that the right of regional action must be generalized so that whatever terms permit regional action by the American nations can also be recognized for other regions. This imperative was brought to bear in the Cuban missile crisis and, as recounted in chapter 2, resulted in informal assurance given to the U.S.S.R. on the removal of U.S. Jupiter missiles in Turkey. The formulation that sanctions a regional security zone for the Americas must be tested also by the consequences of its recognition for regional action in other regions, in Eastern Europe, in the Middle East, in Africa, in Southeast Asia.

Fourth, the U.N. Charter proclaimed new limitations on the use of force in international relations. These limitations must govern regional action involving force just as much as the use of force in other circumstances.

Finally, the problem of regional action requires some accommodation of the authority of regional arrangements and the authority of the United Nations itself. This accommodation is reflected in the provisions of Articles 51, 52, 53, and 54.

Although the legitimacy of the action of the United States and the Organization of American States in the Cuban missile crisis is broadly accepted, the precise formulation of the legitimating principle under the provisions of the United Nations Charter is still a matter of discussion. Louis Henkin has commented that

> as an important action by an important nation, acquiesced in by all other nations (including the Soviet Union, the principal "victim"), what the United States did in the Cuban quarantine became a part of the course of international law and practice. The statements, justifications, and legal interpretations announced by the United States (and others) at the time of the action have influenced and will continue to influence the legal significance of the Cuban case. Unlike the actions at Suez-Sinai, condemned by the United Nations and largely undone, the Cuban quarantine has not been seen and will probably not be seen as a violation leaving the law as it was; probably it made new law, but what that law is cannot yet be told. Much will depend on how the United States itself later interprets what it did and why it was justified, and what other nations seek to make and succeed in making of the incident.[6]

A judicious formulation based on the U.S. position in the Cuban missile crisis provides the foundation for acceptance in international law of the principle of regional security zones.

Some commentators would have grounded the legal basis for U.S. action in the Cuban missile crisis on a right of self-defense, a position our government chose not to take. Others have relied unduly on particular circumstances of the 1962 crisis. In generalizing from that experience it is necessary to reach beyond the particulars of that case. It is essential that the legal basis for a collective right to establish a regional security zone be stated with care.

In the Cuban missile crisis the United States did not rest the ground for action on our exercise of the inherent right of individual or collective self-defense. Accordingly, it did not take a position that introduction of Soviet missiles into Cuba amounted to an "armed attack" on the United States or on other American states within the meaning of Article 51 of the Charter, nor that a right of self-defense exists apart from Article 51 even where no armed attack occurs. Similarly, the collective right to establish a security zone asserted here is not based on Article 51 and does not depend on response to an armed attack.

In the Cuban missile crisis the United States relied on Article 52(1) of the Charter, which provides:

> Nothing in the present Charter precludes the existence of regional arrangements or agencies for dealing with such matters relating to the maintenance of international peace and security as are appropriate for regional action, provided that such arrangements or agencies and their activities are consistent with the Purposes and Principles of the United Nations.

Four points should be observed in the language of Article 52(1) concerning the provision for regional action. First, the article authorizes action only by "regional arrangements or agencies." Second, it authorizes action only in matters "relating to the maintenance of international peace and security." Third, it authorizes action only in matters "appropriate for regional action." Fourth, only activities "consistent with the Purposes and Principles of the United Nations" are permitted. The essential legal position vindicated in the Cuban missile crisis is that Article 52(1) permits regional action "relating to the maintenance of international peace and security," if it (a) is taken under an appropriate "regional arrangement" or by an appropriate "regional agency," (b) is "appropriate for regional action" and (c) is "consistent with the Purposes and Principles of the United Nations."

There is nothing in Article 52 limiting regional action to action not involving the use of force. Indeed, authorization of regional action for "the maintenance of international peace and security" seems to contemplate the use of force if necessary. The language parallels that used in Articles 39, 43, and 48 in relation to such action by the Security Council. This interpretation is confirmed by the requirement in Article 54 that "the Security Council shall at all times be kept fully informed of activities undertaken or in contemplation under regional arrangements or by regional agencies for the maintenance of international peace and security."

This view reflects the purposes of the articles concerning regional arrangements. The purpose of Articles 51 through 54 was not to take the teeth out of the collective policies and developing institutions of the nations of the Americas, but to affirm their role, subject to overriding action by the United Nations. Action for the maintenance of peace and security, potentially involving the use of force, had always been at the root of the Monroe Doctrine and later of the inter-American developments from the Declaration of Lima to the Act of Chapultapec. Such matters had for a long time been recognized as "appropriate for regional action." The Covenant of the League of Nations had provided in Article 21 that nothing in the Covenant should be deemed to affect the validity of "regional understandings like the Monroe Doctrine, for securing the maintenance of peace." The provisions in the U.N. Charter were specifically designed to give approval to the arrangements provided and contemplated in the Act of Chapultepec of 1945.[7]

Regional action under Article 52 is not an exception to the fundamental and essential principle of Article 2(4) of the Charter:

> All Members shall refrain in their international relations from the threat or use of force against the territorial integrity or political independence of any state, or in any other manner inconsistent with the Purposes of the United Nations.

Neither the use of force in self-defense nor the use of force under regional arrangements nor the use of force by members pursuant to Security Council action under Article 42 is treated in the Charter as an exception to the general rule of Article 2(4). Rather they conform to it. It was never supposed, for example, that Article 2(4) denied a right to self-defense.[8] This was true even without the benefit of Article 51, which expressly reserves the inherent right of individual or collective self-defense. The original Dumbarton Oaks Proposals included no counterpart to Article 51, which was inserted at the San Francisco conference only as a means of reconciling action by regional arrangements and action by the Security Council. Not every use of force against a state is "against the territorial integrity or political independence" of the state under Article 2(4). If it were, there would be no occasion for the further prohibition against the use of force "in any other manner inconsistent with the Purposes of the United Nations." Nor, as the words are commonly understood, does the prohibition against the threat or use of force in any manner "inconsistent" with the purposes of the United Nations limit the use of force solely to actions authorized by the United Nations. Regional action that conforms to Article 52 is certainly consistent with the purposes of the United Nations and thus also conforms to Article 2(4).

In the Cuban missile crisis the United States took the position, among others, that the requirement under Article 53(1) that Security Council authorization is necessary for "enforcement action" under regional arrangements or by regional agencies applied only to decisions obligating members to act. The Charter carefully reserves for the Security Council the power to make such decisions. What is at stake is the concern of major powers, including the United States and the Soviet

Union, to avoid becoming committed to military action without their consent. This is the point of reserving authority to make binding decisions to the Security Council, where the powers named as permanent members have a veto. Thus, Article 53(1) of the Charter relating to "enforcement action" seems clearly to be referring to binding Security Council action under Chapter VII. Article 53(1) provides:

> The Security Council shall, where appropriate, utilize such regional arrangements or agencies for enforcement action under its authority. But no enforcement action shall be taken unde regional arrangements or by regional agencies without the authorization of the Security Council.

Thus, the power to take action obligating members to use force is reserved for the Security Council in the case of regional arrangements just as in the case of actions by the United Nations itself. This interpretation is supported by the advisory opinion of the International Court of Justice in *Certain Expenses of the U.N.* There, the court construed the word "action" in Article 11(2), providing that "any such question [relating to the maintenance of international peace and security] on which action is necessary shall be referred to the Security Council by the General Assembly either before or after the discussion." The court held that "the word 'action' must mean such action as is solely within the province of the Security Council. It cannot refer to recommendations which the Security Council might make, as for instance under Article 38, because the General Assembly has a comparable power."[9] The purpose of Article 11(2) as of Article 53(1) was to protect the exclusive authority of the Security Council to make decisions obligating members to take action under Articles 40, 41, or 42. The action by the O.A.S. in the Cuban missile crisis was a recommendation to member states. Regional arrangements can recommend the use of force to defend a regional security zone; they cannot compel it.

The language in the second sentence of Article 53(1) barring "enforcement action" without Security Council authorization does not stand alone. The language by itself presents some difficulty. But it has to be reconciled with Article 52 allowing regional action for "the maintenance of international peace and security." It has to be reconciled with the purpose of Articles 51 through 54 to preserve the regional arrangements of the inter-American system (and others like it), not to nullify them. To read into Article 53 a requirement that allows the big power veto to frustrate regional action would be contrary to the general scheme of Articles 51 through 54. The approach of the Charter to avoiding abuse of regional action is in the limitations embodied in Article 52 and in the right of the Security Council to override, not in the imposition of big power vetoes on legitimate regional action involving force.

The Charter limitations on regional action are vital. Indeed, the concept of regional action has no place in international law without them. Although stated in generalities, as befits a constitutional instrument that has to provide a framework for unforeseeable circumstances, they are nevertheless real.

Regional action under Article 52(1) may be taken only by "regional arrangements" or "regional agencies." The Charter does not define either term, but it clearly contemplates some kind of collective action. This is sound in principle, for if a big power violates the rights of other nations in its region, some or even a majority of the other nations in the region may look upon foreign bases and foreign military involvement as their assurance against aggression by their big-power neighbor. It is not for the U.S.S.R. alone to determine whether Turkey or Iran needs foreign support for protection against domination or aggression by the U.S.S.R. Nor is it for the United States alone to determine whether foreign military power is to be excluded from the Americas. Where, however, jurisdiction to establish a regional security zone has been exercised collectively, implementation action may, in an emergency, have to be taken by a big power alone, pending and subject to further action by nations of the region collectively.

But such collective action does not have to be unanimous. Article 1(1) of the Charter includes as a purpose of the United Nations taking effective collective action for the "prevention and removal" of threats to the peace as well as for the "suppression" of acts of aggression or other breaches of the peace. Article 52 provides for regional action relating to "the maintenance" of international peace and security. It would make a mockery of these provisions for preventive action if collective regional action has to be taken by unanimous consent. Broadly based collective action that is representative of the regional interest should be sufficient. One nation cannot be permitted alone to allow the wolf through the door to the jeopardy of the security of the entire region. This kernel of the 1848 Polk Corollary to the Monroe Doctrine was confirmed in the Cuban missile crisis in the new context of O.A.S. action and in the framework of the U.N. Charter. It is not realistic to base regional jurisdiction in the Cuban missile crisis on the ground that Cuba, as a member of the O.A.S., had consented to the O.A.S. structure, where Cuba had already, in effect, been excluded from the arrangement.

However, where the collective action is not unanimous, especially if it is taken against a nonconsenting state, the requirement of Article 52(1) that the measure taken be one "appropriate for regional action" becomes critical. Article 52(1) does not develop the concept, but it must be based on a community of interest shared by the dissenting state even though it is opposed in the particular case for reasons believed by it to be valid. Regional action is not to be used as a device merely to enforce the will of the many against the few. It is to safeguard the genuine security interests of the region as a whole.

Although the collective right to establish a regional security zone is not based on the right of individual or collective self-defense under Article 51, regional action cannot override a nation's rights under the article. A regional security zone cannot diminish the right of a regional state to seek and receive aid from nations outside the zone if it is itself the victim of aggression.

Article 52(1), as already noted, makes clear that regional arrangments and agencies and all their activities must be "consistent with the Purposes and Principles of the United Nations." There must be full respect for the equal rights, self-determination, and sovereignty of all nations, and the principle of nonintervention must be adhered to.

Regional action under Article 52 is subject to any overriding action that may be taken by the U.N. Security Council. This is implicit in the requirement in Article 54 that the Security Council be kept fully informed of activities undertaken or being contemplated. And the obligation of member states to carry out "decisions" of the Security Council for the maintenance of international peace and security is explicit in Article 48.

In thus defining the right of regional action under Article 52 there is one caution that needs to be stated. We must not exclude the continuing existence of some ultimate residue of right to act with force, unilaterally if need be, where survival of the nation is at stake.[10] We should not try to define that residue of unilateral right for all the unknown contingencies that the future may present. It is sufficient to reserve our right to take unilateral action on such articulable grounds as the law may appropriately be called upon to recognize in giving effect to the underlying premise of our international society—the right of all nations to a viable coexistence.

These are the points that define the collective right to establish a regional security zone. These fundamental points were the basis of the United States position as supported and implemented by the Organization of American States in the Cuban missile crisis. This position received only minimal challenge in the United Nations, no opposing resolution even being brought to a vote. And it was ultimately acceded to by the U.S.S.R. when it withdrew its missiles from Cuba. The authority, where appropriate, to establish a regional security zone by regional action must be taken to be the law of the Charter.[11]

Exclusion of Spheres of Influence

The concept of regional security zones as shaped by principles that can claim recognition in emerging law is clearly different from the claim of spheres of influence asserted in the era of power politics. It is necessarily different in that under Article 52(1) any regional arrangement or agency and all of its actions must be consistent with the purposes and principles of the United Nations.

The differences are fundamental. A regional security zone is justified by its defense of the sovereignty and right of self-determination of the nations of the region. It neither implies nor admits any right of intervention by any nation in the internal or external affairs of any other. The principle of nonintervention is a necesary corollary of the right of self-determination and a part of the international law of the Charter as declared in the 1970 Declaration. Recognition of regional security zones can provide no ground for any big-power veto of the political or social system freely chosen by the people of any nation of the region.

A regional security zone, unlike the sphere of influence of a great power, depends upon and is established only by collective action. It is inconsistent with any notion that special rights inhere in big powers to act unilaterally for their own security or advantage. What the principle permitting establishment of regional security zones does do is to provide a basis for the assertion of genuine regional security interests. It may operate against the government of a particular nation but only in protection of such a genuine regional interest. It gives no legitimacy to the imposition of ideological conformity on the nations of a region.

The foreign policy of the United States is not advanced by the assertion of rights in this hemisphere which on principle cannot be recognized for others in similar circumstances. There is, for one thing, no need of such a claim. There is basis enough for our genuine security needs in the establishment of a regional security zone that can be recognized in law. Furthermore, as seen in chapter 2, our own hemisphere policy has long before now evolved to disclaim any U.S. right to intervene and to provide for hemisphere security by collective action. The political logic of hemisphere relations led us to this point even before adoption of the U.N. Charter.

It must be conceded that our actions have not always conformed to our own principles, despite our attempted justifications and protestations of innocence. This, however, is no reason now to claim rights we cannot justify. Our excesses are also our mistakes and need not lead us into the worse error of claiming untenable rights, an error that is worse because the claim of rights we cannot equally concede to others only causes new damage to the United States.

We have already seen the vital importance to the United States of addressing our regional security concerns on the basis of a community of interest premised on a rule of nonintervention and regional action. The solidarity of the inter-American community represented in the Organization of American States could not exist without our commitment to the principle of nonintervention. That solidarity may well have provided the vital shield that averted significant attack on the quarantine against Soviet missiles in Cuba and enabled us to meet the challenge of the Cuban missile crisis without war. As in so many instances, a position grounded in principle can marshal effective power denied to a naked assertion of force.

Equally damaging is the impact on U.S. interests in other areas from an assertion of unjustifiable claims in this hemisphere. By claiming what we cannot concede to others we not only invite the world to look cynically on our principles, but more important, we allow the U.S.S.R. and other major powers to act with cynical disdain for the constraints of law or principle. The point is not that they are led to disregard law only by our example, but that by our own indifference to law or corruption of its principles we cripple our ability to mount effective pressure to restrain them. We blur the clear distinction between the Brezhnev Doctrine formulated to justify the Soviet invasion of Czechoslovakia in 1968 and the principles embodied in the Charter of the Organization of American States.[12] We make it more difficult to restrain Soviet and Cuban meddling in Africa's troubled waters. Our excesses in the Americas can damage U.S. interests everywhere.

With so much at stake for United States foreign policy it seems curious that notions bordering on a recognition of reciprocal spheres of influence for the United States and the U.S.S.R. should have attained as much currency and approval as may be the case. At least three currents of thought have contributed to this development. It is often stated that coexistence between the United States and the U.S.S.R. requires that the United States must not challenge the U.S.S.R. with force in the area of the special security concerns of the U.S.S.R. and that the Soviets similarly must not challenge us in ours. There is merit to this view. There are, indeed, several considerations against our challenging the U.S.S.R. with force in eastern Europe, including the military disadvantge of the area for us, the fact that no shift in balance of power is involved in Soviet actions in the Warsaw pact nations, and our awareness that such a challenge by us there could easily escalate into a potentially uncontrollable conflict. But it is unjustifiable to jump from rejecting our use of force to acknowledging a right by the U.S.S.R. to act in eastern Europe as it deems necessary for its own security in disregard of the principles of the Charter and the 1970 U.N. Declaration on the Charter principles of international law. The considerations that make our use of force against such Soviet actions imprudent and unadvisable do not make Soviet wrongs right.

A second root of sphere of influence thinking is the idea that in an era when balance of power is based on power blocs intervention may be necessary by a great power within its bloc to keep its bloc in line.[13] Such intervention is, of course, no more permitted than any other under the 1970 Declaration of the United Nations. It was argued in chapter 3 that intervention to maintain the balance of power is no logner a viable course, at least for open societies. And even for the U.S.S.R. the price for its actions in Hungary and Czechoslovakia may have been permanent damage to its former appeal and influence in much of the world. If the Americas are regarded as part of a U.S. power bloc, the argument for the necessity of U.S. intervention to hold the bloc in line flies in the face of our experience in this hemisphere. Here, our efectiveness depends on exactly the reverse approach. The argument for intrabloc intervention can benefit only the U.S.S.R. or another big power dictatorship. Nothing but damage can come to the foreign policy of the United States from an argument that tends to give approval to interventions by the U.S.S.R.

Certainly the flirtation with sphere of influence notions is also aided by the temptation to treat our excesses in Latin America and not our principles as the measure of our policy. Reading our actions as asserting an hegemony of some sort over Latin America leads to judging U.S.S.R. actions in eastern Europe according to the same measure. The admonition against self-righteousness contained in such thinking is undeniably appealing, but there is something upside-down when policy is dictated by error. The United States has not and does not claim such an hegemony over Central America, and there is no need for us to do so now. By claiming it we would only compound the problem of restraining U.S.S.R. domination of eastern Europe, or, if the situation develops, of restraining Chinese domination of southeast Asia.[14]

The issue for U.S. foreign policy is not whether the principle allowing regional security zones is too limited but how to assure its acceptance. The principle is vital to the foreign policy interest of the United States. Any U.S. commitment to the resolution of conflicts by law must be premised on acceptance of this principle as part of emerging law. With that clear understanding, a commitment to law can provide for a more effective U.S. foreign policy than could any attempt to reserve for ourselves a big-power sphere of influence in the western hemisphere.

Eleven
INTERNATIONAL RIGHTS IN STRATEGIC AREAS

The Function of International Rights

Perhaps the most important unfinished business of emerging law is the regime of international rights. They are a part of the power fabric of the rule of law. An understanding of this function of international rights is fundamental to an evaluation of the adequacy of emerging law concerning international rights.

International rights must serve a double function. First, they must provide a basis for nations to coexist, imposing those limitations on sovereignty that are necessary to insure for all nations a viable existence. Second, where sovereignty over strategic areas or resources would threaten the security of others or the world's power balance, international rights must provide the assurances necessary for acceptance of law.

Providing a basis for nations to coexist within a community of nations is, of course, a function of all international law. What international law does is to impose restraints on national sovereignty where necessary for this purpose. The peremptory norms of international law that the Vienna Convention on the Law of Treaties recognizes as binding on all nations are in essence such restraints (see chapter 5). So also are the restraints imposed by the principles of the United Nations Charter.

Much of international law can be conceptualized as an implementation of a principle that the sovereignty of nations is limited to whatever extent may be necessary to avoid encroaching on the equal sovereignty of other nations, but the premise that underlies this accommodation is that the nations of the world must respect the right of each to a viable existence. The ever-increasing interdependence of nations forces on us an increasing awareness of the fact of our existence as parts of a community of nations.

The second equally necessary function of international rights—to provide a basis for acceptance of law—is less obvious but vital where issues concern the sovereignty of a nation over its own territory. It is a point central to consideration of a foreign policy commitment to the resolution of conflicts by law.

The concept that the sovereignty of a nation even over its own territory is limited by rules protecting the community of nations is not new. Perhaps the clearest and most familiar case is the regime of international straits. In *The Corfu Channel Case* the International Court of Justice declared

> It is, in the opinion of the Court, generally recognized and in accordance with international custom that States in time of peace have a right to send their warships through straits used for international navigation between two parts of the high seas without the previous authorization of a coastal State, provided that the passage is *innocent*. Unless otherwise prescribed in an international convention, there is no right for a coastal State to prohibit such passage through straits in time of peace.[1]

In the tentative formulation of the regime of international straits by the Third Conference on the Law of the Sea, provision is made that "the sovereignty or jurisdiction of the States bordering the straits is exercised subject to this Part and to the other rules of international law."[2]

The strategic reliance on the regime of straits came into sharp focus in the Third Conference on the Law of the Sea. The proposed extension of territorial waters from three to twelve miles would have brought under the regime of straits a great many strategic waterways more than six miles wide previously regarded as parts of the high seas. These included the Strait of Gibraltar. To avoid subjecting these straits to a regime permitting only innocent passage the tentative text provides for a distinct right of "transit passage" applicable to straits, extending rights of passage to all ships and aircraft in war as well as in peace.[3] By the special regime for international straits the tentative Law of the Sea text attempts to preclude the territorial sovereignty of a bordering nation being exercised in a manner contrary to the necessary strategic as well as commercial reliance by other nations on the use of the strait.

It is evident, however, that the regime of international straits even as defined in the Law of the Sea text falls short of accomplishing this purpose. Although the text provides for international rights of passage and even some procedures for settlement of disputes,[4] it does not provide for guarantees against violation by a nation bordering the strait. If a bordering nation can in fact close off the strait, even though in violation of international rights, it retains the power to seize other nations at the jugular. The problem of the territorial sovereignty of a bordering nation cannot be solved as long as possession of territory by a bordering nation poses a threat to the viable existence of others.

This deficiency is not just a matter of having to make progress toward law by steps, of learning to crawl before we can walk. If the possession of areas upon whose control the life and security of nations may depend is not effectively neutralized to assure the protection of international rights, an essential basis for nations to accept territorial adjustments based on rights of self-determination or on any principles of law is placed in jeopardy. Each case, no doubt, presents its own issues, but the problem of guarantees underlies all international rights where such rights are to exist under a rule of law.

The practical impacts can readily be seen. The United States was prepared to turn over control of the Panama Canal to the Republic of Panama (without any regime of international control) only in conjunction with a permanent treaty with Panama providing guarantees. That treaty not only provides rights of transit for vessels of war as well as other vessels and in time of war as well as in peace but also gives the United States the right to take direct military action, if necessary, to maintain this regime of neutrality of the canal. The Strait of Gibraltar presents similar considerations. It is probably the most strategically significant waterway in the world. Although Great Britain has not pleaded its own or the world's security concerns to oppose loss of control of Gibraltar, it is easy to understand why it would be reluctant to turn over Gibraltar without effective international arrangements or guarantees to a Spain of doubtful political stability.

The world has moved in fits and starts and with some backtracking to recognize and protect international rights not only in international straits but also in interoceanic canals and in international rivers, to recognize a right of access to the sea for landlocked states, even to recognize general rights of transit over routes of necessity or convenience.

The strategic significance of access to the coal, coke, and steel of the Ruhr even gave rise to the creatin of an international authority to protect the interests of countries dependent on those resources. These developments have to be viewed as indicating directions, not as finished business.

In carrying this unfinished business forward the adequacy of established and emerging international rights has to be tested against their necessary function under a rule of law. What has to be understood is that a necessary function of international rights is to provide a basis for the acceptance of law. International rights have to defuse territorial control as a threat to the community of nations. They have to make it possible for territorial adjustments to be made when required by emerging law with the assurance that international rights will not thereby be jeopardized. Where the security or viable existence of nations is at stake, international rights have to be more than rights on paper, if we are not to return to a world that must rely on the principle that possession is nine-tenths of the law. International rights must function as a kind of territorial disarmament. In short, international rights have to impose those limitations on territorial sovereignty that are necessary to provide a basis for acceptance of law.

Unfortunately, territorial sovereignty is something of a fetish, as jealously guarded by the new nations as by any. We shall have to be clear, therefore, in any commitment to resolution of conflict by law to preserve our rights of independent action wherever nations are unwilling to allow the necessary scope and protection of international rights to be determined by a standard consistent with the rule of law.

Defining Substantive Rights

The principle that international rights must be shaped to provide a basis for acceptance of territorial sovereignty under a rule of law defines the need and provides the measure for the delineation of international rights concerning strategic areas. It must determine the scope of substantive rights and the nature of guarantee arrangements. It must define the kinds of areas that are to be subject to international rights. Thus the term "strategic areas" is used here to refer to all those areas whose control by one nation without protection of international rights would pose a threat to the security or viable existence of others.

The concept of strategic areas obviously covers some very different situations. It includes but is not limited to international straits, canals permanently dedicated to international use, international rivers, and areas whose fortification by one nation would imperil another. Different kinds of areas may clearly present very different issues. Indeed, the circumstances may vary from case to case.

Faced with such diversity, the approach of emerging law must be that taken by Professor Elihu Lauterpacht in 1957 in his pathfinding article, "Freedom of Transit in International Law." After asserting that "the operative principle, it is believed, is that States, far from being free to treat the establishment or regulation of routes of transit as a substantial derogation of their sovereignty which they are entirely free to refuse, are bound to act in this matter in the fulfillment of an obligation to the community of which they form a part,"[5] he formulated a basis for implementation of the principle in particular cases as follows:

> The existence of a right of transit may be said to be dependent on two basic conditions. In the first place, the State claiming the right of transit must be able to justify it by reference to considerations of necessity or convenience. Secondly, the exercise of the right must be such as to cause no harm or prejudice to the transit State.[6]

Lauterpacht's approach and his perceptive and balanced comments have application to issues of international rights on a much broader scale than he originally contemplated. Emerging law must recognize that different situations call for different rules and different arrangements of guarantee shaped by the international necessities on one side and the burdens on the territorial sovereign on the other.

This twofold analysis can be seen in application to one of the vital issues upon which international rights must provide a basis for a commitment to law: the right of passage for naval vessels in wartime. The United States clearly cannot concede to a nation bordering the Straits of Gibraltar or to the Republic of Panama the right to close the strait or the canal to naval vessels of the United States. This applies in time of peace or in time of war and whether or not the nation bordering the strait or the canal is a belligerent. It will be recalled that in *The Corfu Channel Case* the International Court of Justice declared only that "in time of peace" there is a right of "innocent" passage for warships in an international strait. The Montreux Convention of 1936 governing rights in the Turkish Straits provided only limited rights of passage for warships of non-Black Sea Powers even in time of peace, and in time of war, if Turkey was a belligerent, left the passage of warships entirely to the discretion of the Turkish government.[7] But the tentative Law of the Sea text, while protecting provisions of long-standing conventions for specific straits,[8] adopts as a general rule, as noted above, a right of passage for warships of all nations in time of peace or war.

It has been argued that a nation through whose territory an international canal flows should have the right in a time of war or armed conflict to which it it is a party to close the canal to warships or merchant ships of a nation with which it is engaged in war or armed conflict and to ships transporting contraband.[9] However, this position will not provide a basis for acceptance of law. Despite erratic international practice, treaty provisions have always pointed to a more adequate rule.

The Convention of Constantinople of 1888 governing the Suez Canal provided for the canal to be "free and open, in time of war as in time of peace, to every vessel of commerce or of war, without distinction of flag" and that "the Canal shall never be subject to the exercise of the right of blockade."[10] Egypt, however, asserting a state of war existed with Israel, closed the canal to Israeli ships and cargo, relying on a further Article of the Convention providing that Articles IV, V, VII, and VIII (limiting military measures) should not stand in the way of measures that the sultan "might find it necessary to take to assure by their own forces the defense of Egypt and the maintenance of public order."[11] This was a dubious position at best.

The Hay-Pauncefote Treaty of 1901 between the United States and Great Britain contained provisions similar to those of the Convention of Constantinople of 1888, providing that the canal then proposed to connect the Atlantic and the Pacific should "be free and open to vessels of commerce and of war of all nations" and that the canal "shall never be blockaded, nor shall any right of war be exercised nor any act of hostility be committed in it."[12] Notwithstanding these provisions, the United States closed the Panama Canal to the enemy after it became a belligerent in World War I and again in World War II. The unsoundness of this position becomes apparent when the transfer of the canal to Panama is contemplated. As noted, the United States was certainly not prepared to allow Panama to close the canal even in time of a war in which Panama is a belligerent, even if Panama was at war with the United States.

It can be argued that a duty to keep a canal open for the warships of an enemy of the territorial sovereign or of the nation operating the canal is impractical nonsense. It is asking more than can be expected of a country. Furthermore it accomplishes nothing, because the enemy ships could and would be attacked on the high seas before they approached the canal. And it subjects the canal to a risk of damage or blocking by the sacrifice of one enemy vessel. For all the superficial common sense of such arguments, however, one has to recognize that it is not nonsense in the eyes of the United States when transfer of control of the Panama Canal to Panama is at issue. In the larger view of the prospects for law it is never nonsense. For if possession of the territory through which a strategic international canal flows gives a right to close the canal in time of war, possession of that territory becomes an issue that cannot be resolved by law, only by contest or even by force. International canals, at least interoceanic canals, must stand in the same posture as international straits.

International rivers, however, stand on an entirely different footing. Applying Lauterpacht's analysis there is no necessity for nonriparian nations generally to have access to international rivers for their naval vessels in time of peace or in time of war. While regimes for international rivers have sometimes provided rights of navigation to nonriparian states, there is no consistency of practice on this matter even for commercial vessels. The rights and interests that depend most critically on rights of navigation in international rivers are those of the riparian states. This is reflected in the proposed Helsinki Rules on the Uses of Waters of International Rivers adopted by the International Law Association in 1966.[13]

The Problem of Guarantees

The most difficult piece of unfinished business in the emerging law governing strategic areas is the means of guaranteeing international rights. Here too the diversity of situations must be met with a diversity of responses. The spotty history of attempts to protect international rights by specific arrangements suggests that recognition of the need for assurances has been easier than formulation of acceptable and effective means to accomplish the purpose.

Recognition of the need does not have to be deduced solely by the somewhat ambiguous process of interpreting negotiated arrangements, many of which have proved to be temporary. In two cases the international community acting in a quasi-legislative capacity has recognized the need.

In the controversy in 1920 and 1921 between Sweden and Finland over the Aaland Islands the Council of the League of Nations in its resolution of 24 June 1921, after recognizing the sovereignty of Finland over the Islands, further provided:

> Nevertheless, the interests of the world, the future of cordial relations between Finland and Sweden, the prosperity and

> happiness of the Islands themselves cannot be insured unless (a) certain further guarantees are given for the protection of the Islanders [amendment of the autonomy law of May 7, 1920]; and unless (b) arrangements are concluded for the non-fortification and neutralization of the Archipelago. . . .
>
> An international agreement in respect of the non-fortification and neutralization of the Archipelago should guarantee to the Swedish people and to all countries concerned, that the Aaland Islands will never become a source of danger from the military point of view. With this object, the Convention of 1856 should be replaced by a broader agreement, placed under the guarantee of all the Powers concerned, including Sweden. The Council is of opinion that this agreement should conform, in its main lines, with the Swedish draft Convention for the neutralization of the Islands. The Council instructs the Secretary-General to ask the Governments concerned to appoint duly accredited representatives to discuss and conclude the proposed Treaty.[14]

A treaty was promptly concluded between interested nations on October 20, 1921 in accordance with the Council's resolution.[15]

In a second case the international community acted through the Security Council of the United Nations. As recounted in chapter 4, at the height of the Suez Canal crisis, before the attacks by Israel, Britain, and France, the Security Council, with the approval of Egypt, voted six principles to be embodied in a settlement. These included the principle that "the operation of the Canal should be insulated from the politics of any country." In the altered environment created by the ensuing military attacks no implementation was pursued, and any conclusion as to what would have been done is too speculative to be of much value (see chapter 4, p. 38–39). But a principle requiring "insulation" of canal operation from politics was plainly stated.

When one comes to grips with the problem of actually formulating arrangements to protect international rights it is necessary to get beyond the generalized prescription of a meaningless "internationalization." There are four principal options, which may be considered in the alternative or in combination: (1) demilitarization, (2) international guarantees, (3) international participation, and (4) United Nations peacekeeping agreements.

Demilitarization

Demilitarization must be viewed as a device of limited usefulness in assuring international rights. Both history and reason suggest this conclusion. In the case of the Aaland Islands it was useful because the islands were not of strategic significance unless fortified. Demilitarization of international straits, however, has not been a successful device. The Lausanne Convention of 1921 provided for a demilitarized regime for the Turkish Straits with international guarantees to Turkey. Turkey's request in 1936 for a change in the convention to permit fortification of the straits pointed to a change in "the horoscope for the entire international development." Turkey argued: "When the Convention of Lausanne was concluded, Europe was on the road to disarmament, and the international community was on the verge of being transformed into a community based on unalterable principles of law, the available military forces were far less threatening, the situation in the Black Sea was uncertain, etc. In these circumstances Turkey had been in a position to accept the restrictions on her supremacy over the Straits and their coasts imposed by the Convention of Lausanne in consideration of the international guarantees given her in Article 18 of the Convention against infringements of Turkish territory in the Straits."[16] Now the international scene was changed and "the guarantee must be illusory."[17] The realism of Turkey's argument was accepted in the Montreux Convention of 1936[18] permitting Turkey to fortify the Straits.

Bruël argues with cogency that without effective international guarantees an unfortified strait would be too easy a prey to a great belligerent power.[19] He even suggests that the best solution may be control of a strait by a weak power with right to fortify it.[20] Bruël's solution does not meet the test of securing international rights, but he seems clearly right in pointing to the vulnerability of an unfortified strait unless protected by reliable guarantees.

The history of the demilitarized Tangiers Zone on the southern shore of the Strait of Gibraltar somewhat ambiguously looks to the same conclusion. The demilitarization of Tangiers was initiated by the Anglo-French Declaration of April 8, 1904, subsequently confirmed by a Spanish declaration of October 1904, and treaties in 1912, 1923, 1945, and 1952, and was finally abrogated in 1956.[21] There is an inherent ambiguity in the Tangiers experience, however, for the Tangiers Zone cannot be regarded a regime for a demilitarized strait. It applied only to the southern shore, while Great Britain continued her fortifications at Gibraltar.

Bruël's argument against demilitarization of straits applies with equal cogency to demililtarization of an interoceanic canal. It is significant that in the new Panama Canal treaties demilitarization has no role.

International Guarantees

International guarantees have often been tied to a regime of demilitarization, as in the Aaland Islands solution in 1921 and the Lausanne Convention of 1923 governing the Turkish Straits, but they may equally stand alone. The new Panama Canal neutrality treaty is usually thought of in terms of a right by the United States to protect its own rights of transit, but it is in form a guarantee of the rights of all nations. Given the interest of the United States in the Panama Canal it is reasonable to exepct that this approach will provide an effective guarantee of international rights.

There are, however, two problems with the approach of securing international rights through guarantees by other nations. First, the reliability of such guarantees may be undermined by events, such as changes in the domestic political scene of the guaranteeing powers or international developments requiring the commitment of their priorities to other interests. The problem is illustrated by the difference between a Europe in rising crisis in 1936 when Turkey sought amendment of the Lausanne Convention and the Europe of 1923 when the guarantees were given.

In the world as it is now developing the second problem with reliance on international guarantees may be even more serious. There is clearly an increasing sensitivity to big-power intervention in a nation's affairs. When action is taken against a territorial sovereign for failure to uphold international rights, this kind of fulfillment of a guarantee can easily be viewed as an unwarranted intervention when feelings of national pride and independence become involved. The sensitivity can be seen in the controversy that nearly blocked ratification of the new Panama Canal treaties, namely, whether the neutrality treaty gives the United States a right to intervene in Panama's affairs. Assurance of international rights through big-power guarantees invites awkward controversy if those guarantees ever have to be backed up, controversy that can only work against their fulfillment.

International Participation

What is contemplated here by the term international participation does not include a zone under international political administration. Such a zone must now be seen as creating an unstable arrangement. It conflicts with what is regarded as the right of self-determination of the people of the zone and of the people of the nation to which they belong. This issue cannot adequately be met even by separate but democratic institutions for the zone itself. In the long run any international arrangement has to allow national administration of civil and political affairs.

For the same reason even the trusteeship of strategic areas specifically provided for in Articles 82, 83, and 84 of the U.N. Charter does not provide reliable assurance for international rights in strategic areas. In practice all trusteeships have been treated as subject to the goal of fully implementing the right of the people to self-determination.[22] The only trusteeship designated as for a strategic area is that of the United States for the Trust Territory of the Pacific Islands. As it happens, part of the area has opted for a self-governing commonwealth status tied to the United States.[23] But a strategic trusteeship under the U.N. Charter cannot be viewed as an instrument for securing international rights. Even though it vests supervisory authority in the Security Council instead of the General Assembly, it must realistically be assumed that the trusteeship provides at best only a transition arrangement pending a full exercise of the right of self-determination.

International participation as an arrangement to secure international rights has to be addressed not to control of civil or political affairs but to control of operations affecting international rights. The precedent is well established in the administration of international rivers. Many treaties governing international rivers have established international commissions, some with representatives of nonriparian states.[24] Professor R. R. Baxter has argued at length against the applicability of a similar arrangement to interoceanic canals, principally on the ground that insoluble conflicts of interest exist among user, operator, and territorial sovereign. He argues that such conflicts of interest in interoceanic waterways of great strategic and economic importance have to be dealt with in the diplomatic arena. This conclusion is to some extent a reflection of the fact that Baxter subjects essential international needs to the discretion of the territorial sovereign. There is no reason to belileve, if the issues of substantive rights are resolved, as outlined above, that operational responsibilities should be beyond the competence of an international commission.[25]

International participation must be seen as a nonmilitary option unless combined with international guarantees or with a U.N. peacekeeping agreement as discussed below. The important feature of an international participation approach is that at some essential operational level an international instrumentality exists that would have to be not just bypassed or ignored by the territorial sovereign or operator state attempting to deny established international rights, but confronted and ejected. This is not a guarantee against determined military action by the territorial sovereign but a substantial obstacle and deterrent to it. It does not have to be an international commission with complete operational responsibility. But if participation on a partial level is to provide credible assurance, it has to exist at some essential operational level that puts the international instrumentality in a position to create an impasse. International participation should be seen as a nonmilitary buffer against denial of international rights.

United Nations Peace-keeping Arrangements

There is a variety of possible United Nations peace-keeping arrangements, and most of them do not lend themselves to the kind of guarantee of international rights required to provide a basis for acceptance of a rule of law. U.N. peace-keeping arrangements may be established by the General Assembly or the Security Council under their powers to recommend measures or by the Security Council under its power to take mandatory action to deal with a threat to the peace, breach of the peace, or act of aggression. Action under recommendatory powers can provide no meaningful long-term protection of international rights, for the continued presence of U.N. forces on the territory of a nation under a recommendatory vote depends on that nation's continued consent. Nor does reliance on future Security Council action provide realistic assurance, for Security Council action can be frustrated by the veto of any of the permanent members.

One kind of U.N. peace-keeping arrangement that might provide the necessary realistic assurance is an agreement under Article 43. That article provides for agreements to make available to the Security Council "armed forces, assistance, and facilities, including rights of passage, necessary for the purpose of maintaining international peace and security."

Article 43 was undoubtedly designed for a different purpose, to provide for member nations to make forces and facilities available for action against some offending nation. The "rights of passage" referred to presumably were seen as rights for U.N. forces to carry out Security Council enforcement action. But the wording is not limited. It includes agreements to make available any "assistance, and facilities, including rights of passage" necessary for the purpose of maintaining "international peace and security." There is no apparent reason why this could not, for example, include an agreement by the United Nations with a nation bordering an international strait for a right of access by U.N. forces to protect freedom of transit in a strait, a right for a present, expandable U.N. patrol presence to be permanently stationed in the territory, even a right of access by forces of guaranteeing powers in accordance with the terms of the agreement.

Article 43 provides for agreements making forces, assistance, and facilities "available to the Security Council, on its call," and no doubt this contemplates that control of the deployment of U.N. forces must continue to rest with the Security Council, and would be subject therefore to veto by a permanent member of any future action required by the Council. The U.N. presence itself, however, need not be in jeopardy. Indeed, the veto would be available to block action to require its removal. And if the agreement provided for direct action by guaranteeing powers, that action, unless so provided, would not be subject to frustration by veto by a permanent member.

The purpose here is not to advocate an Article 43 approach to the problem of providing protection for international rights but merely to indicate that it appears to provide possibilities that could fill a place in emerging law. What sets it apart from peace-keeping forces established under recommendatory action by the General Assembly is the provision for agreements by which the territorial sovereign could be bound. Article 43 must contemplate agreements upon which the Security Council can rely, agreements that cannot be revoked by the member nation without the Council's consent. This is confirmed by the provision in Article 43(3) attributing to these agreements the solemnity of treaties by making them "subject to ratification by the signatory states in accordance with their respective constitutional processes."

One must conclude from this examination of emerging law that there is clearly much remaining to be accomplished in perfecting a regime for the protection of international rights concerning strategic areas. While the directions in which the law appears to be moving are hopeful and there are foundations on which to build satisfactory solutions, emerging law does not yet provide a basis for a commitment to resolution of conflict by law except upon an explicit understanding that necessary international rights shall be recognized and protected. Nor can we afford to commit our own policy to acceptance of resolution by law without a clear reservation of our rights of independent action where other nations are unwilling to allow for the necessary scope and protection of international rights.

Twelve

INTERNATIONAL RIGHTS OF ACCESS TO RESOURCES

The Implications of Scarcity

Americans are not very different from the citizens of other countries in their instinct that a jealous guarding of the nation's sovereignty is automatically in the nation's interest. But this is a myopic view. In the discussion of international rights in strategic areas the vital stake of the United States in limitations on the sovereignty of nations bordering straits or traversed by an interoceanic canal was clear. The United States has a similar stake in international rights that limit sovereignty over resources, as was brought into dramatic focus by the Arab oil embargo of 1973. The deliberate manipulation of the supply of a raw material absolutely essential to industrial societies faced us starkly with the issue as to how far the sovereignty of a nation to control the disposition of its natural resources can be permitted to extend.

In the Arab oil embargo the United States chose the route of dialogue, looking toward cooperation and not confrontation in dealing with the crisis. Although the embargo ended in 1974, controversy over oil prices continued, and the specter of action that could deny the United States its required supplies through embargo or price action continued to lie behind current events. In 1975 Secretary Kissinger and

President Ford were repeatedly pressed as to whether in any circumstances the nation might resort to military action. They staked out a position in behalf of the United States, which President Ford stated most unequivocally in an interview for NBC television and radio on January 23, 1975:

> I wanted to make as clear as I possibly could that this country, in case of economic strangulation—and the key word is "strangulation"—we had to be prepared, without specifying what we might do, to take the necessary action for our self-preservation.
>
> When you are being strangled, it is a question of either dying or living. And when you use the word "strangulation" in relationship to the existence of the United States or its non-existence, I think the public has to have a reassurance, our people, that we are not going to permit America to be strangled to death. And so, I, in my willingness to be frank—but with moderation—I thought ought to say what I said then. And I hope I have amplified it, I hope clarified it, here.[1]

Both President Ford and Secretary Kissinger took pains to make clear that the position was entirely hypothetical, and the United States has consistently stated that the actual situations it has confronted did not call for military action.

Actually the issue of using military force is a rather narrow one, simply whether force is a legitimate remedy. Force is an extreme remedy, and its use is severely circumscribed under the U.N. Charter. Many actions that cannot lawfully be met with force are nevertheless themselves unlawful. Focus on the issue of the use of force tends to distract attention from the issue of the legitimacy of the actions by the Arab countries themselves. That is the question that must concern us in trying to weigh the implications of a commitment to resolve conflict by law. The issue is as to the extent of the sovereignty of a nation over the disposition of its resources.

The issue is, of course, more than an issue over oil. Our industrialized world depends on limited resources. No nation can be self-sufficient. Ours has become an interdependent world, and this interdependence relates to resources, environment, economic health, financial stability, development, and many other facets of our lives. The fundamental issue raised by the Arab oil embargo is that of a right of access to resources. It is an issue that will press upon us with increasing urgency in the years ahead.

The Emerging Law

As on other vital problems we have considered, there is an emerging law, and although it tends verbally to overemphasize national sovereignty over resources, the emerging law taken as a whole provides the basis for a constructive development of the right of access to resources.[2] What is emerging is not so much an affirmative right to acquire any specific amount or share of resources, but a negative right not to be denied access by certain actions or inaction, which are offenses or defaults on the part of the nation controlling the resources.

The emerging law is forming around four principles: (1) interventionary coercion, (2) unjustifiable discrimination, (3) responsibility to supply needs, and (4) duty to cooperate (General Assembly resolutions bearing on these issues are collected in appendix 5). There is reason in some of the U.N. resolutions for the sense of frustration felt by many of the Western nations. And it would be a mistake to gloss over the apparent ideological division in the concept of the "new international economic order" fervently promoted by the less developed nations. But none of this should blind us to the constructive elements of an emerging law of access to resources.

Interventionary Coercion

It has been argued from time to time that economic coercion is a kind of "force" and its use is governed by the general principles of Article 2(4) of the Charter of the United Nations. However, arguments to the contrary have generally prevailed, and the General Assembly in its landmark 1970 Declaration on Principles of International Law concerning Friendly Relations and Co-operation among States in accordance with the Charter of the United Nations treats economic coercion, not as a use of force in violation of Article 2(4), but as a kind of violation of the principle of nonintervention. This has an important bearing on what kind of action is prohibited. The 1970 Declaration bars economic or any other type of measures "to coerce another State in order to obtain from it the subordination of the exercise of its sovereign rights and to secure from it advantages of any kind."[3] Thus the motive or intended effect of coercive action is an essential part of the offense condemned. Intervention involves some attempted control of the free action of another nation. The language in the 1970 Declaration was derived from Res. 2131 of 1965 and is substantially repeated in Article 32 of the Charter of Economic Rights and Duties of States adopted by Res. 3281 in 1974.

The Arab nations themselves recognize the validity of the principle barring economic coercion for an interventionary purpose. I. F. I. Shihata, legal adviser to the Kuwait Fund for Arab Development, justified the 1973 oil embargo as a limited exception arising out of a state of war with Israel and the alleged encouragement by the United States and other nations to Israel not to return the Arab lands seized in the 1967 war as required by international law.[4] Whatever the case might be for economic coercion applied to Israel on such grounds, it must be rejected as applied to third nations who are guilty of nothing more than failing to coerce Israel, if the rule against interventionary coercion is to have any meaning. But Shihata's attempt to limit the Arab case carefully as an exception to the general rule attests to the acceptance of the rule itself even at a time when it might have been more convenient to downgrade it to a level of policy resting in the discretion of a nation in the exercise of its sovereignty.

A rule that bars economic coercion according to its motive or intended effect has some defects as a rule for practical application. Motive and intent are elusive. But rules of law have to be constructed to apply equally to all situations to which they are applicable by their terms. Even the rule as stated in the 1970 Declaration, unless read in its context as a rule against intervention, could go further than either the United States or the world is ready to go. The United States has long used economic pressure as an instrument of policy. This has not been confined to a denial of foreign aid or credits or other benefits but has extended to trade controls as well.[5] Of course, the governing rule does not necessarily have to be constructed to provide scope for all that the United States has seen fit in the past to do in the pursuit of its own policies. We probably have not always been as circumspect as a sound rule of general application would require of us. But our own experience can demonstrate that under a realistic rule for general application a finding merely that action is coercive cannot be sufficient to condemn it.

The element of intent—the intent to coerce the policy of another nation—is indeed vital, as can readily be seen when we consider the question of sales of arms and other strategic products. The United States, indeed any nation, will certainly insist on the right to ban sale of arms or military supplies or related technology where they might be used against it. This policy may have a powerful, if not coercive, effect on the policy orientation of a nation eager to acquire arms. But if the intent of the nation banning the sale is self-protection, it would clearly be unrealistic and wrong to contemplate a rule against coercion that would deny a nation this means of protecting itself from injury inflicted, so to speak, by its own weapons.

The point involved is in fact broader than this specific and fairly obvious case. Trade controls imposed not to coerce the policy of another nation but to implement one's own policy is not intervention and is not to be condemned as interventionary coercion. In the area of control of strategic products, the rule, for example, does not condemn controls to implement a policy of maintaining a regional power balance, as in the Middle East, or avoiding nuclear proliferation. The fact that application of a rule that depends on intent is elusive and uncertain is a problem, but it does nothing to deny the point that intent must be an element of the offense. If the rule of paragraph C2 of the 1970 Declaration on Principles of International Law is read in its context as a part of a rule of nonintervention, the condemnation of measures "to coerce another State in order to obtain from it the subordination of the exercise of its sovereign rights and to secure from it advantages of any kind" states a sound rule.

R. B. Lillich argues for a general principle "that serious and sustained economic coercion should be accepted as a form of permissible self-help only when it is also compatible with the overall interests of the world community, as manifested in the principles of the U.N. Charter or in decisions taken or documents promulgated thereunder."[6] Thus he argues that not only economic sanctions voted by the United Nations but economic sanctions applied to influence the Soviet Union to permit Soviet Jews to emigrate in accordance with the right affirmed under Article 13(2) of the Universal Declaration of Human Rights and Article 12(2) of the International Covenant on Civil and Political Rights (to which the Soviet Union is a party) should not offend the rule against interventionary coercion. This is not only sound but in accord with the rule of the 1970 Declaration itself, for economic action to influence a nation to comply with international law is not action to obtain from it "the subordination of the exercise of its sovereign rights." A nation's sovereign rights do not extend to actions that violate international law.

Unjustifiable Discrimination

Something like a rule of equal access to resources is evolving in a framework that allows only justifiable distinctions to be made. The rule is looser than the coercion principle in its allowable justifications but tighter in that it applies to discrimination not amounting to coercion.

The most-favored-nation concept has a long history. This history laid the foundation for the generalization of a rule against discrimination in the General Agreement of Tariffs and Trade of October 30, 1947 (GATT).[7] Article XIII established the general rule as to export restrictions in these terms:

> No prohibition or restriction shall be applied by any contracting party . . . on the exportation of any product destined for the territory of any other contracting party, unless . . . the exportation of the like product to all third countries is similarly prohibited or restricted.

Article XX, providing general exceptions to GATT rules, further stated the nondiscrimination principle:

> Subject to the requirement that such measures are not applied in a manner which would constitute a means of arbitrary or unjustifiable discrimination between countries where the same conditions prevail, or as a disguised restriction on international trade, nothing in this Agreement shall be construed to prevent the adoption or enforcement by any contracting party of measures. . . .

Among the restrictive measures permitted are conservation measures "if such measures are made effective in conjunction with restrictions on domestic production and consumption" (Article XX, clause I[g]) and measures "essential to the acquisition or distribution of products in general or short supply; *Provided* that any such measures shall be consistent with any multilateral arrangements directed to an equitable international distribution of such products or, in the absence of such arrangements, with the principle that all contracting parties are entitled to an equitable share of the international supply of such products" (Article XX, clause II[a]).

Article XXI provided a severe limitation on the reliability of the GATT principles in preserving the right of a nation to take "any action which it considers necessary for the protection of its essential security interests . . . taken in time of war or other emergency in international relations."

Not all nations are parties to GATT, and its provisions rest on a treaty basis, but the attempt to generalize a nondiscrimination principle attests to the international sense of a principle that ought to govern all nations. This international sense is reflected in other developments. The Charter of Economic Rights and Duties of States adopted by the U.N. General Assembly in 1974 in Res. 3281 reflects it in Article 26, which provides:

> International trade should be conducted without prejudice to generalized non-discriminatory and non-reciprocal preferences in favour of developing countries, on the basis of mutual advantage, equitable benefits and the exchange of most-favoured-nation treatment.

The notion that preference for developing countries is a justifiable discrimination is not found in GATT, but it pervades the Chareter of Economic Rights and Duties. But it should be noted that even this preference to be justifiable must be applied on a "generalized non-discriminatory and non-reciprocal basis."

The tentative Law of the Sea text contains provisions reflecting a principle against unjustifiable discrimination between nations. Express provisions against discrimination apply to regulations by a coastal state in its territorial sea (Article 24 [1][b]) and regulations by bordering states in an international strait (Article 42[2]). The text also evidences the need to allow for justifiable discrimination, expressly providing that most-favored-nation treatment does not apply to arrangements made to implement the right of transit of a landlocked nation (Article 126).

What we see is not a principle that has acquired the status of binding international law but a principle that has become a part of the sense of obligation of the international community and would have to have a place in any foreign policy commitment to the resolution of conflict by law. It is a principle whose application must be somewhat uncertain, for it has to allow for distinctions recognized as justifiable in the ever-evolving sense of the international community.

Responsibility to Supply Needs.

That the needs of nations give rise to international rights is attested by the historic development of the law governing international straits and the rights accorded at least riparian nations in international rivers. These developments may be seen as implementing the regime of the freedom of the seas, but even viewed in this narrowest perspective their imperative comes from the need of nations dependent on the transit of straits or rivers.

This is, however, too narrow a view. Even rights of transit are not confined to waterways. The covenant of the League of Nations committed the members to "make provision to secure and maintain freedom of communications and of transit and equitable treatment for the commerce of all members of the League" (Article 23[e]). The attempt to implement this provision included a Convention on Freedom of Transit on Land in 1921. After World War II the nations tackled the issue again in 1947 in the context of the General Agreement of Tariffs and Trade, providing for a generalized right of transit in Article V. The 1958 Convention on the High Seas included provision that landlocked states "should" have free access to the sea and that states situated between landlocked states and the sea "shall" furnish rights of transit by agreement.[8] If the 1958 Convention fell short of language of firm obligation, as some have thought,[9] the current tentative Law of the Sea text cures the deficiency in providing: "Land-locked States shall have the right of access to and from the sea for the purpose of exercising the rights provided for in this Convention including those relating to the freedom of the high seas and the common heritage of mankind. To this end, landlocked States shall enjoy freedom of transit through the territories of transit States by all means of transport."[10] As noted above, Professor Elihu Lauterpacht concluded in 1958 that a general right of transit had come to be recognized in international law, developed partly in a course of treaty development but standing independent of treaty obligation. Conceding that this conclusion was a "hesitating one," he pointed out:

> Nevertheless, the fact is that freedom of transit is one of the most fundamental needs of the community. Just as, historically, in municipal law, the right of eminent domain was formulated principally in connection with the construction of roads and railways, so it should not be regarded as particularly surprising if, in international law, the existence of a definable interest of the community came to be recognized by the acknowledgment of a legal right to freedom of transit.[11]

Freedom of transit is an emerging right based on necessity and convenience. It is neither confined to waterways nor grounded on or limited by the right of freedom of the seas.

These evolving international rights stem from considerations more fundamental than anything to do merely with transit. As Lauterpacht intimates, when the necessities of our coexistence in a community of nations come to be identified in some definable interest, that interest in time comes to be recognized by the acknowledgment of a legal right. The same considerations that lie behind international rights in international straits and rivers, which give rights of access to the sea for landlocked states and other rights of transit also give rise to a right of access to resources necessary for a viable coexistence in a community of nations. This is such a compelling and necessary conclusion that even in the heat of controversy over the OPEC oil actions, the Arab countries in substance conceded it. Shihata summarized: "In fact, the continued supply of oil has been officially regarded by the Arab oil-exporting countries as an 'international responsibility' of the highest moral order."[12]

The Charter of Economic Rights and Duties of States, adopted by Res. 3281 in 1974, lists among the governing principles "peaceful co-existence," "mutual and equitable benefit," and "free access to and from the sea by landlocked countries within the framework of the above principles." The International Covenant on Economic, Social and Cultural Rights and the International Covenant on Civil and Political Rights, proposed by Res. 2200 in 1966, each provide in Article 1(2):

> All peoples may, for their own needs, freely dispose of their natural wealth and resources without prejudice to any obligations arising out of international economic co-operation, based on the principles of mutual benefit, and international law. In no case may a people be deprived of its own means of subsistence.

In recognizing a right of access to necessary resources, we are talking about a right that does not by its own operation translate into a right to any specific quantity, at any specific price, on any specific terms. Much must turn upon equitable considerations and rest in the exercise of some measure of justifiable discretion on the part of the nation that has sovereignty over the territory in which the resources exist. But the fact that a discretion exists, the fact even that the right is implemented by terms that must be agreed upon, does not, as Lauterpacht points out, deny the right or preclude its implementation by an adjudicative process in case of an abuse of discretion, failure to bargain in good faith, or insistence on inadmissible positions.[13]

Duty to Cooperate

Current developments clearly acknowledge a final level of duty by which a right of access to resources may be defined in emerging law—a duty of economic cooperation. The 1970 Declaration on Principles of International Law asserts this as a duty under the international law of the Charter (par. D1). The resolutions collected in appendix 5 demonstrate that the duty to cooperate has been repeatedly asserted. The 1974 Charter on the Economic Rights and Duties of States, adopted by Res. 3281, makes clear that a major format for such cooperation is contemplated to be "by means of arrangements and by the conclusion of long-term multilateral commodity agreements, where appropriate, and taking into account the interests of producers and consumers"

(Article 6). The resolution further states that "all States have the duty to conduct their mutual economic relations in a manner which takes into account the interests of other countries" (Article 24; see also the provisions of Articles 9, 14, and 28 excerpted in appendix 5).

One can regard the responsibility to supply needs discussed above as a separate principle or as an aspect of the duty to cooperate, although it seems useful to identify it as a separate principle since it relates to a specific definable interest of compelling necessity. If the world does in fact move down the road of cooperation contemplated by the U.N. resolutions, it may well be that the right of access to necessary resources will be implemented by multilateral agreements.

It remains to consider the terms under which the sovereignty of nations over their resources is stated in U.N. resolutions. These resolutions are collected and excerpted in appendix 5. It is evident from a reading of these resolutions that the language is often modified to reflect duties existing under international law. And even when it is not, the affirmation of sovereignty can hardly be intended as a denial of the principles concerning coercion, nondiscrimination, necessity, and cooperation, which resolutions, often the same ones, equally assert. National sovereignty over resources, like other aspects of sovereignty, refers to rights to be exercised in accordance with and subject to applicable principles imposed in the interest of the community of nations.

In brief, these developments evidencing an evolution of law on four levels of restraint provide a basis for an emerging right of access to resources. It is a part of the unfinished business of emerging law, but there is a foundation on which to build.

The right of access to resources must be viewed as a part of the larger issue, the limiting of territorial sovereignty to the extent necessary for the protection of international rights. The conclusions stated at the end of chapter 11 dealing with strategic areas apply here too. Any commitment to resolve conflict by law must be based on an explicit understanding that necessary international rights shall be recognized and protected and on a reservation of freedom of action where other nations are unwilling to allow for the necessary scope and protection of such rights.

These cautious conclusions do little to suggest the stake that the United States has in a process of adjudication, if one should become available, to define and implement a right of access to resources. The discussion of the role for adjudication in United States foreign policy is the subject of part three.

Part Three

ADJUDICATION IN THE REAL WORLD

Thirteen

THE NATIONAL INTEREST IN A PROCESS OF ADJUDICATION

The Role of an Adjudication Option

The argument has brought us to this point—that our realistic foreign policy choice is not between law and power but between making the most of the power of law and grudgingly accepting its restraints while losing its constructive potential. We are often blind to the role of law in foreign policy. When we perceive law only as a set of sometimes embarrassing restraints at the periphery of policy, we fail to see in law the only successful strategy for the resolution of conflict, a strategy that lies at the center of our foreign policy concerns. When the importance of national security and vital interests lead us to think that foreign policy must be shaped by considerations of power and not of law, we ignore the political logic that has shaped our fundamental foreign policy positions to reflect legal concepts. When we assign priority to maintaining a balance of power as an alternative to law, we fail to understand that the balance of power is in fact not an alternative to law but its underpinning, something that realistically can be preserved only by actions which accord with law. When a supposedly tough-minded realism leads us to act in disregard of law, we have had to learn that this is instead the path of weakness and failure. It is only with law that we marshal the complex of the elements of power that work for success. Not the least of these is the capacity of law to unite the nation behind action and sustain the support and sacrifice that may be necessary if the action is challenged in a test of power and will.

We have also seen that the kind of law that is the business of foreign policy, the kind of law that serves the historic mission of law, is law that has the capacity to change to implement the felt necessities of the time. This is dictated not only by the strategy of law, but by the facts of international life. As no realistic foreign policy could have ignored the emerging law of self-determination, so foreign policy cannot be tied to the status quo against any change identified in emerging principles that have become a part of the operating reality of the time. Developing law, as it is seen in General Assembly resolutions, is a part of the reality by which even the major powers find they have to shape their policies and their actions.

But the argument for law is not just that it is inescapable or that it can be pursued without jeopardy to our national security and other vital interests. Looking to the future the more important point is the constructive potential of law. Thus, the principle of self-determination can work to provide a discipline to the powerful aspirations it articulates. The rule of nonintervention—based on reciprocal abstention and backed by the corollary right of counterintervention—is the alternative to escalation of local conflict into big-power conflagration. The principle of regional security zones not only provided the rationale that enabled us to secure the removal of Soviet missiles from Cuba without actual armed conflict, but avoids the counterproductive logic of claiming or recognizing spheres of influence. And, finally, we have seen that our national security, even our viable economic existence, depend on the recognition of international rights—rights in strategic areas and rights of access to resources.

How then are the possibilities of law to be realized? Before turning to the proposal to be made in this part, some preliminary observations will help to define the problem.

We should have no illusions that the United States can make the world a safe place by the simple declaration of our own commitment to the resolution of internatinal conflict by rules of law. Foreign policy is bound to be a frustrating business in any circumstances, for we cannot control the actions of other nations. And though it is true that nothing is more likely to destroy our capacity to influence the policies of other nations or developments within them than an attempt to coerce them, it does not follow that our dedication to rules of law will automatically or immediately transform the behavior of others.

There are, nevertheless, unique virtues to policies based on law. First, they have the capacity to attract support from nations with diverse histories and cultures, conflicting ideologies, and disparate domestic policies. As such they provide the basis on which coalitions for order and peaceful change can be built. Even though such coalitions can be built only by patience and consistent commitment, one can easily foresee that the United States can achieve a greater influence over the behavior of other nations through a shared sense of law than through the raw assertion of power.

Policies based on law also possess a second source of strength. They identify with those aspirations and convictions that are the most fundamental articles of belief, to which peoples hold with the greatest tenacity, which peoples demand as their right because they believe them to be right. These are the special concerns of law. They are "the felt necessities of the time" to which the reconciling strategy of law is applied. A policy that would frustrate instead of fulfill a legitimate right of self-determination, a policy that would attempt to excuse the coercive intervention by one nation in the affairs of another, is bound to be in permanent danger. Its temporary success is not a building block of future strength but instead a source of resentment, rejection, instability, and ineffectiveness.

Finally, the effectiveness of foreign policy in influencing other nations must reflect in some measure our own national commitment to it. As we look to the future, we must not forget what I have suggested may be the real lesson of Vietnam (above, pp. 46–47), that for foreign policy to command the commitment of the people, to sustain the unity of the people, it must be grounded in law.

We should be able to recognize the validity of these sources of strength from our own failings. In the United States we have been somewhat ambivalent even about the basis for the use of our own power. It should not be surprising that we are often perceived by others as we often see ourselves—simply as using power to support governments viewed by us as friendly and to oppose those viewed by us as unfriendly. This perception is damaging to us, for it limits our ability to influence events. It contributes to anti-American resentments. These resentments even provide a cover for the machinations of others. The damage to us is a price we pay without any compensating gain, for in practice our freedom to use our power to implement such a policy is limited anyway.

Our inclination to take a friends-and-enemies approach to foreign policy is damaging even to our own sense of leadership. When we seem to fail in this policy, as when the government in South Vietnam succumbed, or seem to let down a friendly government, as in Iran, we are left in frustration and confusion. We seem to be unable to influence the courses of events that are supposed to be of vital importance to us despite our superior military and economic power.

If we are going to restore our sense of leadership, if we are going to recover the momentum of an effective, sustainable initiative, if we are going to make the most of law in serving our national interest, we must find the most effective means of asserting a leadership based on law. We should not expect to change the world at the stroke of a pen, but we need to assert a leadership that can make effective use of the building blocks of law.

With these preliminary observations out of the way, it is time to consider what a leadership based on commitment to the resolution of conflict by rules of law entails. If it is in our national interest to ground our foreign policy in a genuine commitment to law, it is also in our national interest to implement that commitment by acceptance of some process for adjudication of disputes that cannot be resolved by negotiation and diplomacy. This is not a self-evident proposition, although everyone will, I think, concede that there cannot be a rule of law without a process of adjudication. Adjudication provides the third-party decision process identified in chapter 1 as one of the three essential elements of law as a strategy for the resolution of conflict. No nation can necessarily expect its determination of its own rights and obligations to be accepted by other nations who disagree with it.

The issue here, however, is not whether we must sooner or later come to acceptance of some process of adjudication but whether it is desirable and prudently feasible to do so now. There are several reasons why it is important to fashion a process of adjudication that we can accept now. First, our commitment to law is going to suffer much in credibility and effectiveness if we are not prepared to let the law be determined and applied on an impartial basis. Even when our purposes are genuine, it is not difficult for others to misrepresent them to a skeptical world. And, candidly, our record, like those of all other nations, many of which are worse than ours, provides ample evidence of the temptation to use a subjective tactics-oriented interpretation of law to serve other ends. A declaration of our dedication to law, even if genuine, will not give our policies the power and respect abroad and support at home that could be expected from the credibility to be derived from our willingness to adjudicate as a last resort.

Second, a standing offer to adjudicate would inevitably shape the negotiation of specific disputes. It would not only discipline our own negotiating positions but influence those of other parties as well. Even those unwilling to adjudicate would have to react to the negotiating pressure by some accommodation to meritorious legal positions.

Third, we have seen that on many of the Cold War/balance-of-power issues of the world, our interest is not in particular terms of settlement but in avoiding a shift in power accomplished by the unilateral use or threat of force (see chapter 3). Such was the issue in Vietnam, and, as argued in chapter 4, we had everything to gain and nothing to lose from an offer to adjudicate the issues involved. We would have accomplished our purposes if an adjudication had taken place, and fortified our position if the offer had been rejected.

Fourth, in issues of self-determination some determination by international process is often an essential preliminary to a legitimate exercise of the right (see chapter 8). The issues for determination call for a process that is adjudicative in nature. Forces of division are at work in the world, and the right of self-determination is their battle cry. The right has to be implemented by some process of adjudication, or it only adds impetus to the potential for chaos and conflict. With a process of adjudication, the principle of self-determination can be a principle for legitimacy and peaceful change. If we are to make our weight felt toward a constructive development of the principle of self-determination, we must support and be ready to accept its implementation by a process of adjudication.

Fifth, where exercise of a right of counterintervention becomes necessary, we strengthen and clarify our position and help to avoid the charge that the United States is the offending intervenor if our counterintervention is made subject to adjudication, provided other affected parties will agree, and is subject to interim determinations the adjudicatory tribunal may make (see chapter 9). By offering to adjudicate we do not compromise our power to act before an adjudication can take place if the circumstances require it. Rather we fortify the basis for that action.

Sixth, if we mean to mount effective pressure against Soviet or Cuban intervention in Africa or elsewhere, we need to come to the fray with a policy of nonintervention as unequivocal and distortion-proof as we can make it (see chapter 9). As long as the right of counterintervention is preserved, we have nothing to lose and everyting to gain from being willing to adjudicate issues of intervention. In some cases our willingness to adjudicate may itself provide an important element of the counter-pressure against intervention. When interventions are hidden or justified by fabricated claims, as they often are, our willingess to adjudicate issues of intervention can help to expose the hypocrisy of those nations that will not subject their own claims to the same test. If our willingness to adjudicate becomes an accepted fact in the calculations of other nations, it can give them cause for restraint.

Seventh, the United States may need a process of adjudication to protect its own interests. We depend absolutely on recognition of international rights by other nations, and not least upon recognition of the emerging rights that provide some access to resources (see chapter 12). The Arab oil embargo reminds us that, powerful as we are, the United States is no different from the weak in having a direct stake in the enforcement of rights through legal process rather than force.

Finally, even in issues where the interest of the United States is only in assisting a peaceful, just, and stable solution, our ability to exert influence on the shape of the settlement is limited by fear of being perceived as partial. We can support principles of law without losing our standing of impartiality, but only if our own attachment to law is beyond question. The traditional role of conciliation, which by being blind to the application of legal principles lends a color of respectability to intransigent positions that reject or misapply law, may no longer provide the path to peace. The dispute between Israel and her Arab neighbors may be a case where only acceptance of legal principles can resolve the intractable issues and only a strong influence from a United States whose impartial dedication to law is beyond question can bring about a settlement.[1] The older role of conciliation may still be appropriate in many situations, but if law does provide the best strategy for the resolution of conflict, then peace requires that we position ourselves to use our influence strongly for resolutions based on law.

There is an essential point to be made about all these reasons. They are reasons why the United States must offer to adjudicate issues that cannot be resolved by negotiation and diplomacy. It is our willingness to adjudicate that is important. The reasons do not depend on the willingness of other nations to adjudicate. The impact of our offer to adjudicate does not derive from the number of cases that may in fact be adjudicated. Our declared willingness to adjudicate can serve its function, even if no case is ever adjudicated.

The current role of an option for adjudication is not to keep tribunals busy. It is not to substitute adjudication for negotiation or diplomacy. It is not to dispense with armed forces or balance of power. Rather it is to make a foreign policy grounded in law a more effective foreign policy.

Our choice in foreign policy is between making the most effective use of the power of law and losing the opportunity to do so. It is in our national interest to fashion a realistic process of adjudication that we can accept now.

The Problems that Shape the Option

The challenge is to construct terms for an adjudication option that are realistic for us and for others. What is required is in fact a real option. The Permanent Court of International Justice commented that "the judicial settlement of international disputes . . . is simply an alternative to the direct and friendly settlement of such disputes between the Parties. . . ."[2] Any third-party decision process has to be shaped as such an alternative if it is to bear on the real world at all.

The adjudication option does not have to be a preferred alternative. It does not have to provide the normal basis for resolving disputes. Litigation normally is and should be a last resort. Negotiation and diplomacy provide nations the security of retaining control over the process to assure a result that will be satisfactory to them. Nor should the law-generating capacity of the negotiating process be disparaged. Compromises and accommodations hammered out in negotiation have often provided the roots of law.

What is required is an adjudication option that provides a reasonable alternative. This is vital if the option is to serve its foreign-policy purpose. If our terms for adjudication are loaded one way or hedged with unacceptable conditions, they will be seen as a sham. Holding out that kind of an adjudication option will only boomerang and add to cynicism about our protestations of commitment to law and even to cynicism about law itself.

The terms of an adjudication option have to reflect considerations that stem from three problems inherent in the context in which it is to be offered: (1) the necessity of giving effect to emerging law; (2) the uncertainties of law on some critical issues; and (3) the absence of any assurance that other nations will be willing to accept adjudication.

Since foreign policy cannot disregard emerging law that may not yet qualify as law that the International Court of Justice can recognize under Section 38 of the Statue of the Court (see chapter 5), so an adjudication option designed to support and implement foreign policy must also provide some means of giving effect to emerging law. The adjudicating tribunal must be directed to base its decision on established law and on principles commanding widespread international acceptance that the tribunal determines to be appropriate for acceptance as law.

The tribunal cannot, however, be given a strictly legislative competence. Neither the United States nor other nations will be prepared to hand over to a tribunal the authority to make law in that sense. Its function is not to invent principles, but to sift out of the political and diplomatic process those principles that are appropriate for acceptance as law.[3] Like all law those principles must be legal in character in that they apply equally to all according to their terms and they must respond to and implement the felt necessities of the times. Like any adjudicating body, the tribunal must have a wide discretion in fashioning remedies for proven violation, but issues that are not judicable by established law or by emerging principles appropriate for acceptance as law must be referred back to the parties for negotiation or other appropriate disposition, within such guidelines or limitations as legal principles may provide (further implications of the necessity of giving effect to emerging law are considered in chapters 13 and 14).

An adjudication giving effect to emerging law must not be confused with arbitration. International arbitration is unlike most other arbitrations in that it contemplates a decision by legal principles only without authority in the arbitrator to provide his own principles of decision where the law fails to supply the answers.[4] International arbitration simply calls for a judicial determination by a tribunal that is not a court. Most other arbitrations call for a determination by the arbitrator according to law insofar as there is law and otherwise by whatever principles the arbitrator deems appropriate. Foreign policy calls for an option that contemplates an adjudication, not an arbitration in this latter sense. In providing for decision by principles of emerging law it does not call for a determination out of the tribunal's head. This is a necessary premise for an adjudication option to be declared as general policy by the United States, and ordinarily would be necessary for any voluntary acceptance of the jurisdiction of a tribunal by other parties.

The second kind of problem that shapes the adjudication option is the uncertainty of law or emerging law on some critical issues. Two examples will make the point. The United States is certainly not going to agree to an adjudication that might deny the American nations the right to act as they did in the Cuban missile crisis. The United States set forth a cogent legal position at the time, which was not widely challenged and to which in effect the U.S.S.R. acquiesced. That position provides the basis as outlined in chapter 10 for regional security zones established by regional collective action. The issue is, however, so vital to the United States, that it would not be prudent for the United States to leave acceptance of our reading of events and our understanding of principles to chance. A second example is the right of counterintervention. Although sound in principle and supported by legal writers, it is not spelled out in terms in the 1970 Declaration or other binding documents. Again, it is too vital a matter to be left to chance. These examples are intended only to indicate the problem. The consideration of a full and balanced statement of necessary understandings will require a careful exploration of problem areas and consultation with other nations.

There is nothing new in the concept that the premises for consent to the jurisdiction of a tribunal should include an explicit agreement on certain provisions of governing law. The Charter of the Nuremberg Tribunal for the trial of war ciriminals is a prominent example. In a declaration that backs our commitment to resolution of conflicts by law with a standing option to adjudicate, some stated understandings as to governing law must be spelled out, those understandings that form the minimum premises for our consent to adjudicate.

This is a precaution, however, that can be carried too far. An excess of hedge clauses and one-sided understandings can undercut our declared commitment to law and cause our whole effort to boomerang as already suggested. It can also limit the possibilities for the evolution of law, a development in which the United States also has a stake. While it is the offer to adjudicate that is itself of most immediate significance, we should recognize also the possibilities of the process for the growth of law. If adjudications do take place, they will provide a means by which law can be declared and defined by the cumulative course of decisions as in the growth of the common law.

Finally, a policy of allowing an adjudication option has to face the fact that there is absolutely no assurance the option will be accepted by the other necessary parties to a dispute. This has several implications. Obviously, it has to be made absolutely clear that the United States reserves it rights to act as its interests may require, if other parties necessary for an adjudication of all interlocking issues decline to proceed for adjudication. But more than this, the procedure has to be capable of operating where necessary parties are willing to adjudicate without waiting for all nations to accept such a process for all issues. The provision has to be for a voluntary process of adjudication that is not dependent on universal acceptance or on acceptance of compulsory jurisdiction by any nation. There has to be careful provision (considered further in chapter 14) that the interests of nations consenting to the jurisdiction of a tribunal are not prejudiced by the absence of other nations who have not consented.

Perspectives on Emerging Law

It became clear in the discussion of emerging law in part two that an evaluation of it must be seen as a mixed result. On some points emerging law was seen to be reasonably clear and satisfactory. On others only the potential for satisfactory solutions could fairly be said to exist. This seems inevitable at any stage in history. At any time some principles will have reached a point of precision and acceptance little short of what the International Court of Justice can apply under its statute as the Court reads it; some will be little more than embryonic; and others will lie in that middle ground where, although not recognizable as binding law by the Court, they will have reached a point of definition and acceptance that makes them functionally operative as law for foreign policy purposes. Emerging law is a reality with which foreign policy has to deal, and it will always present principles in different stages of development.

Although emerging law is a reality that we cannot ignore, our evaluation of it is important in deciding how to deal with it. When we are considering the feasibility of an adjudication option, as we are here, it is important to recognize that the perspective of our evaluation is not the same as when we were considering only the desirability of an explicit commitment of foreign policy to law.

In part two we were largely considering emerging law in the latter perspective. Does the law governing nonintervention, for example, provide a sound basis for foreign policy? Does the U.N. rule of nonintervention coupled with a right of counterintervention provide a sound basis for confronting Soviet actions in Africa? Does it provide a prudent measure for U.S. actions in Latin America? In this perspective, ongoing developments for which sound foundations have been laid and sound directions set are only slightly less satisfactory than more advanced development, for they are consistent with a foreign policy commitment to law. In the implementation of that commitment we can lean upon those foundations and directions and use our substantial weight to help to shape their constructive development.

Consideration of a standing adjudication option requires a different perspective. It is a difference that cuts two ways. On the one hand, insufficiently formed or accepted principles present a greater risk of an adverse determination, one contrary to the way we choose to read and move emerging law. On the other hand, however, the process of adjudication, where it is accepted by others, can present a more advantageous forum in which to shape developments than the cruder arena of contention and power in which principles are otherwise hammered out. It is almost inconceivable, for example, that international rights in straits, canals, and other strategic areas and international rights providing access to necessary resources would not be at least as well protected in an adjudication as they are in the maelstrom of contention directed by considerations of national pride and national power in which foreign policy is otherwise conducted. There clearly are elements of risk in a process of adjudication, but there are reasons to prefer them to the risks that otherwise can block or distort the development of the law.

Two of the suggestions made in the previous section have an important bearing on the evaluation of these risks. The risks of an adjudication option must be seen in the context of an option that (a) includes stipulations of substantive law on a limited number of critical issues necessary for consent and (b) leaves the United States free to act if other parties necessary for an adjudication of all interlocking issues do not consent to proceed.

Fourteen

A PROPOSED DECLARATION FOR LAW AND ACCEPTANCE OF ADJUDICATION

Proposed Declaration

Our argument points to the conclusion that the foreign policy of the United States would be strengthened and progress toward a rule of law aided by a declaration of a policy commitment to law. Such a declaration must obviously be made only after the most careful consideration and discussion and only after full consultation with the U.S. Senate and with other nations. This, however, is a situation in which discussion is most likely to be advanced by outlining a concrete proposal. The best way to consider the feasibility of a declaration of policy is to propose one. It is in that spirit, making no claim to final answers, that a proposal is offered here.

I propose that the United States, with other like-minded nations, if feasible, should issue a Declaration for Law and Acceptance of Adjudication covering the following points:

> 1. The United States, reaffirming its dedication to equal justice under law, declares that the foreign policy of the United States shall reflect our commitment to law; law whose principles apply equally to all nations according to their terms; law which is capable of effecting necessary change and which itself has the

capacity to change according to the changing needs of mankind; law which respects and safeguards the esential rights and interests of all nations; law whose impartial application is assured by the availability of a process of independent adjudication.

2. Accordingly, it is the policy of the United States to seek resolution of international disputes according to principles of law, including those widely accepted principles not yet established as binding law that have the character of law and are appropriate for acceptance as law.

3. When resolution in accordance with such principles cannot be achieved through negotiation and diplomacy after a genuine and full effort has been made to do so, the United States is prepared to seek a resolution according to such principles through a voluntary process of adjudication upon terms specified in a proposed Charter for a Voluntary Adjudication Tribunal, which is made a part of the Declaration.

4. The United States reserves the right to take all appropriate measures to protect its interests and the interests of the international community, if any of the parties necessary for an adjudication of all interlocking issues involved in a dispute is unwilling to proceed for an adjudication or fails to proceed in good faith and with due diligence or fails to comply with any interlocutory or final determination by the Tribunal, or if the Tribunal declines to act. Where a dispute is to be determined by adjudication, the United States reserves the right to take all appropriate measures to require others to desist from or reverse actions that may be prejudicial to an adjudicated resolution, subject, however, to any interim order the Tribunal may make in accordance with its Charter.

5. The Declaration is a statement of the policy of the United States. It is made unilaterally and not as part of any treaty or other agreement and is not intended to create or add to any legally binding obligation of the United States. A submission for a binding adjuciation of a specific dispute is subject to the requirements of the U.S. constitution.[1] The policy of accepting adjudication does not apply to issues arising under the laws of warfare during the continuation of hostilities.

Proposed Charter for a Voluntary Adjudication Tribunal

As appears from point 2 of the proposed Declaration, the proposed Charter for a Voluntary Adjudication Tribunal is contemplated as an integral part of the Declaration. The proposed Charter would cover the following points:

A. Unless the parties otherwise agree, the Tribunal shall be an ad hoc tribunal of not less than five members appointed by the International Court of Justice by not less than a majority of the full Court.[2]

B. The Tribunal shall not exercise jurisdiction unless it has jurisdiction over all parties determined by it to be necessary for an adjudication of all issues involved in the dispute, including all matters necessary for it to make a determination without jeopardy to the national security or vital interests of any party. All parties shall accept the jurisdiction of the Tribunal in all matters determined by the Tribunal to be necessary for a determination.

C. The Tribunal shall provide an opportunity to intervene or to be heard to all nations whose security or other interests may be substantially affected by a determination.

D. When necessary to accomplish the purposes of the Charter of the Tribunal, individuals, groups, and other entities may be recognized as parties.[3]

E. The Tribunal may not exercise jurisdiction as to matters that are essentially within the domestic jurisdiction of any nation.[4]

F. The Tribunal shall make its determination on the basis of law, which shall not be limited by the terms of Article 38(1) of the Statute of the International Court of Justice and shall include such other widely accepted principles as it determines to have the character of law and to be appropriate for acceptance as law. Issues that are not justiciable by law as so understood must be referred back to the parties for negotiation or other appropriate action, within such guidelines or limitations determined by the Tribunal as applicable principles may provide.

G. A corresponding rule shall determine the effect to be given to treaties. The Vienna Convention on the Law of Treaties governs and shall apply to past as well as to future treaties. A widely accepted principle that the Tribunal determines to be appropriate for acceptance as a peremptory norm of general international law shall be given effect as such in the application of the terms of the Convention. The principle of self-determination shall be respected as a peremptory norm of general international law under Articles 53 and 64 of the Convention.[5]

H. All interlocutory and final decisions by the Tribunal shall be in writing with findings of fact and statement of reasons.

I. All government parties agree to arrange for the use of local process by all parties and by the Tribunal.

J. The Tribunal may: (a) grant necessary temporary relief

pending final adjudication on the merits, including establishment of truce lines, ordering withdrawal of forces or weapons, or cessation of aid (see I.C.J. Statute Article 41); (b) employ the procedure of a commission of inquiry (see I.C.J. Statute Article 50); (c) employ the procedure of a plebiscite and for this purpose determine the procedure and terms of plebiscite, define the area or areas by which a vote shall be taken and fix the conditions to assure a free and informed expression of the wishes of the people involved.

K. The Tribunal shall be bound by the following stipulations of substantive law:

1. The right of self-determination does not apply to an area whose inhabitants are accorded full civil and political rights without discrimination and in substantial compliance with the Universal Declaration of Human Rights, unless the territory was annexed and is held under circumstances making the annexation currently voidable under international law.

2. The right of nations in a region, by appropriate collective action, and subject to preemptive action by the U.N. Security Council, to establish a regional security zone on appropriate terms shall be respected.

3. The rights of the community of nations necessary for their peaceful, secure, and viable coexistence shall be respected and protected by appropriate measures.

L. Decisions of the Tribunal shall not be reviewable by the International Court of Justice on their merits but shall be reviewable as to noncompliance with the terms of the Charter of the Tribunal, exceeding its authority, or failure to observe requirements of procedural due process.

The Role of the International Court of Justice

It is apparent that a rather limited role is contemplated for the International Court of Justice in the proposed Charter for a Voluntary Adjudication Tribunal. The Court would only appoint the Tribunal (if the parties did not otherwise agree) and provide a strictly limited review of the Tribunal's decisions relating only to the Tribunal's compliance with its Charter, its authority, and with requirements of procedural due process. At a time when the caseload of the Court is minimal and years of thought and effort have been devoted to ways of providing a greater use of the Court this certainly warrants some comment. The limited functions proposed for the Court imply no criticism of the Court or its decisions, given the difficulty of its position. They derive rather from the nature of the responsibility to be given to the Tribunal.

For the reasons discussed earlier, the Tribunal is to apply not just established law but also what has been termed here emerging law. This is an assignment for which the I.C.J. is not an appropriate tribunal. The statute of the Court, like the earlier provision for the Permanent Court of International Justice, is actually broad enough to permit it. Article 38(2) provides that the limitation of categories of established law in Article 38(1) "shall not prejudice the power of the Court to decide a case *ex aequo et bono,* if the parties agree thereto." However, the prospects for the Court ever acting *ex aequo et bono* even when the parties agree is under some cloud. In the much discussed *Free Zones Case* in 1930 the Permanent Court of International Justice, in a case where the submission was at least arguably for a decision *ex aequo et bono,* declined to act, giving the parties an opportunity to negotiate instead. The Court commented that "although the Court, being a Court of Justice, cannot disregard rights recognized by it and base its decision on considerations of pure expediency, nevertheless there is nothing to prevent it, having regard to the advantages which a solution of this kind might present, to offer the Parties, who alone can bring it about, a further opportunity for achieving this end," that is, a settlement "even though departing from strict law."[6]

There is no more reason to think that the present International Court of Justice would find acceptable a reference requiring it to give effect to principles not yet recognizable as binding law in modification of rights under established law. Indeed, the current international climate makes the role of the I.C.J. a far more delicate one than was the role of the P.C.I.J. in 1930. Some of the world openly rejects adjudication by the Court and even the idea of third-party adjudication. The Court has reason to be very cautious in trying to build the confidence of some parts of the international community. It can be argued that the role assigned to the proposed voluntary tribunal is a more promising path to build that confidence, since part of the skepticism is based on a perception that the Court's kind of law is the law of the status quo. But the Court is clearly in an awkward position and is not likely to move into a new mission without general acceptance of its new role.

But something more than the sensitivity of the Court to the current international situation is involved and something more than the logical inconsistency that disturbed the court in the *Free Zones Case.* A dual role for the I.C.J. would present a conflict of commitment. The proposed voluntary ad hoc tribunal contemplates a tribunal that will implement the desire of willing nations to extend the role of law. A tribunal that in one role is committed to apply rules that are not but ought to be law would be involved in a process of implied criticism of its other function of determining cases by rules that already are established law. The I.C.J. would be likely to be inhibited in its voluntary adjudication function by the responsibilities of its function under Article 38(1). A foreign policy commitment to law needs to be implemented by an adjudication option employing a tribunal that can share that commitment.

The vareity of I.C.J. reform proposals coming out of the activity stimulated by General Assembly Res. 2723 (XXV) of December 15, 1970 and Res. 2818 (XXVI) of December 15, 1971 has not met the central problem involved here. However useful many of the reform proposals may be in facilitating the use of the Court in its own role, they do not provide the basis for assigning to it the mission contemplated for the proposed voluntary ad hoc adjudication tribunals. Res. 3232 (XXIX) of November 12, 1974 attempted to go further, drawing attention to the potential role of General Assembly resolutions in the Court's consideration of developments in law and to the opportunity for I.C.J. adjudication *ex aequo et bono* under its statute. The words of the resolution do nothing to solve the problem. The I.C.J. is not in a position to commit itself to the task contemplated.

The limited role contemplated in the proposal for the I.C.J. stands on a different footing. Giving the appointing authority to the Court builds upon the long-standing practice of giving the president of the I.C.J. the function of appointing arbitrators.[7] Because of the importance of the contemplated role of an ad hoc tribunal and the kinds of issues it may be called upon to decide, it is proposed that appointment should be made by the full Court rather than the president.

The limited review of decisions of an ad hoc tribunal presents strictly legal issues to the Court consistent with its traditional role. This review provides an appropriate safeguard to the parties without undercutting the function of the tribunal.

The Problem of Interlocking Issues

A policy providing to others a general standing option to adjudicate disputes with the United States has to make clear that an adjudication must determine all interlocking issues or none. The United States, for example, could not prudently have accepted an adjudication of Panama's claim for control of the Canal on grounds of self-determination and sovereignty without the issues of rights of passage in peace and war and the means of their protection, as well as the issue of treaty-acquired rights and recognition of investment, being adjudicated at the same time. Or to take another example, activity charged to be prohibited intervention and defended as legitimate counterintervention cannot be adjudicated without the activities of both nations coming before the tribunal for adjudication.

The problem has two aspects and requires assurance on two points: (a) that the adjudication between the parties shall extend to all issues involved, and (b) that the tribunal has jurisdiction over all nations necessary to enable it to make a determination of all issues.[8] Both points are covered in point B of the proposed Charter. Although much is left to the determination of the Tribunal as to what issues and parties are necessary for a determination, the principle is simple. The Tribunal must act, if it is to act at all, on a basis that enables its determination to resolve the real issues involved.

There is a temptation to extend the principle to include what may be characterized as parallel rather than interlocking issues. Our instinct is likely to be that we should not create a process that enables the U.S.S.R., say, (assuming it has "standing"[9] for this issue) to hold the United States to a nonintervention principle in Guatemala or the Dominican Republic without submitting itself to the same process for Czechoslovakia or Angola. Our instinct is to rebel against something that causes us to accept an adjudicated solution in Panama while Egypt refuses to do so in Suez and the Strait of Tiran and Great Britain refuses in Gibraltar. The instinct has its roots in the concept of law itself, in its reciprocality. The essence of law is that it applies equally to all. When a nation refuses to submit for adjudication against itself a principle it invokes against another, our instinct to balk has roots also in the principle expressed in common law jurisdictions in the maxim that "he who seeks equity must do equity."

Despite these understandable impulses, it seems clear that we should not try to extend the requirement that interlocking issues be determined together to require that parallel situations also be adjudicated together. There are a number of reasons why we should not do so. We are really dealing with an aspect of a problem familiar in most movements of reform. Those whose affairs are affected in the beginning stages usually feel put upon, and there is some justice to their feeling. But progress has to start somewhere. If no problem can be tackled until all problems are tackled, we are likely never to begin.

This is especially the case when we are talking about a process of adjudication that depends on consent. What is proposed is a voluntary process of adjudication. To return to the example of the Panama Canal, even though it is now resolved (at least for a time) by the new treaties, if the United States could not accept a process of adjudication for Panama until Egypt did likewise for Suez and the Strait of Tiran, and Turkey and Russia for the Turkish Straits, and Spain and Great Britain for Gibraltar, and so on and so on, the world would never move at all. To offer an adjudication option based on such a requirement would be a farce. It would advance nothing and would put the seriousness of our purposes in doubt. It would be better to forego any adjudication option at all.

Turning the question around, why do we need to insist on consent to adjudication of parallel situations? One situation does not really depend on another. If it did, it would not be just parallel but interlocking. Our willingness to adjudicate parallel situations separately does more to advance our ends than insisting on tieing them together. If in 1957 we had been willing to adjudicate the Panama Canal problem, that would certainly have put more pressure on Egypt to adjudicate Suez than any other posture we could have taken. Do we really have to worry if the U.S.S.R. (assuming again it has "standing") should choose to push us to an adjudication of alleged U.S. intervention in Nicaragua? If we have learned to behave ourselves better than we have sometimes done in the past, that Soviet move could strengthen our hand in controlling Soviet and Cuban intervention in Angola and Ethiopia. Even if the U.S.S.R. did not by seeking an adjudication of alleged U.S. intervention accept jurisdiction for an adjudication of its own intervention elsewhere, the whole world sees the validity of the principle that the rule the Soviets invoke must apply to them as well. We probably ought to be delighted to have the U.S.S.R. put itself in such an embarassing situation. It would certainly give us more leverage than we now enjoy.

Finally, one has to keep in mind what, realistically, our alternatives are. We have seen how our foreign policy evolves to reflect law. Political logic has committed us to respect law. We cannot long go on insisting on indefensible positions or using power illegitimately. We are a democratic nation, and we find it difficult to maintain a power-oriented position against strongly asserted claims of justice and law, even without any process of adjudication. The United States is in the position of having to accept the risk of peaceful change and the implementation of legal principles. Realistically, parallel situations have to be dealt with separately; if need be, even now. We negotiated ourselves out of Panama without any tieing in of Suez or any other parallel issue. And we did so even without adjudication.

For us the alternatives are not adjudication or standing pat. Nor are the alternatives separate resolutions or package deals. Realistically, we have to address the demands for peaceful change and to meet each situation on its own merits, with or without adjudication. Adjudication must be seen as a way to structure change. By and large, where it is accepted, it may cause us less anguish and more success than negotiating the same issues in a framework in which law is not necessarily destined to play a dominant role.

Part Four

THE CHOICE

Fifteen
ACTION AND RISK

The hardest decisions an individual or a nation has to make, in the end, after all the evidence is in and the analysis is done, have to be made in the face of uncertainties and unknowns. It seems no important decisions can ever be made without risk. On the major issues there are risks involved in all our options.

Nor will the issues yield simply to a policy of minimizing risks. We reject that choice as human beings. Indeed, in issues of values and goals there are no purely scientific routes to answers. There are different kinds of considerations that cannot be quantified against one another. We have to make choices, and those choices depend on casting up the pros and cons to be measures by the only scale by which they can be related, the values we affirm as human beings.

Americans have always counted as a part of our strength that we were on the side of history. Standing for ideals sought by all peoples is one of the sources of our strength. We have never feared the risks of competition in the marketplace of ideas. We welcome that competition in the confident belief that our creed will claim the future. We stand for what we believe in, and this act of faith is a source of our strength.

The choice of committing the foreign policy of the nation to law involves the same kinds of imponderables. We know as a nation that it is right that rules which govern nations must apply equally to all. We know that law must change as a changing world presents new needs and new perceptions. We know that the impartiality of law cannot be accepted in practice if each nation is free to define the facts and interpret the law to serve its own ends. If we put our beliefs to work, our commitment to law, like our dedication to democracy and freedom and constitutionalism, can also be a part of our strength. And if we mean to win in the marketplace of ideas, we will have to translate our beliefs into policy and action.

We are, indeed, not very good at policy that runs contrary to our beliefs. We have taken careful account of our strategic interests from Washington's advice to avoid entangling alliances to the Monroe Doctrine to aid to Greece and Turkey in 1947, but the policies we proclaimed have been framed by principles we believed in. We have by and large been able to encompass the necessity from time to time of making alliances with dictators in support of our higher ends, although, short of wartime, there are always many who are unable to swallow what they see as compromising our principles. We have been through enough in the 1930s and since World War II to enable most of us to understand that the balance of power is the indispensable underpinning of law. But it is as the underpinning of law that it will command our support, not as an alternative to law. It seems unlikely that the United States can effectively pursue a policy that disregards our sense of law. We are not all pure in heart, but we are a nation that stands for something. Most of us have a sense of America as something more than a piece of geography. We are defined by what we stand for, and no amount of Machiavellian justification is likely to bring us to support the use of our power against what we perceive to be the rights of another people.

Much of the skepticism about international law has stemmed from some false ideas about law, which I hope the previous chapters will have helped to put to rest. Some leaders, whose policies in the era of the Cold War in fact provided essential support for law, contributed by their statements to the confusion. In a celebrated lecture George Kennan argued against trying to approach foreign policy issues in legal terms, characterizing the effort as one based on the belief that "instead of taking the awkward conflicts of national interest and dealing with them on their merits with a view to finding solutions least unsettling to the stability of international life, it would be better to find some formal criteria of a juridical nature by which the permissible behavior of states could be defined."[1] Happily, with the help of Kennan and others and the hard realities of the Cold War, the naïve view of law as a set of principles that can simply be laid upon the nations and allows us to put behind us concerns with contention and power is a view that is now largely buried in the past. But, unfortunately, Kennan and many others saw no other view of law. His assumption that law is not concerned with "taking the awkward conflicts of national interest and dealing with them on their merits with a view to finding solutions least unsettling to the stability of international life" could not be further from the truth. The relevance of law to the foreign policy enterprise is precisely as a strategy for the resolution of conflict. It does not ignore the conflicts of national interest. It attempts to reconcile them on the only basis they can possibly be reconciled, on a basis of reciprocity by principles that apply equally to all. It does so not by principles that come out of the head of Zeus but by principles that come out of the real world and are in fact defined in the process of reconciling claims for the recognition of interests that compete or conflict.

The disembodied concept of law that Kennan attacked is further revealed in his references to law's concern with "preservation of the juridical tidiness of international life,"[2] to law "imposing a legal straight-jacket" on the process of change,[3] to law ignoring the device of the puppet state and "the set of techniques by which states can be converted into puppets with no formal violation, or challenge to, the outward attributes of their sovereignty and their independence."[4] He helps to teach but fails to see that his lesson in fact points to a different kind of law when he sees those arguing for law as failing to realize that "even under a system of world law the sanction against disruptive international behavior might continue to rest, basically, as it has in the past, on the alliances and relationships among the great powers themselves"[5] or that somehow the law is responsible for the concept of "total victory."[6] Kennan's argument is an argument against the wrong kind of law.[7] The challenge of our time, as was stated at the beginning of this book, is to move the world toward the kind of rule of law that takes account of the realities of power and contention.

Another constructive leader of foreign policy who in fact provided leadership in support of law also contributed to the confusion about the nature of law. Dean Acheson, in one of the statements most quoted by those who argue that national interest rather than law must govern foreign policy, contended that the quarantine imposed in the Cuban missile crisis was "not a legal issue or an issue of international law as those terms should be understood."[8] He argued that in the Cuban missile crisis "the power, position and prestige of the United States had been challenged by another state; and law simply does not deal with such questions of ultimate power—power that comes close to the sources of sovereignty. I cannot believe that there are principles of law that say we must accept destruction of our way of life."[9]

Acheson's notion of law, like Kennan's, as some disembodied set of abstract principles is reflected in his tacit assumption that, if law applied to the quarantine issue it would prohibit rather than permit the quarantine action, even though the action was required to avoid "destruction of our way of life." The mission of law is rather to respond to and to reconcile competing interests. If our vital interests were such that in the circumstances we had to be permitted to act in imposing the Cuban quarantine, as Acheson believed we did, then a framework of law responsive to reality would have to recognize grounds that supported our right to act. The irony is that the United States at the time was supported by and publicly articulated a sound legal case for O.A.S. action, as outlined in chapter 10 above. The Cuban missile crisis and the nature of our response to it provided, indeed, a significant step in the evolution of emerging law.[10]

The issues on which a decision on grounding our foreign policy on a commitment to law must turn are not those raised by Kennan or Acheson. The only kind of law worthy of our commitment is one that adheres to the mission of law as a strategy for the resolution fo conflict. The issues on which decisions must turn are those involving our evaluation of emerging law. Even the risks of adjudication turn largely on that evaluation.

Although it may have come as a surprise to many, the fact is that while we have been struggling with what seems and undoubtedly is a chaotic world, the pieces providing the basis of emerging law have been falling into place. The Cuban missile crisis revealed that there is a sound basis for regional security zones, one that avoids the untenable position of claiming special rights of hegemony for us or any other great power. The 1970 Declaration on the Charter principles of international law resolved many of the controverted issues of the emerging law and by its unanimous adoption commands a special authority. It resolved the problem of secession. It fixed a rule of nonintervention that is as sound for foreign policy as for law. It and the 1974 definition of aggression established a prohibition on indirect aggression. Even the widely criticized 1974 Charter of the Economic Rights and Duties of States laid some basis for dealing with the great issue of access to resources, a problem on which we clearly need the leverage of law. The Law of the

Sea conference, although still struggling with problems concerning the deep sea bed, has agreed on recognition of necessary international rights in straits. The new Panama Canal treaties point the way to necessary international rights in interoceanic canals.

Even the intellectual underpinnings have been falling into place. In 1969 the Vienna Convention on the Law of Treaties affirmed the existence of principles of law that are binding on nations without their consent and cannot be abrogated by them. The Convention affirmed not only the existence of such principles (peremptory norms) but also the capacity of new principles of the same binding character to emerge out of the world's international experience. Law has now joined fact to recognize the concept of emerging law.

What it comes to is this. The United States has very little choice but to accept law, because we believe in it. And as developments have put the pieces into place we can see that we have less to fear from it than to gain by it. It can be a source of our strength and a force for the kind of world we believe in.

One would always rather negotiate than risk adjudication, but willingness to adjudicate can help us to negotiate. The risk inherent in declaring our willingness to adjudicate arises only when the option is accepted, not when it is rejected. It is a risk that may be a happy one, indeed. It is hard to see that we did better over Suez in 1957 than we would have through adjudication. Vietnam may carry many lessons, and we may still be too close to read them clearly, but it is difficult to see how an adjudication, if the contestants had accepted it, could have been anything but an advantage. It is hard to see that we are now dealing with Soviet and Cuban interventions in Africa any better than we would by adjudication, if one were accepted.

Realisticcally, we are not likely to be taken up on an adjudication option very often. But a policy of providing the option helps to defend our commitment to law against disparagement and misrepresentation, and it strengthens our foreign policy hand. When negotiations become deadlocked, we shall probably have reason to wish the option would be accepted. Adjudication has risks, but so does stalemate. If law is our policy, adjudication risks only a wrong determination or wrong application of law. Stalemate may risk its rejection and denial.

The risks of a commitment to law also have to be placed against the emptiness at the roots of a policy based merely on a calculation of our supposed interests. That is a policy which tends to be suspect at home and abroad, to create confusion about our purposes, and in the end often is denied the capacity to shape the very events for which it is framed. If we wish to revive the dedication of the American people, if we wish to lay hold on an initiative to move events, we shall have to build a policy on firmer ground than calculation of the kinds of interests that lack the capacity of law to resolve conflict. The world is likely to remain stuck on its dead center until its nations are provided a leadership capable of commanding their belief and support.

Our decision in the end has to be made against our view of the world. One has to weigh the risks and potentials of law against the alternative. What is realism, what is prudence, in the world we know? Is it to settle for a system of international relations that cannot provide real security to any nation, even the most powerful, that requires us all to live under the risk of catastrophe, that provides no basis for either a just or a stable peace? I suggest it is to chart our course to a rule of law, to recognize the reality and the power of the concept of law, to shape our policy to put that power to work for us and for all nations. If we can move the world toward law by our commitment and our influence, that is the wisest and safest course we can take. If we will fashion the instruments to implement that policy with understanding and care, the risks need not deter us from the path of law.

APPENDIX 1[1]

Declaration on Principles of International Law Concerning Friendly Relations and Co-operation among States in Accordance with the Charter of the United Nations

RESOLUTION 2625 (XXV)

THE GENERAL ASSEMBLY,

Recalling its resolutions 1815 (XVII) of 18 December 1962, 1966 (XVIII) of 16 December 1963, 2103 (XX) of 20 December 1965, 2181 (XXI) of 12 December 1966, 2327 (XXII) of 18 December 1967, 2463 (XXIII) of 20 December 1968 and 2533 (XXIV) of 8 December 1969, in which it affirmed the importance of the progressive development and codification of the principles of international law concerning friendly relations and co-operation among States,

Having considered the report of the Special Committee on Principles of International Law concerning Friendly Relations and Co-operation among States, which met in Geneva from 31 March 1970 to 1 May 1970,

Emphasizing the paramount importance of the Charter of the United Nations for the maintenance of international peace and security and for the development of friendly relations and co-operation among States,

Deeply convinced that the adoption of the Declaration on Principles of International Law concerning Friendly Relations and Co-operation among States in accordance with the Charter of the United Nations during the celebration of the twenty-fifth anniversary of the United Nations would contribute to the strengthening of world peace and constitute a landmark in the development of international law and of relations among States, in promoting the rule of law among nations and particularly the universal application of the principles embodied in the Charter,

Considering the desirability of the wide dissemination of the text of the Declaration,

1. *Approves* the Declaration on Principles of International Law concerning

Friendly Relations and Co-operation among States in accordance with the Charter of the United Nations, the text of which is annexed to the present resolution;

2. *Expresses* its appreciation to the Special Committee for its work resulting in the elaboration of the Declaration;

3. *Recommends* that all efforts be made so that the Declaration becomes generally known.

ANNEX

Declaration on Principles of International Law concerning Friendly Relations and Co-operation among States in accordance with the Charter of the United Nations

Preamble

THE GENERAL ASSEMBLY,

[1] *Reaffirming* in the terms of the Charter that the maintenance of international peace and security and the development of friendly relations and co-operation between nations are among the fundamental purposes of the United Nations,

[2] *Recalling* that the peoples of the United Nations are determined to practise tolerance and live together in peace with one another as good neighbours,

[3] *Bearing in mind* the importance of maintaining and strengthening international peace founded upon freedom, equality, justice and respect for fundamental human rights and of developing friendly relations among nations irrespective of their political, economic and social systems or the levels of their development,

[4] *Bearing in mind also* the paramount importance of the Charter of the United Nations in the promotion of the rule of law among nations,

[5] *Considering* that the faithful observance of the principles of international law concerning friendly relations and co-operation among States, and fulfillment in good faith of the obligations assumed by States, in accordance with the Charter, is of the greatest importance for the maintenance of international peace and security, and for the implementation of the other purposes of the United Nations,

Noting that the great political, economic and social changes and scientific progress which have taken place in the world since the adoption of the Charter of the United Nations give increased importance to these principles and to the need for their more effective application in the conduct of States wherever carried on, [6]

Recalling the established principle that outer space, including the Moon and other celestial bodies, is not subject to national appropriation by claim of sovereignty by means of use or occupation or by any other means, and mindful of the fact that consideration is being given in the United Nations to the question of establishing other appropriate provisions similarly inspired, [7]

Convinced that the strict observance by States of the obligation not to intervene in the affairs of any other State is an essential condition to ensure that nations live together in peace with one another since the practice of any form of intervention not only violates the spirit and letter of the Charter of the United Nations but also leads to the creation of situations which threaten international peace and security, [8]

Recalling the duty of States to refrain in their international relations from military, political, economic or any other form of coercion aimed against the political independence or territorial integrity of any State, [9]

Considering it essential that all States shall refrain in their international relations from the threat or use of force against the territorial integrity or political independence of any State, or in any other manner inconsistent with the purposes of the United Nations, [10]

Considering it equally essential that all States shall settle their international dis- [11]

putes by peaceful means in accordance with the Charter,

[12] Reaffirming, in accordance with the Charter, the basic importance of sovereign equality and stressing that the purposes of the United Nations can be implemented only if States enjoy sovereign equality and comply fully with the requirements of this principle in their international realtions,

[13] Convinced that the subjection of peoples to alien subjugation, domination and exploitation constitutes a major obstacle to the promotion of international peace and security,

[14] Convinced that the principle of equal rights and self-determination of peoples constitutes a significant contribution to contemporary international law, and that its effective application is of paramount importance for the promotion of friendly relations among States, based on respect for the principle of sovereign equality,

[15] Convinced in consequence that any attempt aimed at the partial or total disruption of the national unity and territorial integrity of a State or country or at its political independence is incompatible with the purposes and principles of the Charter,

[16] Considering the provisions of the Charter as a whole and taking into account the role of relevant resolutions adopted by the competent organs of the United Nations relating to the content of the principles,

[17] Considering that the progressive development and codification of the following principles:

(a) The principle that States shall refrain in their international relations from the threat or use of force against the territorial integrity or political independence of any State, or in any other manner inconsistent with the purposes of the United Nations,

(b) The principle that States shall settle their international disputes by peaceful means in such a manner that international peace and security and justice are not endangered,

(c) The duty not to intervene in matters within the domestic jurisdiction of any State, in accordance with the Charter,

(d) The duty of States to co-operate with one another in accordance with the Charter,

(e) The principle of equal rights and self-determination of peoples,

(f) The principle of sovereign equality of States,

(g) The principle that States shall fulfil in good faith the obligations assumed by them in accordance with the Charter, so as to secure their more effective application within the international community would promote the realization of the purposes of the United Nations,

Having considered the principles of international law relating to friendly relations and co-operation among States, [18]

1. Solemnly proclaims the following principles:

The principle that States shall refrain in their international relations from the threat or use of force against the territorial integrity or political independence of any State, or in any other manner inconsistent with the purposes of the United Nations [A]

Every State has the duty to refrain in its international relations from the threat or use of force against the territorial integrity or political independence of any State, or in any other manner inconsistent with the purposes of the United Nations. Such a threat or use of force constitutes a violation of international law and the Charter of the United Nations and shall never be employed as a means of settling international issues. [1]

[2] A war of aggression constitutes a crime against the peace, for which there is responsibility under international law.

[3] In accordance with the purposes and principles of the United Nations, States have the duty to refrain from propaganda for wars of aggression.

[4] Every State has the duty to refrain from the threat or use of force to violate the existing international boundaries of another State or as a means of solving international disputes, including territorial disputes and problems concerning frontiers of States.

[5] Every State likewise has the duty to refrain from the threat or use of force to violate international lines of demarcation, such as armistice lines, established by or pursuant to an international agreement to which it is a party or which it is otherwise bound to respect. Nothing in the foregoing shall be construed as prejudicing the positions of the parties concerned with regard to the status and effects of such lines under their special regimes or as affecting their temporary character.

[6] States have a duty to refrain from acts of reprisal involving the use of force.

[7] Every State has the duty to refrain from any forcible action which deprives peoples referred to in the elaboration of the principle of equal rights the self-determination of their right to self-determination and freedom and independence.

[8] Every State has the duty to refrain from organizing or encouraging the organization of irregular forces or armed bands, including mercenaries, for incursion into the territory of another State.

[9] Every State has the duty to refrain from organizing, instigating, assisting or participating in acts of civl strife or terrorist acts in another State or acquiescing in organized activities within its territory directed towards the commission of such acts, when the acts referred to in the present paragraph involve a threat or use of force.

The territory of a State shall not be the object of military occupation resulting from the use of force in contravention of the provisions of the Charter. The territory of a State shall not be the object of acquisition by another State resulting from the threat or use of force. No terriotial acquisition resulting from the threat or use of force shall be recognized as legal. Nothing in the foregoing shall be construed as affecting: [10]

(a) Provisions of the Charter or any international agreement prior to the Charter regime and valid under international law; or

(b) The powers of the Security Council under the Charter.

All States shall pursue in good faith negotiations for the early conclusion of a universal treaty on general and complete disarmament under effective international control and strive to adopt appropriate measures to reduce international tensions and strengthen confidence among States. [11]

All States shall comply in good faith with their obligations under the generally recognized principles and rules of international law with respect to the maintenance of international peace and security, and shall endeavour to make the United Nations security system based upon the Charter more effective. [12]

Nothing in the foregoing paragraphs shall be construed as enlarging or diminishing in any way the scope of the provisions of the Charter concerning cases in which the use of force is lawful. [13]

The principle that States shall settle their international disputes by peaceful means in such a manner that international peace and security and justice are not endangered [B]

Every State shall settle its international disputes with other States by peaceful means, in such a manner that international peace and security, and justice, are not endangered. [1]

[2] States shall accordingly seek early and just settlement of their international disputes by negotiation, inquiry, mediation, conciliation, arbitration, judicial settlement, resort to regional agencies or arrangements or other peaceful means of their choice. In seeking such a settlement, the parties shall agree upon such peaceful means as may be appropriate to the circumstances and nature of the dispute.

[3] The parties to a dispute have the duty, in the event of failure to reach a solution by any one of the above peaceful means, to continue to seek a settlement of the dispute by other peaceful means agreed upon by them.

[4] States parties to an international dispute, as well as other States, shall refrain from any action which may aggravate the situation so as to endanger the maintenance of international peace and security, and shall act in accordance with the purposes and principles of the United Nations.

[5] International disputes shall be settled on the basis of the sovereign equality of States and in accordance with the principle of free choice of means. Recourse to, or acceptance of, a settlement procedure freely agreed to by States with regard to existing or future disputes to which they are parties shall not be regarded as incompatible with sovereign equality.

[6] Nothing in the foregoing paragraphs prejudices or derogates from the applicable provisions of the Charter, in particular those relating to the pacific settlement of international disputes.

[C] The principle concerning the duty not to intervene in matters within the domestic jurisdiction of any State, in accordance with the Charter

[1] No State or group of States has the right to intervene, directly or indirectly, for any reason whatever, in the internal or external affairs of any other State. Consequently, armed intervention and all other forms of interference or attempted threats against the personality of the State or against its political, economic and cultural elements, are in violation of international law.

No State may use or encourage the use of economic, political or any other type of measures to coerce another State in order to obtain from it the subordination of the exercise of its sovereign rights and to secure from it advantages of any kind. Also, no State shall organize, assist, foment, finance, incite or tolerate subversive, terrorist or armed activities directed towards the violent overthrow of the regime of another State, or interference in civil strife in another State. [2]

The use of force to deprive peoples of their national identity constitutes a violation of their inalienable rights and of the principle of non-intervention. [3]

Every State has an inalienable right to choose its political, economic, social and cultural systems, without interference in any form by another State. [4]

Nothing in the foregoing paragraphs shall be construed as affecting the relevant provisions of the Charter relating to the maintenance of international peace and security. [5]

The duty of States to co-operate with one another in accordance with the Charter [D]

States have the duty to co-operate with one another, irrespective of the differences in their political, economic and social systems, in the various spheres of international relations, in order to maintain international peace and security and to promote international economic stability and progress, the general welfare of nations and international co-operation free from discrimination based on such differences. [1]

To this end: [2]

(a) States shall co-operate with other States in the maintenance of international peace and security;

(b) States shall co-operate in the promotion of universal respect for and observance of human rights and fundamental freedoms for all, and in the elimination of all forms of racial discrimination and all forms of religious intolerance;

(c) States shall conduct their international relations in the economic, social, cultural, technical and trade fields in accordance with the principles of sovereign equality and non-intervention;

(d) States Members of the United Nations have the duty to take joint and separate action in co-operation with the United Nations in accordance with the relevant provisions of the Charter.

[3] States should co-operate in the economic, social and cultural fields as well as in the field of science and technology and for the promotion of international cultural and educational progress. States should co-operate in the promotion of economic growth throughout the world, especially that of the developing countries.

[E] The principle of equal rights and self-determination of peoples

[1] By virtue of the principle of equal rights and self-determination of peoples enshrined in the Charter, all peoples have the right freely to determine, without external interference, their political status and to pursue their economic, social and cultural development, and every State has the duty to respect this right in accordance with the provisions of the Charter.

[2] Every State has the duty to promote, through joint and separate action, the realization of the principle of equal rights and self-determination of peoples, in accordance with the provisions of the Charter, and to render assistance to the United Nations in carrying out the responsibilites entrusted to it by the Charter regarding the implementation of the principle in order:

(a) To promote friendly relations and co-operation among States; and

(b) To bring a speedy end to colonialism, having due regard to the freely expressed will of the peoples concerned;

and bearing in mind that subjection of peoples to alien subjugation, domination and exploitation constitutes a violation of the principle, as well as a denial of fundamental human rights, and is contrary to the Charter of the United Nations.

Every State has the duty to promote [3]
through joint and separate action universal respect for and observance of human rights and fundamental freedoms in accordance with the Charter.

The establishment of a sovereign and [4]
independent State, the free association or integration with an independent State or the emergence into any other political status freely determined by a people constitute modes of implementing the right of self-determination by that people.

Every State has the duty to refrain from [5]
any forcible action which deprives peoples referred to above in the elaboration of the present principle of their right to self-determination and freedom and independence. In their actions against and resistance to such forcible action in pursuit of the exercise of their right to self-determination, such peoples are entitled to seek and to receive support in accordance with the purposes and principles of the Charter of the United Nations.

The territory of a colony or other non- [6]
self-governing territory has, under the Charter of the United Nations, a status separate and distinct from the territory of the State administering it; and such separate and distinct status under the Charter shall exist until the people of the colony or non-self-governing territory

have exercised their right of self-determination in accordance with the Charter, and particularly its purposes and principles.

[7] Nothing in the foregoing paragraphs shall be construed as authorizing or encouraging any action which would dismember or impair, totally or in part, the territorial integrity or political unity of sovereign and independent States conducting themselves in compliance with the principle of equal rights and self-determination of peoples as described above and thus possessed of a government representing the whole people belonging to the territory without distinction as to race, creed or colour.

[8] Every State shall refrain from any action aimed at the partial or total disruption of the national unity and territorial integrity of any other State or country.

[F] The principle of sovereign equality of States

[1] All States enjoy sovereign equality. They have equal rights and duties and are equal members of the international community, notwithstanding differences of an economic, social, political or other nature.

[2] In particular, sovereign equality includes the following elements:

(a) States are juridically equal;
(b) Each State enjoys the rights inherent in full sovereignty;
(c) Each State has the duty to respect the personality of other States;
(d) The territorial integrity and political independence of the State are inviolable;
(e) Each State has the right freely to choose and develop its political, social, economic and cultural systems;
(f) Each State has the duty to comply fully and in good faith with its international obligations and to live in peace with other States.

The principle that State shall fulfil in good faith the obligations assumed by them in accordance with the Charter [G]

Every State has the duty to fulfil in good faith the obligations assumed by it in accordance with the Charter of the United Nations. [1]

Every State has the duty to fulfil in good faith its obligations under the generally recognized principles and rules of international law. [2]

Every State has the duty to fulfil in good faith its obligations under international agreements valid under the generally recognized principles and rules of international law. [3]

Where obligations arising under international agreements are in conflict with the obligations of Members of the United Nations under the Charter of the United Nations, the obligations under the Charter shall prevail. [4]

GENERAL PART

2. Declares that:

In their interpretation and application the above principles are interrelated and each principle should be construed in the context of the other principles, [i]

Nothing in this Declaration shall be construed as prejudicing in any manner the provisions of the Charter or the rights and duties of Member States under the Charter or the rights of peoples under the Charter taking into account the elaboration of these rights in this Declaration, [ii]

3. Declares further that:

The principles of the Charter which are embodied in this Declaration constitute basic principles of international law, and consequently appeals to all States to be guided by these principles in their international conduct and to develop their mutual relations on the basis of their strict observance.

APPENDIX 2[1]

Definition of Aggression

Resolution 3314 (XXIX)

The General Assembly,

Having considered the report of the Special Committee on the Question of Defining Aggression, established pursuant to its resolution 2330 (XXII) of 18 December 1967, covering the work of its seventh session held from 11 March to 12 April 1974, including the draft Definition of Aggression adopted by the Special Committee by consensus and recommended for adoption by the General Assembly,

Deeply convinced that the adoption of the Definition of Aggression would contribute to the strengthening of international peace and security,

1. Approves the Definition of Aggression, the text of which is annexed to the present resolution;

2. Expresses its appreciation to the Special Committee on the Question of Defining Aggression for its work which resulted in the elaboration of the Definition of Aggression;

3. Calls upon all States to refrain from all acts of aggression and other uses of force contrary to the Charter of the United Nations and the Declaration on Principles of International Law concerning Friendly Relations and Co-operation among States in accordance with the Charter of the United Nations;

4. Calls the attention of the Security Council to the Definition of Aggression, as set out below, and recommends that it should, as appropriate, take account of that Definition as guidance in determining, in accordance with the Charter, the existence of an act of aggression.

Annex
Definition of Aggression

The General Assembly,

Basing itself on the fact that one of the [1]
fundamental purposes of the United Na-

tions is to maintain international peace and security and to take effective collective measures for the prevention and removal of threats to the peace, and for the suppression of acts of aggression or other breaches of the peace,

[2] Recalling that the Security Council, in accordance with Article 39 of the Charter of the United Nations, shall determine the existence of any threat to the peace, breach of the peace or act of aggression and shall make recommendations, or decide what measures shall be taken in accordance with Articles 41 and 42, to maintain or restore international peace and security,

[3] Recalling also the duty of States under the Charter to settle their international disputes by peaceful means in order not to endanger international peace, security and justice,

[4] Bearing in mind that nothing in this Definition shall be interpreted as in any way affecting the scope of the provisions of the Charter with respect to the functions and powers of the organs of the United Nations,

[5] Considering also that, since aggression is the most serious and dangerous form of the illegal use of force, being fraught, in the conditions created by the existence of all types of weapons of mass destruction, with the possible threat of a world conflict and all its catastrophic consequences, aggression should be defined at the present stage,

[6] Reaffirming the duty of States not to use armed force to deprive peoples of their right to self-determination, freedom and independence, or to disrupt territorial integrity,

[7] Reaffirming also that the territory of a State shall not be violated by being the object, even temporarily, of military occupation or of other measures of force taken by another State in contravention of the Charter, and that it shall not be the object of acquisition by another State resulting from such measures or the threat thereof,

[8] Reaffirming also the provisions of the Declaration on Principles of International Law concerning Friendly Relations and Co-operation among States in accordance with the Charter of the United Nations,

[9] Convinced that the adoption of a definition of aggression ought to have the effect of deterring a potential aggressor, would simplify the determination of acts of aggression and the implementation of measures to suppress them and would also facilitate the protection of the rights and lawful interests of, and the rendering of assistance to, the victim,

[10] Believing that, although the question whether an act of aggression has been committed must be considered in the light of all the circumstances of each particular case, it is nevertheless desirable to formulate basic principles as guidance for such determination,

Adopts the following Definition of Aggression:[2]

Article 1

Aggression is the use of armed force by a State against the sovereignty, territorial integrity or political independence of another State, or in any other manner inconsistent with the Charter of the United Nations, as set out in this Definition.

Explanatory note: In this Definition the term "State":

(a) Is used without prejudice to questions of recognition or to whether a State is a Member of the United Nations;

(b) Includes the concept of a "group of States" where appropriate.

Article 2

The first use of armed force by a State in contravention of the Charter shall constitute prima facie evidence of an act of aggression although the Security Council may, in conformity with the Charter, conclude that a determination that an act of aggression has been committed would not be justified in the light of other relevant circumstances, including the fact that the acts concerned or their consequences are not of sufficient gravity.

Article 3

Any of the following acts, regardless of a declaration of war, shall, subject to and in accordance with the provision of article 2, qualify as an act of aggression:

(a) The invasion or attack by the armed forces of a State of the territory of another State, or any military occupation, however temporary, resulting from such invasion or attack, or any annexation by the use of force of the territory of another State or part thereof;

(b) Bombardment by the armed forces of a State against the territory of another State or the use of any weapons by a State against the territory of another State;

(c) The blockade of the ports or coasts of a State by the armed forces of another State;

(d) An attack by the armed forces of a State on the land, sea or air forces, or marine and air fleets of another State;

(e) The use of armed forces of one State which are within the territory of another State with the agreement of the receiving State, in contravention of the conditions provided for in the agreement or any extension of their presence in such territory beyond the termination of the agreement;

(f) The action of a State in allowing its territory, which it has placed at the disposal of another State, to be used by that other State for perpetrating an act of aggression against a third State;

(g) The sending by or on behalf of a State of armed bands, groups, irregulars or mercenaries, which carry out acts of armed force against another State of such gravity as to amount to the acts listed above, or its substantial involvement therein.

Article 4

The acts enumerated above are not exhaustive and the Security Council may determine that other acts constitute aggression under the provisions of the Charter.

Article 5

1. No consideration of whatever nature, whether political, economic, military or otherwise, may serve as a justification for aggression.

2. A war of aggression is a crime against international peace. Aggression gives rise to international responsibility.

3. No territorial acquisition or special advantage resulting from aggression is or shall be recognized as lawful.

Article 6

Nothing in this Definition shall be construed as in any way enlarging or diminishing the scope of the Charter, including its provisions concerning cases in which the use of force is lawful.

Article 7

Nothing in this Definition, and in particular article 3, could in any way prejudice the right to self-determination, freedom and independence, as derived from the Charter, of peoples forcibly deprived of that right and referred to in the Declaration on Principles of International Law concerning Friendly Relations and Co-operation among States in accordance with the Charter of the United Nations, particularly peoples under colonial and racist régimes or other forms of alien domination; nor the right of these peoples to struggle to that end and to seek and receive support, in accordance with the principles of the Charter and in conformity with the above-mentioned Declaration.

Article 8

In their interpretation and application the above provisions are interrelated and each provision should be construed in the context of the other provisions.

Explanatory Notes from the Report of the Special Committee on the Question of Defining Aggression

1. With reference to article 3, paragraph (b), the Special Committee agreed that the expression "any weapons" is used without making a distinction between conventional weapons, weapons of mass destruction and any other kind of weapon.

2. With reference to article 5, paragraph 1, the Committee had in mind, in particular, the principle contained in the Declaration on Principles of International Law concerning Friendly Relations and Co-operation among States in accordance with the Charter of the United Nations according to which "No State or group of States has the right to intervene, directly or indirectly, for any reason whatever, in the internal or external affairs of any other State".

3. With reference to article 5, paragraph 2, the words "international responsibility" are used without prejudice to the scope of this term.

4. With reference to article 5, paragraph 3, the Committee states that this paragraph should not be construed so as to prejudice the established principles of international law relating to the inadmissibility of territorial acquisition resulting from the threat or use of force.

APPENDIX 3

United Nations Resolutions Concerning Self-determination

The following resolutions affirm, apply, or otherwise bear on the principle of self-determination.

General Assembly

Res. 9 (I) Feb. 9, 1946. Non-Self-Governing Peoples.

Res. 39 (I) Dec. 12, 1946. Spain.

Res. 65 (I) Dec. 14, 1946. South West Africa.

Res. 66 (I) Dec. 14, 1946. Transmission of information under Art. 73e.

Res. 112 (II) Nov. 14, 1947. Korea.

Res. 181 (II) Nov. 29, 1947. Future Government of Palestine.

Res. 194 (III) Dec. 11, 1948. Palestine—Holy Places, Jerusalem.

Res. 195 (III) Dec. 12, 1948. Korea.

Res. 217 (III) Dec. 10, 1948. Universal Declaration of Human Rights, Art. 21.

Res. 222 (III) Nov. 3, 1948. Cessation of transmission of information under Art. 73e.

Res. 226 (III) Nov. 18, 1948. Progressive development of Trust Territories.

Res. 289 (IV) Nov. 21, 1949. Disposal of former Italian Colonies—Libya, Italian Somaliland, Eritrea.

Res. 291 (IV) Dec. 8, 1949. China.

Res. 293 (IV) Oct. 21, 1949. Korea.

Res. 303 (IV) Dec. 9, 1949. Palestine-Holy Places, Jerusalem.

Res. 320 (IV) Nov. 15, 1949. Political advancement of Trust Territories.

Res. 334 (IV) Dec. 2, 1949. Territories to which Ch. XI applies.

Res. 376 (V) Oct. 7, 1950. Korea.

Res. 387 (V) Nov. 17, 1950. Libya.

Res. 390 (V) Dec. 2, 1950. Eritrea, federation with Ethiopia.

Res. 392 (V) Dec. 15, 1950. Procedure to delimit boundaries of former Italian colonies.

Res. 441 (V) Dec. 2, 1950. Ewe, Togoland.

Res. 510 (VI) Dec. 20, 1951. Free elections throughout Germany.

Res. 545 (VI) Feb. 5, 1952. Provisions for Covenant on Human Rights.

Res. 555 (VI) Jan. 18, 1952. Ewe, Togoland.

Res. 558 (VI) Jan. 18, 1952. Attainment by trust territories of objective of self-government or independence.

Res. 567 (VI) Jan. 18, 1952. Factors for Application of Article 73c.

Res. 611 (VII) Dec. 17, 1952. Tunis.

Res. 612 (VII) Dec. 17, 1952. Morocco.

Res. 617 (VII) Dec. 17, 1952. Eritrea.

Res. 637 (VII) Dec. 16, 1952. Right of Peoples and Nations to Self-Determination.

Res. 648 (VII) Dec. 10, 1952. Factors for Application of Article 73c.

Res. 652 (VII) Dec. 20, 1952. Ewe, Togoland.

Res. 738 (VII) Nov. 28, 1953. Requesting Recommendation by Commission on Human Rights.

Res. 742 (VII) Nov. 27, 1953. Factors for Application of Article 73c.

Res. 747 (VII) Nov. 27, 1953. Netherlands and Surinam.

Res. 748 (VII) Nov. 27, 1953. Determining Status of full self-government of Puerto Rico.

Res. 750 (VIII) Dec. 8, 1953. Togoland Unification.

Res. 755 (VIII) Dec. 9, 1953. Italian Somaliland.

Res. 811 (IX) Dec. 11, 1954. Korea.

Res. 837 (IX) Dec. 14, 1954. Requesting Recommendation by Commission on Human Rights.

Res. 849 (IX) Nov. 22, 1954. Greenland into Denmark.

Res. 860 (IX) Dec. 14, 1954. Togoland.

Res. 944(X) Dec. 15, 1955. Togoland.

Res. 945 (X) Dec. 15, 1955. Netherland Antilles and Surinam into Netherlands.

Res. 946 (X) Dec. 15, 1955. Attainment by Trust Territories of self-government or independence.

Res. 1010 (XI) Jan. 11, 1957. Korea.

Res. 1012 (XI) Feb. 15, 1957. Algeria.

Res. 1013 (XI) Feb. 26, 1957. Cyprus.

Res. 1044 (XI) Dec. 13, 1956. Togoland under British administration.

Res. 1046 (XI) Jan. 23, 1957. Togoland under French administration.

Res. 1064 (XI) Feb. 26, 1957. Tanganyika, Cameroons, Togoland, Ruanda-Urundi.

Res. 1065 (XI) Feb. 26, 1957. Tanganyika.

Res. 1131 (XI) Jan. 10, 1957. Hungary.

Res. 1180 (XII) Nov. 29, 1957. Korea.

Res. 1182 (XII) Nov. 29, 1957. Togoland under French administration.

Res. 1184 (XII) Dec. 10, 1957. Algeria.

Res. 1188 (XII) Dec. 11, 1957. Reaffirming right of self-determination.

Res. 1207 (XII) Dec. 13, 1957. Attainment by Trust Territories of self-government or independence.

Res. 1253 (XIII) Nov. 14, 1958. Togoland under French administration.

Res. 1264 (XIII) Nov. 14, 1958. Korea.

Res. 1274 (XIII) Dec. 5, 1958. Attainment of self-government or independence by Trust Territories.

Res. 1287 (XIII) Dec. 5, 1958. Cyprus.

Res. 1314 (XIII) Dec. 12, 1957. Establishing Commission to study permanent sovereignty over natural wealth and resources as basic constituent of right of self-determination.

Res. 1349 (XIII) Mar. 13, 1959. Cameroons under French administration.

Res. 1350 (XIII) Mar. 13, 1959. Cameroons under U.K. administration.

Res. 1352 (XIV) Oct. 16, 1959. Cameroons under U.K. administration.

Res. 1353 (XIV) Oct. 21, 1959. Tibet.

Res. 1413 (XIV) Dec. 5, 1959. Attainment of self-government or independence by Trust Territories.

Res. 1418 (XIV) Dec. 5, 1959. Italian Somaliland.

Res. 1419 (XIV) Dec. 5, 1959. Ruanda-Urundi.

Res. 1455 (XIV) Dec. 9, 1959. Korea.

Res. 1469 (XIV) Dec. 12, 1959. Alaska and Hawaii into U.S.

Res. 1473 (XIV) Dec. 12, 1959. Cameroons under U.K. administration.

Res. 1474 (ES-IV) Sept. 20, 1960. Congo.

Res. 1497 (XV) Oct. 31, 1960. The German speaking element of the Province of Bolzano.

Res. 1514 (XV) Dec. 14, 1960. On granting independnece to dependent peoples.

Res. 1537 (XV) Dec. 15, 1960. Progress achieved in Non-Self-Governing Territories (especially par. 5).

Res. 1541 (XV) Dec. 15, 1960. Principles for application of Article 73c.

Res. 1542 (XV) Dec. 15, 1960. Determining application of Article 73c to territories under the administration of Portugal.

Res. 1568 (XV) Dec. 18, 1960. South West Africa (last par. of preamble).

Res. 1569 (XV) Dec. 18, 1960. Western Samoa.

Res. 1573 (XV) Dec. 19, 1960. Algeria.

Res. 1579 (XV) Dec. 20, 1960. Ruanda-Urundi.

Res. 1596 (XV) Apr. 7, 1961. South West Africa.

Res. 1599 (XV) Apr. 15, 1961. Congo.

Res. 1600 (XV) Apr. 15, 1961. Congo.

Res. 1603 (XV) Apr. 20, 1961. Angola.

Res. 1605 (XV) Apr. 21, 1961. Ruanda-Urundi.

Res. 1608 (XV) Apr. 21, 1961. Cameroons under U.K. administration.

Res. 1609 (XV) Apr. 21, 1961. Tanganyika.

Res. 1626 (XVI) Oct. 18, 1961. Western Samoa.

Res. 1642 (XVI) Nov. 6, 1961. Tanganyika.

Res. 1650 (XVI) Nov. 15, 1961. Algeria.

Res. 1654 (XVI) Nov. 27, 1961. Establishing Sepcial Committee to examine and make recommendations as to implementation of Res. 1514.

Res. 1695 (XVI) Dec. 19, 1961. Dissemination of Res. 1514.

Res. 1698 (XVI) Dec. 19, 1961. On racial discrimination in non-self-governing territories.

Res. 1699 (XVI) Dec. 19, 1961. Territories under Portuguese administration.

Res. 1702 (XVI) Dec. 19, 1961. South West Africa.

Res. 1723 (XVI) Dec. 20, 1961. Tibet.

Res. 1724 (XVI) Dec. 20, 1961. Algeria.

Res. 1740 (XVI) Dec. 20, 1961. Korea.

Res. 1742 (XVI) Jan. 30, 1962. Angola.

Res. 1743 (XVI) Feb. 23, 1962. Ruanda-Urundi. (Seeking union with internal autonomy.)

Res. 1745 (XVI) Feb. 23, 1962. Southern Rhodesia.

Res. 1746 (XVI) June 27, 1962. Ruanda-Urundi. (Acceding to separate independence for Rwanda and Burundi.)

Res. 1747 (XVI) June 28, 1962. Southern Rhodesia.

Res. 1755 (XVII) Oct. 12, 1962. Southern Rhodesia.

Res. 1760 (XVII) Oct. 31, 1962. Southern Rhodesia.

Res. 1805 (XVII) Dec. 14, 1962. South West Africa.

Res. 1807 (XVII) Dec. 14, 1962. Territories under Portuguese administration.

Res. 1810 (XVII) Dec. 17, 1962. Reaffirming Res. 1514 and 1654 and enlarging Special Committee.

Res. 1811 (XVII) Dec. 17, 1962. Zanzibar.

Res. 1812 (XVII) Dec. 17, 1962. Kenya.

Res. 1815 (XVII) Dec. 18, 1962. Principles of international law embodied in the Charter.

Res. 1817 (XVII) Dec. 18, 1962. Basutoland, Bechuanaland and Swaziland.

Res. 1818 (XVII) Dec. 18, 1962. Nyasaland.

Res. 1819 (XVII) Dec. 18, 1962. Angola.

Res. 1850 (XVII) Dec. 19, 1962. Racial discrimination in non-self-governing territories.

Res. 1855 (XVII) Dec. 19, 1962. Korea.

Res. 1883 (XVIII) Oct. 14, 1963. Southern Rhodesia.

Res. 1889 (XVIII) Nov. 6, 1963. Southern Rhodesia.

Res. 1899 (XVIII) Nov. 13, 1963. South West Africa.

Res. 1904 (XVIII) Nov. 20, 1963. Declaration on the Elimination of All Forms of Racial Discrimination (Arts. 8, 11).

Res. 1913 (XVIII) Dec. 3, 1963. Territories under Portuguese administration.

Res. 1948 (XVIII) Dec. 11, 1963. Oman.

Res. 1949 (XVIII) Dec. 11, 1963. Aden.

Res. 1950 (XVIII) Dec. 11, 1963. Malta.

Res. 1951 (XVIII) Dec. 11, 1963. Fiji.

Res. 1952 (XVIII) Dec. 11, 1963. Northern Rhodesia.

Res. 1953 (XVIII) Dec. 11, 1963. Nyasaland.

Res. 1954 (XVIII) Dec. 11, 1963. Basutoland etc.

Res. 1955 (XVIII) Dec. 11, 1963. British Guiana.

Res. 1956 (XVIII) Dec. 11, 1963. Reaffirming Res. 1514, 1654 and 1810 and Special Committee.

Res. 1964 (XVIII) Dec. 13, 1963. Korea.

Res. 1972 (XVIII) Dec. 16, 1963. Aden.

Res. 1979 (XVIII) Dec. 17, 1963. South West Africa.

Res. 2005 (XIX) Feb. 18, 1965. Cook Islands.

Res. 2012 (XX) Oct. 12, 1965. Southern Rhodesia.

Res. 2022 (XX) Nov. 5, 1965. Southern Rhodesia.

Res. 2023 (XX) Nov. 5, 1965. Aden.

Res. 2024 (XX) Nov. 11, 1965. Southern Rhodesia.

Res. 2063 (XX) Dec. 16, 1965. Basutoland etc.

Res. 2064 (XX) Dec. 16, 1965. Determining status of full internal self-government of Cook Islands.

Res. 2065 (XX) Dec. 16, 1965. Falkland Islands.

Res. 2066 (XX) Dec. 16, 1965. Mauritius.

Res. 2067 (XX) Dec. 16, 1965. Equatorial Guinea.

Res. 2068 (XX) Dec. 16, 1965. Fiji.

Res. 2069 (XX) Dec. 16, 1965. American Samoa, Antigua, etc., some involving "special circumstances of geographic isolation and economic conditions."

Res. 2070 (XX) Dec. 16, 1965. Gibraltar.

Res. 2071 (XX) Dec. 16, 1965. British Guiana.

Res. 2072 (XX) Dec. 16, 1965. Ifni and Spanish Sahara.

Res. 2073 (XX) Dec. 17, 1965. Oman.

Res. 2074 (XX) Dec. 17, 1965. South West Africa.

Res. 2077 (XX) Dec. 18, 1965. Cyprus.

Res. 2079 (XX) Dec. 18, 1965. Tibet.

Res. 2105 (XX) Dec. 20, 1965. Reaffirming Res. 1514 etc. Requests Special Committee to recommend steps for "small territories" (part. 8). Invites all states "to provide material and moral assistance to the national liberation movements in colonial territories" (par. 10). Requests colonial powers "to dismantle the military bases installed in colonial territories and to refrain from establishing new ones" (par. 12).

Res. 2106 (XX) Dec. 21, 1965. International Convention on the Elimination of all Forms of Racial Discrimination.

Res. 2107 (XX) Dec. 21, 1965. Territories under Portuguese administration.

Res. 2111 (XX) Dec. 21, 1965. Nauru.

Res. 2112 (XX) Dec. 21, 1965. New Guinea and Papua.

Res. 2131 (XX) Dec. 21, 1965. Declaration on the inadvisability of intervention.

Res. 2132 (XX) Dec. 21, 1965. Korea.

Res. 2134 (XXI) Sept. 29, 1966. Basutoland etc.

Res. 2138 (XXI) Oct. 22, 1966. Southern Rhodesia.

Res. 2145 (XXI) Oct. 27, 1966. South West Africa.

Res. 2151 (XXI) Nov. 17, 1966. Southern Rhodesia.

Res. 2160 (XXI)) Nov. 30, 1966. Forcible action depriving people of right to self-determination.

Res. 2183 (XXI) Dec. 12, 1966. Aden.

Res. 2184 (XXI) Dec. 12, 1966. Territories under Portuguese administration.

Res. 2185 (XXI) Dec. 12, 1966. Fiji.

Res. 2189 (XXI) Dec. 13, 1966. Reaffirming Res. 1514 etc.

Res. 2200 (XXI) Dec. 16, 1966. International Covenant on Economic, Social and Cultural Rights, Art. 1; International Covenant on Civil and Political Rights, Art. 1.

Res. 2224 (XXI) Dec. 19, 1966. Korea.

Res. 2226 (XXI) Dec. 20, 1966. Nauru.

Res. 2227 (XXI) Dec. 20, 1966. Papua and New Guinea.

Res. 2228 (XXI) Dec. 20, 1966. French Somaliland.

Res. 2229 (XXI) Dec. 20, 1966. Ifni and Spanish Sahara.

Res. 2230 (XXI) Dec. 20, 1966. Equatorial Guinea.

Res. 2231 (XXI) Dec. 20, 1966. Gibraltar.

Res. 2232 (XXI) Dec. 20, 1966. American Samoa, Antigua, etc.

Res. 2238 (XXI) Dec. 20, 1966. Oman.

Res. 2248 (S-V) May 19, 1967. South West Africa.

Res. 2253 (ES-V) July 4, 1967. Jerusalem.

Res. 2254 (ES-V) July 14, 1967. Jerusalem.

Res. 2262 (XXII) Nov. 3, 1967. Southern Rhodesia.

Res. 2269 (XXII) Nov. 16, 1967. Korea

Res. 2270 (XXII) Nov. 17, 1967. Territories under Portuguese administration.

Consensus Nov. 30, 1967. Aden.

Res. 2288 (XXII) Dec. 7, 1967. Activities of foreign economic and other interests implementation of Res. 1514.

Res. 2302 (XXII) Dec. 12, 1967. Oman.

Res. 2311 (XXII) Dec. 14, 1967. Implementation of Res. 1514 by U.N. agencies.

Res. 2325 (XXII) Dec. 16, 1967. South West Africa.

Res. 2326 (XXII) Dec. 16, 1967. Reaffirming Res. 1514, etc.

Res. 2347 (XXII) Dec. 19, 1967. Nauru.

Res. 2348 (XXII) Dec. 19, 1967. Papua and New Guinea.

Res. 2350 (XXII) Dec. 19, 1967. Fiji.

Res. 2353 (XXII) Dec. 19, 1967. Gibraltar, applying principle that "any colonial situation which partially or completely destroys the national unity and territorial integrity of a country is incompatible" with the Charter and par. 6. of Res. 1514.

Res. 2354 (XXII) Dec. 19, 1967. Ifni and Spanish Sahara. Affirming separate right of self-determination for each.

Res. 2355 (XXII) Dec. 19, 1967. Equatorial Guinea.

Res. 2356 (XXII) Dec. 19, 1967. French Somilaland.

Res. 2357 (XXII) Dec. 19, 1967. American Samoa, Antigua, etc.

Consensus Dec. 19, 1967. Falkland Islands.

Res. 2372 (XXII) June 12, 1968. South West Africa.

Res. 2379 (XXIII) Oct. 25, 1968. Southern Rhodesia.

Res. 2383 (XXIII) Nov. 7, 1968. Southern Rhodisia.

Res. 2395 (XXIII) Nov. 29, 1968. Territories under Portuguese administration.

Res. 2396 (XXIII) Dec. 2, 1968. Apartheid as denial of self-determination (par. 3).

Res. 2403 (XXIII) Dec. 16, 1968. Namibia.

Res. 2422 (XXIII) Dec. 18, 1968. Information under Article 73c as to certain territories (pars. 3 and 4).

Res. 2424 (XXIII) Dec. 18, 1968. Oman.

Res. 2425 (XXIII) Dec. 18, 1968. Activities of foreign economic and other interests.

Res. 2426 (XXIII) Dec. 18, 1968. Implementation of Res. 1514 by U.N. agencies.

Res. 2427 (XXIII) Dec. 18, 1968. Papua and New Guinea.

Res. 2428 (XXIII) Dec. 18, 1968. Ifni and Spanish Sahara.

Res. 2429 (XXIII) Dec. 18, 1968. Gibraltar.

Res. 2430 (XXIII) Dec. 18, 1968. American Samoa, Antigua, etc.

Res. 2465 (XXIII) Dec. 20, 1968. Reaffirming Res. 1514, etc.

Res. 2466 (XXIII) Dec. 20, 1968. Korea.

Res. 2498 (XXIV) Oct. 31, 1969. Namibia.

Res. 2505 (XXIV) Nov. 20, 1969. Concerning O.A.U. manifesto on Southern Africa.

Res. 2507 (XXIV) Nov. 21, 1969. Territories under Portuguese administration.

Res. 2508 (XXIV) Nov. 21, 1969. Southern Rhodesia.

Res. 2516 (XXIV) Nov. 25, 1969. Korea.

Res. 2517 (XXIV) Dec. 1, 1969. Namibia.

Res. 2535B (XXIV) Dec. 10, 1969. People of Palestine.

Res. 2547A (XXIV) Dec. 11, 1969. Racial discrimination and apartheid in southern Africa.

Res. 2548 (XXIV) Dec. 11, 1969. Reaffirming Res. 1514, etc.

Res. 2554 (XXIV) Dec. 12, 1969. Activities of foreign economic and other interests.

Res. 2555 (XXIV) Dec. 12, 1969. Implementation of Res. 1514 by U.N. agencies.

Res. 2558 (XXIV) Dec. 12, 1969. Information under Art. 73c.

Res. 2559 (XXIV) Dec. 12, 1969. Oman.

Res. 2590 (XXIV) Dec. 16, 1969. Papua and New Guinea.

Res. 2591 (XXIV) Dec. 16, 1969. Spanish Sahara.

Res. 2592 (XXIV) Dec. 16, 1969. American Samoa, Antigua, etc.

Consensus Dec. 16, 1969. Falkland Islands.

Res. 2621 (XXV) Oct. 12, 1970. Programme for implementation of Res. 1514.

Res. 2625 (XXV) Oct. 24, 1970. Declaration on Principles of International Law, etc.

Res. 2628 (XXV) Nov. 4, 1970. Middle East.

Res. 2649 (XXV) Nov. 30, 1970. Emphasizing importance of universal realization of self-determination and condemning denial especially to people of southern Africa and Palestine.

Res. 2652 (XXV) Dec. 3, 1970. Southern Rhodesia.

Res. 2668 (XXV) Dec. 7, 1970. Korea.

Res. 2672 C (XXV) Dec. 8, 1970. People of Palestine.

Res. 2678 (XXV) Dec. 9, 1970. Namibia.

Res. 2700 (XXV) Dec. 14, 1970. Papua and New Guinea.

Res. 2701 (XXV) Dec. 14, 1970. Information under Art. 73e.

Res. 2702 (XXV) Dec. 14, 1970. Oman.

Res. 2703 (XXV) Dec. 14, 1970. Activities of foreign economic and other interests.

Res. 2704 (XXV) Dec. 14, 1970. Implementation of Res. 1514 by U.N. agencies.

Res. 2707 (XXV) Dec. 14, 1970. Territories under Portuguese administration.

Res. 2708 (XXV) Dec. 14, 1970. Reaffirming Res. 1514, etc.

Res. 2709 (XXV) Dec. 14, 1970. American Samoa, Antigua, etc.

Res. 2710 (XXV) Dec. 14, 1970. Antigua, Dominica, etc.

Res. 2711 (XXV) Dec. 14, 1970. Spanish Sahara.

Res. 2714 (XXV) Dec. 15, 1970. Racial discrimination and apartheid in southern Africa (par. 2).

Res. 2734 (XXV) Dec. 16, 1970. On strengthening international security (par. 18).

Res. 2758 (XXVI) Oct. 25, 1971. Restoration of the lawful rights of the People's Republic of China in the United Nations. No reference to self-determination.

Res. 2769 (XXVI) Nov. 22, 1971. Southern Rhodesia.

Res. 2787 (XXVI) Dec. 6, 1971. Importance of self-determination.

Res. 2793 (XXVI) Dec. 7, 1971. East Pakistan.

Res. 2795 (XXVI) Dec. 10, 1971. Territories under Portuguese administration.

Res. 2796 (XXVI) Dec. 10, 1971. Southern Rhodesia.

Res. 2799 (XXVI) Dec. 13, 1971. Middle East.

Res. 2865 (XXVI) Dec. 20, 1971. Papua New Guinea, implementing desire "for national unity and independence as a single political and territorial entity."

Res. 2866 (XXVI) Dec. 20, 1971. Seychelles.

Res. 2867 (XXVI) Dec. 20, 1971. Antigua, Dominica, etc.

Res. 2868 (XXVI) Dec. 20, 1971. Niue and the Tokelau Islands.

Res. 2869 (XXVI) Dec. 20, 1971. American Samoa, Bahamas, etc.

Res. 2870 (XXVI) Dec. 20, 1971. Information under 73e.

Res. 2871 (XXVI) Dec. 20, 1971. Namibia.

Res. 2873 (XXVI) Dec. 20, 1971. Activities of foreign economic and other interests.

Res. 2874 (XXVI) Dec. 20, 1971. Implementation of Res. 1514 by U.N. agencies.

Res. 2877 (XXVI) Dec. 20, 1971. Southern Rhodesia.

Res. 2878 (XXVI) Dec. 20, 1971. Reaffirming Res. 1514, etc.

Consensus Dec. 20, 1971. Falkland Islands.

Res. 2880 (XXVI) Dec. 21, 1971. On strengthening international security.

Res. 2908 (XXVII) Nov. 2, 1972. Reaffirming Res. 1514, etc.

Res. 2918 (XXVII) Nov. 14, 1972. Territories under Portuguese administration.

Res. 2923E (XXVII) Nov. 15, 1972. South Africa, esp. preamble 6.

Res. 2945 (XXVII) Dec. 7, 1972. Southern Rhodesia.

Res. 2949 (XXVII) Dec. 8, 1972. Middle East.

Res. 2955 (XXVII) Dec. 12, 1972. Importance of self-determination.

Res. 2963C (XXVII) Dec. 13, 1972. Israeli action in Gaza Strip.

Res. 2963D (XXVII) Dec. 13, 1972. Territories occupied by Israel.

Res. 2963E (XXVII) Dec. 13, 1972. People of Israel.

Res. 2977 (XXVII) Dec. 14, 1972. Papua New Guinea.

Res. 2978 (XXVII) Dec. 14, 1972. Information under Art. 73e.

Res. 2979 (XXVII) Dec. 14, 1972. Activities of foreign economic and other interests.

Res. 2980 (XXVII) Dec. 14, 1972. Implementation of Res. 1514 by U.N. agencies.

Res. 2983 (XXVII) Dec. 14, 1972. Spanish Sahara.

Res. 2984 (XXVII) Dec. 14, 1972. American Samoa, Bahamas, etc.

Res. 2985 (XXVII) Dec. 14, 1972. Seychelles.

Res. 2986 (XXVII) Dec. 14, 1972. Niue and Tokelau Islands.

Res. 2987 (XXVII) Dec. 14, 1972. Antigua, Dominica, etc.

Res. 2993 (XXVII) Dec. 15, 1972. Sovereignty over resources (par. 4).

Res. 3005 (XXVII) Dec. 15, 1972. Territories occupied by Israel.

Res. 3031 (XXVII) Dec. 18, 1972. Namibia.

Res. 3050 (XXVIII) Sept. 18, 1973. Admission of both Germanys to membership in the U.N.

Res. 3061 (XXVIII) Nov. 2, 1973. Guinea-Bissau.

A/9341 Consensus Nov. 28, 1973. Korea.

Res. 3070 (XXVIII) Nov. 30, 1973. Importance of self-determination.

Res. 3089D (XXVIII) Dec. 7, 1973. People of Palestine.

Res. 3092B (XXVIII) Dec. 7, 1973. Territories occupied by Israel.

Res. 3103 (XXVIII) Dec. 12, 1973. Legal status of combatants struggling against colonial and alien domination and recist régimes.

Res. 3109 (XXVIII) Dec. 12, 1973. Papua New Guinea.

Res. 3110 (XXVIII) Dec. 12, 1973. Information under Art. 73E.

Res. 3111 (XXVIII) Dec. 12, 1973. Namibia.

Res. 3113 (XXVIII) Dec. 12, 1973. Territories under Portuguese administration.

Res. 3115 (XXVIII) Dec. 12, 1973. Southern Rhodesia.

Res. 3117 (XXVIII) Dec. 12, 1973. Activities of foreign aconomic and other interests.

Res. 3118 (XXVIII) Dec. 12, 1973. Implementation of Res. 1514 by U.N. agencies.

Res. 3151G (XXVIII) Dec. 14, 1973. South Africa, esp. pars. 11, 14

Res. 3155 (XXVIII) Dec. 14, 1973. Niue.

Res. 3156 (XXVIII) Dec. 14, 1973. American Samoa, Gilbert and Ellice Islands, etc.

Res. 3157 (XXVIII) Dec. 14, 1973. Bermuda, British Virgin Is., etc.

Res. 3158 (XXVIII) Dec. 14, 1973. Seychelles.

Res. 3159 (XXVIII) Dec. 14, 1973. Brunei.

Res. 3160 (XXVIII) Dec. 14, 1973. Falkland Islands.

Res. 3161 (XXVIII) Dec. 14, 1973. Comoro Archipelago.

Res. 3162 (XXVIII) Dec. 14, 1973. Spanish Sahara.

Res. 3163 (XXVIII) Dec. 14, 1973. Reaffirming Res. 1514, etc.

Consensus. Dec. 14, 1973. Cocos (Keeling) Islands and Tokelau Islands.

Consensus. Dec. 14, 1973. Gibraltar.

Res. 3175 (XXVIII) Dec. 17, 1973. Sovereignty over resources of occupied territories.

Res. 3181 (XXVIII) Dec. 17, 1973. Angola, etc.

Res. 3212 (XXIX) Nov. 1, 1974. Cyprus.

Res. 3236 (XXIX) Nov. 22, 1974. The Palestinian people.

Res. 3240A (XXIX) Nov. 29, 1974. Territories occupied by Israel.

Res. 3246(XXIX) Nov. 29, 1974. Importance of self-determination.

Res. 3285 (XXIX) Dec. 13, 1974. Niue.

Res. 3286 (XXIX) Dec. 13, 1974. Gibraltar.

Res. 3287 (XXIX) Dec. 13, 1974. Seychelles.

Res. 3288 (XXIX) Dec. 13, 1974. Gilbert and Ellice Islands.

Res. 3289 (XXIX) Dec. 13, 1974. Bermuda, etc.

Res. 3290 (XXIX) Dec. 13, 1974. American Samoa, etc.

Res. 3291 (XXIX) Dec. 13, 1974. Comoro Archipelago.

Res. 3292 (XXIX) Dec. 13, 1974. Spanish Sahara.

Res. 3293 (XXIX) Dec. 13, 1974. Information under Art. 73e.

Res. 3294 (XXIX) Dec. 13, 1974. Territories under Portuguese administration.

Res. 3295 (XXIX) Dec. 13, 1974. Namibia.

Res. 3297 (XXIX) Dec. 13, 1974. Southern Rhodesia.

Res. 3299 (XXIX) Dec. 13, 1974. Activities of foreign economic and other interests.

Res. 3300 (XXIX) Dec. 13, 1974. Implementation of Res. 1514 by U.N. agencies.

Res. 3324C (XXIX) Dec. 16, 1974. South Africa, esp. par. 1 (c).

Res. 3324E (XXIX) Dec. 16, 1974. South Africa, esp. par. 10.

Res. 3328 (XXIX) Dec. 16, 1974. Reaffirming Res. 1514, etc.

Res. 3333 (XXIX) Dec. 17, 1974. Korea.

Res. 3336 (XXIX) Dec. 17, 1974. Sovererignty over resources of occupied territories.

Res. 3340 (XXIX) Dec. 17, 1974. Mozambique.

Res. 3375 (XXX) Nov. 10, 1975. The Palestinian people.

Res. 3376 (XXX) Nov. 10, 1975. The Palestinian people.

Res. 3382 (XXX) Nov. 10, 1975. Importance of self-determination.

Res. 3390A, B (XXX) Nov. 18, 1975. Korea.

Res. 3395 (XXX) Nov. 20, 1975. Cyprus.

Res. 3396 (XXX) Nov. 21, 1975. Southern Rhodesia (Zimbabwe).

Res. 3398 (XXX) Nov. 21, 1975. Activities of foreign economic and other interests.

Res. 3399 (XXX) Nov. 26, 1975. Namibia.

Res. 3411D (XXX) Nov. 28, 1975. South Africa-bantustans.

Res. 3411F (XXX) Nov. 28, 1975. South Africa, esp. preamble 4 and par. 1 (d).

Res. 3411G (XXX) Dec. 10, 1975. South Africa (pars. 5, 6).

Res. 3414 (XXX) Dec. 5, 1975. Middle East. Palestinian people.

Res. 3420 (XXX) Dec. 8, 1975. Information under Art. 73e.

Res. 3421 (XXX) Dec. 8, 1975. Implementation of Res. 1514 by U.N. agencies.

Res. 3424 (XXX) Dec. 8, 1975. Brunei.

Res. 3425 (XXX) Dec. 8, 1975. Montserrat.

Res. 3426 (XXX) Dec. 8, 1975. Gilbert Islands.

Res. 3427 (XXX) Dec. 8, 1975. Bermuda, etc.

Res. 3428 (XXX) Dec.8, 1975. Tokelau Islands.

Res. 3429 (XXX) Dec. 8, 1975. American Samoa, etc.

Res. 3430 (XXX) Dec. 8, 1975. Seychelles.

Res. 3431 (XXX) Dec. 8, 1975. Solomon Islands.

Res. 3432 (XXX) Dec. 8, 1975. Belize.

Res. 3433 (XXX) Dec. 8, 1975. New Hebrides, etc.

Res. 3458A (XXX) Dec. 10, 1975. Spanish (Western) Sahara.

Res. 3458B (XXX) Dec. 10, 1975. Saharan populations of Western Sahara.

Res. 3480 (XXX) Dec. 11, 1975. French Somaliland (Djibouti).

Res. 3481 (XXX) Dec. 11, 1975. Reaffirming Res. 1514, etc. Namibia, Zimbabwe.

Res. 3485 (XXX) Dec. 12, 1975. Portuguese Timor.

Res. 3525A (XXX) Dec. 15, 1975. Territories occupied by Israel.

Res. 31/4 Oct. 21, 1976. Comorian island of Mayotte.

Res. 31/6A Oct. 21, 1976. Bantustan of Transkei.

Res. 31/6C, I, J Nov. 9, 1976. South Africa.

Res. 31/7 Nov. 5, 1976. Activities of foreign economic and other interests.

Res. 31/12 Nov. 9, 1976. Cyprus.

Res. 31/20 Nov. 24, 1976. Palestinian people.

Res. 31/29 Nov. 29, 1976. Information under Art. 73e.

Res. 31/30 Nov. 29, 1976. Implementation of Res. 1514 by U.N. agencies.

Res. 31/33 Nov. 30, 1976. Regimes in southern Africa.

Res. 31/34 Nov. 30, 1976. Importance of self-determination.

Res. 31/45 Dec. 1, 1976. Western Sahara.

Res. 31/46 Dec. 1, 1976. Solomon Islands.

Res. 31/47 Dec. 1, 1976. Gilbert Islands.

Res. 31/48 Dec. 1, 1976. Tokelau Islands.

Res. 31/49 Dec. 1, 1976. Falkland Islands.

Res. 31/50 Dec. 1, 1976. Belize.

Res. 31/51 Dec. 1, 1976. New Hebrides.

Res. 31/52 Dec. 1, 1976. Bermuda, etc.

Res. 31/53 Dec. 1, 1976. East Timor.

Res. 31/54 Dec. 1, 1976. British Virgin Islands.

Res. 31/55 Dec. 1, 1976. American Samoa.

Res. 31/56 Dec. 1, 1976. Brunei.

Res. 31/57 Dec. 1, 1976. U.S. Virgin Islands.

Res. 31/58 Dec. 1, 1976. Guam.

Res. 31/59 Dec. 1, 1976. French Somaliland (Djbouti).

Consensus 31/406A Dec. 1, 1976. St. Helena.

Consensus 31/406B Dec. 1, 1976. Tuvalu.

Consensus 31/406C Dec. 1, 1976. Gibraltar.

31/406D Dec. 1, 1976. Cocos (Keeling) Islands.

Res. 32/5 Oct. 28, 1977. Territories occupied by Israel.

Res. 32/7 Nov. 1, 1977. Comorian isalnd of Mayotte.

Res. 32/9A-H Nov. 4, 1977. Namibia.

Res. 32/14 Nov. 7, 1977. Importance of self-determination.

Res. 32/15 Nov. 9, 1977. Cyprus.

Res. 32/20 Nov. 25, 1977. Territories occupied by Israel.

Res. 32/22 Nov. 28, 1977. Western Sahara.

Res. 32/23 Nov. 28, 1977. Gilbert Islands.

Res. 32/24 Nov. 28, 1977. American Samoa.

Res. 32/25 Nov. 28, 1977. Solomon Islands.

Res. 32/26 Nov. 28, 1977. New Hebrides.

Res. 32/27 Nov. 28, 1977. Brunei.

Res. 32/28 Nov. 28, 1977. Guam.

Res. 32/29 Nov. 28, 1977. Bermuda, etc.

Res. 32/30 Nov. 28, 1977. Cayman Islands.

Res. 32/31 Nov. 28, 1977. U.S. Virgin Islands.

Res. 32/32 Nov. 28, 1977. Belize.

Res. 32/33 Nov. 28, 1977. Information under Art. 73e.

Res. 32/34 Nov. 28, 1977. East Timor.

Res. 32/35 Nov. 28, 1977. Activities of foreign economic and other interests.

Res. 32/36 Nov. 28, 1977. Implementation of Res. 1514 by U.N. agencies.

Consensus 32/407 Nov. 28, 1977. Tuvalu.

Consensus 32/409 Nov. 28, 1977. Tokelau Islands.

Consensus 32/410 Nov. 28, 1977. St. Helena.

Consensus 32/411 Nov. 28, 1977. Gibraltar.

Res. 32/40A Dec. 2, 1977. Palestinian people.

Res. 32/41 Dec. 7, 1977. Zimbabwe and Namibia.

Res. 32/42 Dec. 7, 1977. Reaffirming Res. 1514, etc.

Res. 32/91C Dec. 13, 1977. Territories occupied by Israel.

Res. 32/105 J, K, N Dec. 14, 1977. South Africa and bantustan policy.

Res. 32/116A Dec. 16, 1977. Southern Rhodesia.

Res. 32/147 Dec. 16, 1977. On international terrorism.

Res. 32/154 Dec. 19, 1977. On strengthening international security.

Res. 32/155 Dec. 19, 1977. International détente.

Res. 32/161 Dec. 19, 1977. Sovereignty over resources of occupied territories.

Res. S-9/2 May 3, 1978. Namibia.

Res. 33/15 Nov. 9, 1978. Cyprus.

Res. 33/23 Nov. 29, 1978. Regimes in southern Africa.

Res. 33/24 Nov. 29, 1978. Importance of self-determination.

Res. 33/28 Dec. 7, 1978. Palestine.

Res. 33/29 Dec. 7, 1978. Middle East.

Res. 33/30 Dec. 13, 1978. New Hebrides.

Res. 33/31A Dec. 13, 1978. Western Sahara.

Res. 33/32 Dec. 13, 1978. American Samoa.

Res. 33/33 Dec. 13, 1978. Guam.

Res. 33/34 Dec. 13, 1978. U.S. Virgin Islands.

Res. 33/35 Dec. 13, 1978. Bermuda, etc.

Res. 33/36 Dec. 13, 1978. Belize.

Res. 33/37 Dec. 13, 1978. Information under Art. 73e.

Res. 33/38A Dec. 13, 1978. Southern Rhodesia.

Res. 33/39 Dec. 13, 1978. East Timor.

Res. 33/41 Dec. 13, 1978. Implementation of Res. 1514 by U.N. agencies.

Res. 33/44 Dec. 13, 1978. Decolonization.

Consensus Dec. 13, 1978. Gibraltar.

Consensus Dec. 13, 1978. Tokelau Islands.

Consensus Dec. 13, 1978. St. Helena.

Consensus Dec. 13, 1978. Cocos (Keeling) Islands.

Res. 33/206 May 31, 1979. Namibia.

Res. 34/10 Nov. 2, 1979. New Hebrides.

Res. 34/21 Nov. 9, 1979. Co-operation with Organization of African Unity. (Par. 4).

Res. 34/24 Nov. 15, 1979. Apartheid and racism.

Res. 34/30 Nov. 20, 1979. Cyprus.

Res. 34/33 Nov. 21, 1979. Information under Art. 73e.

Res. 34/34 Nov. 21, 1979. Bermuda, etc.

Res. 34/35 Nov. 21, 1979. American Samoa.

Res. 34/36 Nov. 21, 1979. U.S. Virgin Islands.

Res. 34/37 Nov. 21, 1979. Western Sahara.

Res. 34/38 Nov. 21, 1979. Belize.

Res. 34/39 Nov. 21, 1979. Guam.

Res. 34/40 Nov. 21, 1979. East Timor.

Res. 34/41 Nov. 21, 1979. Activities of foreign economic and other interests.

Res. 34/42 Nov. 21, 1979. Implementation of Res. 1514 by U.N. agencies.

Consensus Nov. 21, 1979. St. Helena.

Consensus Nov. 21, 1979. Gibraltar.

Consensus Nov. 21, 1979. Tokelau.

Consensus Nov. 21, 1979. Cocos (Keeling) Islands.

Res. 34/44 Nov. 23, 1979. Implementation of Res. 1514 by states.

Res. 34/65A, B Dec. 12, 1979. Palestinian people.

Res. 34/69 Dec. 6, 1979. Comorian Island of Mayotte.

Res. 34/70 Dec. 6, 1979. Middle East.

Res. 34/90A, C Dec. 12, 1979. Settlements in occupied territories.

Res. 34/91 Dec. 12, 1979. Islands of Glorieuses, Juan de Nova, Europa and Basas da India.

Res. 34/92A-G Dec. 12, 1979. Namibia.

Res. 34/93A, G, O Dec. 12, 1979. South Africa including bantustans.

Res. 34/94 Dec. 13, 1979. Decolonization.

Res. 34/100 Dec. 14, 1979. On strengthening international security.

Res. 34/103 Dec. 14, 1979. Hegemonism.

Res. 34/136 Dec. 14, 1979. Sovereignty over resources of occupied Arab territories.

Res. 34/145 Dec. 17, 1979. Terrorism.

Res. 34/192 Dec. 18, 1979. Zimbabwe (Southern Rhodesia).
[Through December 31, 1979]

Security Council

Res. 21 (1947) Apr. 2, 1947. Trusteeship of the Territory of the Pacific Islands.
Res. 47 (1948) Apr. 21, 1948. Jammu and Kashmir.
Res. 67 (1949) Jan. 28, 1949. Indonesia.
Res. 80 (1950) Mar. 14, 1950. Jammu and Kashmir.
Res. 82 (1950) June 25, 1950. Korea.
Decision Aug. 1, 1950. Representation of China.
Res. 87 (1950) Sept. 29, 1950. Taiwan.
Res. 91 (1951) Mar. 30, 1951. Jammu and Kashmir.
Res. 98 (1952) Dec. 23, 1952. Jammu and Kashmir.
Res. 118 (1956) Oct. 13, 1956. Suez.
Res. 122 (1957) Jan. 24, 1957. Jammu and Kashmir.
Res. 126 (1957) Dec. 2, 1957. Jammu and Kashmir.
Res. 145 (1960) July 22, 1960. Congo.
Res. 146 (1960) Aug. 9, 1960. Congo.
Res. 161 (1961) Feb. 21, 1961. Congo.
Res. 163 (1961) June 9, 1961. Territories under Portuguese administration.
Res. 169 (1961) Nov. 24, 1961. Congo.
Res. 180 (1963) July 31, 1963. Territories under Portuguese administration.
Res. 183 (1963) Dec. 11, 1963. Territories under Portuguese administration.
Res. 186 (1964) Mar. 4, 1964. Cyprus.
Res. 191 (1964) June 18, 1964. South Africa.
Res. 192 (1964) June 20, 1964. Cyprus.
Res. 193 (1964) Aug. 9, 1964. Cyprus.
Res. 198 (1964) Dec. 18, 1964. Cyprus.
Res. 199 (1964) Dec. 30, 1964. Congo.
Res. 202 (1965) May 6, 1965. Southern Rhodesia.
Res. 206 (1965) June 15, 1965. Cyprus.
Res. 207 (1965) Aug. 10, 1965. Cyprus.
Res. 216 (1965) Nov. 12, 1965. Southern Rhodesia.
Res. 217 (1965) Nov. 20, 1965. Southern Rhodesia.
Res. 218 (1965) Nov. 23, 1965. Territories under Portuguese administration.
Res. 219 (1965) Dec. 17, 1965. Cyprus.
Res. 220 (1966) Mar. 16, 1966. Cyprus.
Res. 221 (1966) Apr. 9, 1966. Southern Rhodesia.
Res. 222 (1966) June 16, 1966. Cyprus.
Res. 231 (1966) Dec. 15, 1966. Cyprus.
Res. 232 (1966) Dec. 16, 1966. Southern Rhodesia.
Res. 238 (1967) June 19, 1967. Cyprus.
Res. 242 (1967) Nov. 22, 1967. Middle East.
Res. 244 (1967) Dec. 22, 1967. Cyprus.
Res. 246 (1968) Mar. 14, 1968. South West Africa.
Res. 247 (1968) Mar. 18, 1968. Cyprus.
Res. 252 (1968) May 21, 1968. Jerusalem.
Res. 253 (1968) May 20, 1968. Southern Rhodesia.
Res. 254 (1968) June 18, 1968. Cyprus.
Res. 258 (1968) Sept. 18, 1968. Middle East.
Res. 261 (1968) Dec. 10, 1968. Cyprus.
Res. 264 (1969) Mar. 20, 1969. Namibia.
Res. 266 (1969) June 10, 1969. Cyprus.
Res. 267 (1969) July 3, 1969. Jerusalem.
Res. 269 (1969) Aug. 12, 1969. Namibia.
Res. 274 (1969) Dec. 11, 1969. Cyprus.
Res. 276 (1970) Jan. 30, 1970. Namibia.
Res. 277 (1970) Mar. 18, 1970. Southern Rhodesia.
Res. 281 (1970) June 9, 1970. Cyprus.
Res. 283 (1970) July 29, 1970. Namibia.
Res. 288 (1970) Nov. 17, 1970. Southern Rhodesia.
Res. 290 (1970) Dec. 8, 1970. Angola, etc.
Res. 291 (1970) Dec. 10, 1970. Cyprus.
Res. 293 (1971) May 26, 1971. Cyprus.

Res. 295 (1971) Aug. 3, 1971. Guinea (Bissau).

Res. 298 (1971) Sept. 25, 1971. Jerusalem.

Res. 301 (1971) Oct. 20, 1971. Namibia.

Res. 302 (1971) Nov. 24, 1971. Guinea (Bissau).

Res. 305 (1971) Dec. 13, 1971. Cyprus.

Res. 309 (1972) Feb. 4, 1972. Namibia.

Res. 310 (1972) Feb. 4, 1972. Namibia.

Res. 312 (1972) Feb. 4, 1972, Angola, etc.

Res. 314 (1972) Feb. 28, 1972. Southern Rhodesia.

Res. 315 (1972) June 15, 1972. Cyprus.

Res. 318 (1972) July 28, 1972. Southern Rhodesia.

Res. 319 (1972) Aug. 1, 1972. Namibia.

Res. 322 (1972) Nov. 22, 1972. Angola, etc.

Res. 323 (1972) Dec. 6, 1972. Namibia.

Res. 324 (1972) Dec. 12, 1972. Cyprus.

Res. 326 (1973) Feb. 2, 1973. Southern Rhodesia.

Res. 328 (1973) Mar. 10, 1973. Southern Rhodesia.

Res. 334 (1973) June 15, 1973. Cyprus.

Res. 343 (1973) Dec. 14, 1973. Cyprus.

Res. 349 (1974) May 29, 1974. Cyprus.

Res. 364 (1974) Dec. 13, 1974. Cyprus.

Res. 365 (1974) Dec. 13, 1976. Cyprus.

Res. 366 (1974) Dec. 17, 1974. Namibia.

Res. 367 (1975) Mar. 12, 1975. Cyprus.

Res. 370 (1975) June 13, 1975. Cyprus.

Res. 377 (1975) Oct. 22, 1975. Western Sahara.

Res. 379 (1975) Nov. 2, 1975. Western Sahara.

Res. 383 (1975) Dec. 13, 1975. Cyprus.

Res. 384 (1975) Dec. 22, 1975. East Timor.

Res. 385 (1976) Jan. 30, 1976. Namibia.

Res. 386 (1976) Mar. 17, 1976. Southern Rhodesia and Mozambique.

Res. 388 (1976) Apr. 6, 1976. Southern Rhodesia.

Res. 389 (1976) Apr. 22, 1976. East Timor.

Res. 391 (1976) June 15, 1976. Cyprus.

Res. 392 (1976) June 19, 1976. South Africa.

Agreed statement Nov. 11, 1976. Territories occupied by Israel.

Res. 401 (1976) Dec. 14, 1976. Cyprus.

Res. 402 (1976) Dec. 22, 1976. Lesotha and the bantustan Transkei.

Res. 403 (1977) Jan. 14, 1977. Southern Rhodesia.

Res. 407 (1977) May 25, 1977. Lesotha and the bantustan Transkei.

Res. 409 (1977) May 25, 1977. Southern Rhodesia.

Res. 410 (1977) June 15, 1977. Cyprus.

Res. 411 (1977) June 30, 1977. Southern Rhodesia.

Res. 414 (1977) Sept. 15, 1977. Cyprus.

Res. 415 (1977) Sept. 29, 1977. Southern Rhodesia.

Res. 417 (1977) Oct. 31, 1977. South Africa.

Res. 422 (1977) Dec. 15, 1977. Cyprus.

Res. 423 (1978) Mar. 14, 1978. Southern Rhodesia.

Res. 424 (1978) Mar. 17, 1978. Southern Rhodesia.

Res. 428 (1978) May 6, 1978. Angola and Namibia.

Res. 431 (1978) July 27, 1978. Namibia.

Res. 432 (1978) July 27, 1978. Namibia.

Res. 435 (1978) Sept. 29, 1978. Namibia.

Res. 439 (1978) Nov. 13, 1978. Namibia.

Res. 440 (1978) Nov. 27, 1978. Cyprus.

Res. 445 (1979) Mar. 8, 1979. Southern Rhodesia.

Res. 446 (1979) Mar. 22, 1979. Territories occupied by Israel.

Res. 447 (1979) Mar. 28, 1979. Angola and Namibia.

Res. 448 (1979) Apr. 30, 1979. Southern Rhodesia.

Res. 451 (1979) June 15, 1979. Cyprus.

Res. 452 (1979) July 20, 1979. Territories occupied by Israel.

Decision Sept. 21, 1979. The bantustan Venda.

Res. 458 (1979) Dec. 14, 1979. Cyprus.

Res. 460 (1979) Dec. 21, 1979. Zimbabwe (Southern Rhodesia).

[Through December 21, 1979]

APPENDIX 4

United Nations Resolutions Concerning Nonintervention

The following resolutions affirm, apply, or otherwise bear on the principle of nonintervention.

General Assembly

Res. 109 (II) Oct. 21, 1947. Threats to the political independence and territorial integrity of Greece.

Res. 110 (II) Nov. 3, 1947. Propaganda to provoke or encourage threat to the peace, etc.

Res. 112 (II) Nov. 14, 1947. Independence of Korea. Par. 7 of Part B.

Res. 193 A, B (III) Nov. 27, 1948. Threats to the political independnece and territorial integrity of Greece.

Res. 288A (IV) Nov. 18, 1949. Threats to the political independence and territorial integrity of Greece.

Res. 290 (IV) Dec. 1, 1949. Essentials of peace. See especially pars. 2, 3.

Res. 291 (IV) Dec. 8, 1949. Political independence of China.

Res. 292 (IV) Dec. 8, 1949. Political independnece of China.

Res. 375 (IV) Dec. 6, 1949. Draft Declaration on Rights and Duties of States. See especially Arts. 3, 4, 9.

Res. 378A (V) Nov. 17, 1950. Outbreak of hostilities. First par. of preamble.

Res. 380 (V) Nov. 17, 1950. Peace through deeds.

Res. 381 (V) Nov. 17, 1950. Progapanda against peace.

Res. 382 A, B (V) Dec. 1, 1950. Threats to the political independence and territorial integrity of Greece.

Res. 498 (V) Feb. 1, 1952. Intervention by People's Republic of China in Korea.

Res. 505 (VI) Feb. 1, 1952. Soviet violations of treaty of Aug. 14, 1945 with China.

Res. 509 (VI) Dec. 14, 1951. Yugoslavia complaints against U.S.S.R., Bulgaria, Hungary, Romania, Albania, Czechoslovakia, and Poland.

Res. 707 (VII) Apr. 23, 1953. Complaint of Burma against Republic of China.

Res. 717 (VIII) Dec. 8, 1953. Complaint of Burma against Republic of China.

Res. 815 (IX) Oct. 29, 1954. Complaint of Burma against Republic of China.

Res. 997 (ES-1) Nov. 2, 1956. Suez.

Res. 999 (ES-1) Nov. 4, 1956. Reaffirming Res. 997, etc.

Res. 1002 (ES-1) Nov. 7, 1956. Reaffirming Res. 997, etc.

Res. 1004 (ES-II) Nov. 4, 1956. Hungary.

Res. 1005 (ES-II) Nov. 9, 1956. Hungary.

Res. 1127 (XI) Nov. 21, 1956. Hungary.

Res. 1130 (XI) Dec. 4, 1956. Hungary.

Res. 1131 (XI) Dec. 12, 1956. Hungary.

Res. 1133 (XII) Sept. 14, 1957. Hungary.

Res. 1236 (XII) Dec. 14, 1957. On Peaceful relations.

Res. 1312 (XIII) Dec. 12, 1958. Hungary.

Res. 1454 (XVI) Dec. 9, 1959. Hungary.

Res. 1474 (ES-IV) Sept. 20, 1960. Congo.

Res. 1514 (XV) Dec. 14, 1960. On grantinig independence to dependent peoples (par. 3).

Res. 1741 (XVI) Dec. 20, 1961. Hungary.

Res. 1815 (XVII) Dec. 18, 1962. Principles of international law embodied in the Charter.

Res. 1857 (XVII) Dec. 20, 1962. Hungary.

Res. 2077 (XX) Dec. 18, 1965. Cyprus.

Res. 2131 (XX) Dec. 21, 1965. Declaration on the Inadmisibility of Intervention.

Res. 2160 (XXI) Nov. 30, 1966. Prohibition of the threat or use of force.

Res. 2181 (XXI) Dec. 12, 1966. Request Special Committee consider proposal to widen area of agreement expressed in Res. 2131.

Res. 2225 (XXI) Dec. 19, 1966. Reaffirming Res. 2131 etc.

Res. 2307 (XXII) Dec. 13, 1967. Policies of apartheid in S. Africa. Appeal for assistance to people in their struggle (par. 8).

Res. 2396 (XXIII) Dec. 2, 1968. Policies of apartheid in S. Africa. Appeal for assistance in par. 7.

Res. 2625 (XXV) Oct. 24, 1970. Declaration on principles of international law etc.

Res. 2734 (XXV) Dec. 16, 1970. On strengthening international security.

Res. 2880 (XXVI) Dec. 21, 1971. On strengthening international security.

Res. 2936 (XXVII) Nov. 29, 1972. Non-use of force in international relations.

Res. 2993 (XXVII) Dec. 15, 1972. Measure or pressure directed against sovereign right to dispose of national resources (par. 4).

Res. 3212 (XXIX) Nov. 1, 1974. Cyprus.

Res. 3238 (XXIX) Nov. 28, 1974. Cambodia.

Res. 3314 (XXIX) Dec. 14, 1974. Definition of aggression.

Res. 3395 (XXX) Nov. 20, 1975. Cyprus.

Res. 31/12 Nov. 12, 1976. Cyprus.

Res. 31/53 Dec. 1, 1976. East Timor.

Res. 31/84 Dec. 13, 1976. Choice of objectives of social development "without any external interference" (par. 1).

Res. 31/91 Dec. 14, 1976. Non-interference in internal affairs.

Res. 31/92 Dec. 14, 1976. On strengthening international security.

Res. 32/15 Nov. 9, 1977. Cyprus.

Res. 32/153 Dec. 19, 1977. Non-interference in internal affairs.

Res. 32/154 Dec. 19, 1977. On strengthening international security.

Res. 32/155 Dec. 19, 1977. International détente.

Res. S-8/2 Apr. 21, 1978. Lebanon.

Res. 34/22 Nov. 14, 1979. Kampuchea (Cambodia).

Res. 34/30 Nov. 20, 1979. Cyprus.

Res. 34/93A, P Dec. 12, 1979. Condemning collaboration with regime in South Africa.

Res. 34/100 Dec. 14, 1979. On strengthening international security.

Res. 34/101 Dec. 14, 1979. Non-interference in internal affairs.

Res. 34/103 Dec. 14, 1979. Hegemonism.

[Through December 31, 1979]

Many resolutions affirm the right, within the scope of the Charter, to assist peoples in their legitimate exercise of a right of self-determination. The following are examples:

Res. 2022 (XX) Nov. 5, 1965. Par. 10: "moral and material help."

Res. 2974 (XX) Dec. 17, 1965. Par. 12: "moral and material support."

Res. 2105 (XX) Dec. 20, 1965. Par. 10: "material and moral assistance."

Res. 2131 (XX) Dec. 21, 1965. Par. 6: "contribute to" elimination of colonialism.

Res. 2151 (XXI) Nov. 17, 1966. Par. 10: "moral and material support."

Res. 2160 (XXI) Nov. 30, 1966. Preamble, par. 4: "all support in their struggle which is in accordance with the purposes and principles of the Charter."

Res. 2184 (XXI) Dec. 12, 1966. Par. 6: "moral and material support."

Res. 2189 (XXI) Dec. 13, 1966. Par. 7: "material and moral assistance."

Res. 2326 (XXII) Dec. 16, 1967. Par. 6: "moral and material assistance."

Res. 2383 (XXIII) Nov. 7, 1968. Par. 14: "moral and material assistance."

Res. 2395 (XXIII) Nov. 29, 1968. Par. 5: "moral and material assistance."

Res. 2465 (XXIII) Dec. 20, 1968. Par. 5: "moral and material assistance."

Res. 2548 (XXIV) Dec. 11, 1969. Par. 5: "moral and material assistance."

Res. 2625 (XXV) Oct. 24, 1970. Par. E5 of Declaration:"support in accordance with the purposes and principles of the Charter" in response to "forcible action."

Res. 2708 (XXV) Dec. 14, 1970. Par. 6: "moral and material assistance."

Res. 2734 (XXV) Dec. 16, 1970. Par. 18: "assistance . . . in accordance with the Charter."

Res. 2878 (XXVI) Dec. 20, 1971. Par. 7: "moral and material assistance."

Res. 2908 (XXVII) Nov. 2, 1972. Par. 8: "moral and material assistance."

Res. 2945 (XXVII) Dec. 7, 1972. Par. 7: "moral and material assistance."

Res. 2983 (XXVII) Dec. 14, 1972. Par. 2: "moral and material assistance."

Res. 3031 (XXVII) Dec. 18, 1972. Par. 10(b): "moral and material assistance."

Res. 3163 (XXVIII) Dec. 14, 1973. Par. 7: "moral and material assistance."

Res. 3314 (XXIX) Dec. 14, 1974. Art. 7 of Definition of Aggression: right of peoples "forcibly deprived" to seek and receive "support in accordance with the principles of the Charter and in conformity with the above-mentioned Declaration [Res. 2625]."

Res. 3324C (XXIX) Dec. 16, 1974. Par. 2: "moral and material assistance."

Res. 3328 (XXIX) Dec. 16, 1974. Par. 7: "moral and material assistance."

Res. 3481 (XXX) Dec. 11, 1975. Par. 10: "moral and material assistance."

Res. 31/146 Dec. 20, 1976. Namibia. Par. 4: "all necessary support and assistance" to SWAPO.

Res. 32/42 Dec. 7, 1977. Par. 12: "moral and material assistance."

Res. 33/206 May 31, 1979. Namibia. Par. 9: "increased and sustained support and material, financial, military and other assistance to SWAPO."

[Through December 31, 1979]

Security Council

Res. 118 (1956) Oct. 13, 1956. Suez.

Res. 138 (1960) June 23, 1960. Eichman case.

Res. 143 (1960) July 14, 1960. Congo.

Res. 145 (1960) July 22, 1960. Congo.

Res. 146 (1960) Aug. 9, 1960. Congo.

Res. 156 (1960) Sept. 9, 1960. Dominican Republic.

Res. 161 (1961) Feb. 21, 1961. Congo.

Res. 169 (1961) Nov. 24, 1961. Congo.

Res. 178 (1963) Apr. 24, 1963. Senegal.

Res. 186 (1964) Mar. 4, 1964. Cyprus.

Res. 187 (1964) Mar. 13, 1964. Cyprus.

Res. 192 (1964) June 20, 1964. Cyprus.

Res. 193 (1964) Aug. 9, 1964. Cyprus.

Res. 194 (1964) Sept. 25, 1964. Cyprus.

Res. 198 (1964) Dec. 18, 1964. Cyprus.

Res. 199 (1964) Dec. 30, 1964. Cyprus.

Res. 201 (1965) Mar. 19, 1965. Cyprus.

Res. 204 (1965) May 19, 1965. Senegal.

Res. 206 (1965) June 15, 1965. Cyprus.

Res. 207 (1965) Aug. 10, 1965. Cyprus.

Res. 216 (1965) Nov. 12, 1965. Southern Rhodesia.

Res. 217 (1965) Nov. 20, 1965. Southern Rhodesia.

Res. 219 (1965) Dec. 17, 1965. Cyprus.

Res. 221 (1966) Apr. 9, 1966. Southern Rhodesia.

Res. 226 (1966) Oct. 14, 1966. Congo.
Res. 232 (1966) Dec. 16, 1966. Southern Rhodesia.
Res. 239 (1967) July 10, 1967. Congo.
Res. 241 (1967) Nov. 15, 1967. Congo.
Res. 253 (1968) May 29, 1968. Southern Rhodesia.
Res. 268 (1969) July 28, 1969. Zambia.
Res. 273 (1969) Dec. 9, 1969. Senegal.
Res. 275 (1969) Dec. 22, 1969. Guinea.
Res. 277 (1970) Mar. 18, 1970. Southern Rhodesia.
Res. 288 (1970) Nov. 17, 1970. Southern Rhodesia.
Res. 294 (1971) July 15, 1971. Senegal.
Res. 300 (1971) Oct. 12, 1971. Zambia.
Res. 302 (1971) Nov. 24, 1971. Senegal.
Res. 313 (1972) Feb. 28, 1972. Lebanon.
Res. 316 (1972) June 26, 1972. Lebanon and Syria.
Res. 317 (1972) July 21, 1972. Lebanon and Syria.
Res. 321 (1972) Oct. 23, 1972. Senegal.
Res. 328 (1973) Mar. 10, 1973. Southern Rhodesia.
Res. 332 (1973) Apr. 21, 1973. Lebanon.
Res. 337 (1973) Aug. 15, 1973. Lebanon.
Res. 347 (1974) Apr. 24, 1974. Lebanon.
Res. 353 (1974) July 20, 1974. Cyprus.
Res. 357 (1974) Aug. 14, 1974. Cyprus.
Res. 360 (1974) Aug. 16, 1974. Cyprus.
Res. 364 (1974) Dec. 13, 1974. Cyprus.
Res. 365 (1974) Dec. 13, 1974. Cyprus.
Res. 367 (1975) Mar. 12, 1975. Cyprus.
Res. 370 (1975) June 13, 1975. Cyprus.
Res. 383 (1975) Dec. 13, 1975. Cyprus.
Res. 384 (1975) Dec. 22, 1975. East Timor.
Res. 386 (1976) Mar. 17, 1976. Mozambique.
Res. 387 (1976) Mar. 31, 1976. Angola.
Res. 389 (1976) Apr. 22, 1976. East Timor.
Res. 393 (1976) July 30, 1976. Zambia.
Res. 403 (1977) Jan. 14, 1977. Botswana.
Res. 404 (1977) Feb. 8, 1977. Benin.
Res. 405 (1977) Apr. 14, 1977. Benin.
Res. 406 (1977) May 25, 1977. Botswana.
Res. 411 (1977) June 30, 1977. Mozambique.
Res. 418 (1977) Nov. 4,, 1977. South Africa.
Res. 419 (1977) Nov. 24, 1977. Benin.
Res. 425 (1978) Mar. 19, 1978. Lebanon.
Res. 427 (1978) May 3, 1978. Lebanon.
Res. 428 (1978) May 6, 1978. Angola and Namibia.
Res. 434 (1978) Sept. 18, 1978. Lebanon.
Res. 437 (1978) Oct. 6, 1978. Lebanon.
Res. 444 (1979) Jan. 19, 1979. Lebanon.
Res. 447 (1979) Mar. 28, 1979. Angola and Namibia.
Res. 450 (1979) June 14, 1979. Lebanon.
Res. 451 (1979) June 15, 1979. Cyprus.
Res. 454 (1979) Nov. 2, 1979. Angola.
Res. 455 (1979) Nov. 23, 1979. Zambia.
Res. 458 (1979) Dec. 14, 1979. Cyprus.
Res. 459 (1979) Dec. 19, 1979. Lebanon.

[Through December 31, 1979]

APPENDIX 5

United Nations Resolutions Concerning Access to Resources

General Assembly

Res. 523 (VI) Jan. 12, 1952. Recommending commercial agreements and recognizing "the sovereign rights of the under-developed countries, including the right to determine their own plans for economic development."

Res. 626 (VII) Dec. 21, 1952. Recommends member states "in the exercise of their right freely to use and exploit their natural wealth and resources wherever deemed desirable by them for their own progress and economic development, to have due regard, consistently with their sovereignty, to the need for maintaining the flow of capital in conditions of security, mutual confidence and economic cooperation among nations."

Res. 837 (IX) Dec. 14, 1954. Requesting Commission on Human Rights to complete recommendations on right of self-determination "including sovereignty over their natural wealth and resources, having due regard to the rights and duties of States under international law and to the importance of encouraging international co-operation in the economic development of under-developed countries."

Res. 1314 (XIII) Dec. 12, 1958. Establishing commission to survey status of permanent sovereignty over material wealth and resources and deciding that "in the conduct of the full survey of the status of permanent sovereignty of peoples and nations over their natural wealth and resources, due regard shall be paid to the rights and duties of States under international law and to the importance of encouraging international co-operation in the economic development of under-developed countries."

Res. 1514 (XV) Dec. 14, 1960. Affirming in preamble "that peoples may, for their own ends, freely dispose of their natural wealth and resources without prejudice to any obligations arising out of international economic co-operation, based upon the principle of mutual benefit, and international law."

Res. 1515 (XV) Dec. 15, 1960. Affirming (preamble) "the solemn undertaking embodied in the Charter to employ international machinery for the promotion of the economic and social development of all peoples" and recommending (par. 5) "that the sovereign right of every State to dispose of its wealth and its natural resources should be respected in conformity with the rights and duties of States under international law."

Res. 1721A (XVI) Dec. 20, 1961. Outer space and celestial bodies not subject to "national appropriation."

Res. 1803 (XVII) Dec. 14, 1962. Declaration concerning permanent sovereignty over natural resources, declaring "the right of peoples and nations to permanent sovereignty over their natural wealth and resources must be exercised in the interest of their national development and of the well-being of the people of the State concerned." Requests Secretary-General to continue study taking into account the desire of members "to ensure protection of their sovereign rights while encouraging international co-operation in the field of economic development."

Res. 1962 (XVIII) Dec. 13, 1963. Outer space and celestial bodies not subject to "national appropriation."

Res. 2131 (XX) Dec. 21, 1965. "No State may use or encourage the use of economic, political or any other type of measures to coerce another State in order to obtain from it the subordination of the exercise of its sovereign rights or to secure from it advantages of any kind" (par. 2).

Res. 2158 (XXI) Nov. 25, 1966. Reaffirms "the inalienable right of all countries to exercise permanent sovereignty over their natural resources in the interest of their national development, in accordance with the spirit and principles of the Charter of the United Nations and as recognized in General Assembly resolution 1803 (XVII)" (par. 1).

Res. 2200 (XXI) Dec. 16, 1966. International Covenant on Economic, Social and Cultural Rights, Art. 1(2). International Covenant on Civil and Political Rights, Art. 1(2). Both covenants provide: "All peoples may, for their own ends, freely dispose of their natural wealth and resources without prejudice to any obligations arising out of international economic co-operation, based on the principle of mutual benefit, and international law. In no case may a people be deprived of its own means of subsistence."

Res. 2222 (XXI) Dec. 19, 1966. Commending Treaty on Principles Governing the Activities of States in the Exploration of Outer Space, including the Moon and Other Celestial Bodies.

Res. 2288 (XXII) Dec. 7, 1967. Reaffirms the inalienable right of the peoples of colonial Territories "to the natural resources of their Territories, as well as the right to dispose of these resources in their best interests" (par. 2).

Res. 2386 (XXIII) Nov. 19, 1968. Reaffirming Res. 2158.

Res. 2425 (XXIII) Dec. 18, 1968. Par. 2 reaffirms par. 2 of Res. 2288.

Res. 2625 (XXV) Oct. 24, 1970. Declaration on Principles of International Law, etc. (appears in full in appendix 1). "No State may use or encourage the use of economic, political or any other type of measures to coerce another State in order to obtain from it the subordination of the exercise of its sovereign rights and to secure from it advantages of any kind" (par. C2). Compare Preamble 9). "States have the duty to co-operate with another . . . to promote international economic stability and progress" (par. D1).

Res. 2692 (XXV) Dec. 11, 1970. Reaffirms "the right of peoples and nations to permanent sovereignty over their natural wealth and resources, which must be exercised in the interest of their national development and of the well-being of the people of the State concerned" (par. 2.)

Res. 2749 (XXV) Dec. 17, 1970. Seabed lying beyond limits of national jurisdiction and its resources are "the common heritage of mankind."

Res. 2880 (XXVI) Dec. 21, 1971. Par. 9.

Res. 2993 (XXVII) Dec. 15, 1972. Par. 4.

Res. 3005 (XXVII) Dec. 15, 1972. "Affirms the principle of the sovereignty of the population of the occupied territories [i.e., occupied by Israel] over their national wealth and resources (par. 4).

Res. 3016 (XXVII) Dec. 18, 1972. Reaffirms "the right of States to permanent sovereignty over all their natural resources, on land within their international boundaries as well as those found in the sea-bed and subsoil thereof within their national jurisdiction and in the superjacent waters" (par. 1). Reaffirms the provision of Res. 2625 against economic, political, or other measures "to coerce another State in order to obtain from it the subordination of the exercise of its sovereign rights and to secure from it advantages of any kind" (par. 2).

Res. 3041 (XXVII) Dec. 19, 1972. Endorsed (by par. 16) Res. 88 (XII) of Oct. 19, 1972 by the Trade and Development Board (A/8715/Rev. 1 of 71) which reaffirms "the sovereign right of all countries freely to dispose of their natural resources for the benefit of their national development in the spirit and in accordance with the principles, of the Charter of the United Nations, as recognized and stated in the aforementioned resolutions of the General Assembly and in those of the United Nations Conference on Trade and Development" (par. 1).

Res. 3171 (XXVIII) Dec. 17, 1973. Reaffirming par. 1 of Res. 3016 as "inalienable rights" (par. 1). Emphasizes "the duty of all States to refrain in their international relations from military, political, economic or any other form of coercion aimed against the territorial integrity of any State and the exercise of its national jurisdiction."

Res. 3201 (S-VI) May 1, 1974. Declaration on the Establishment of a New International Economic Order.

Res. 3202 (S-VI) May 1, 1974. Programme of Action on the Establishment of a New International Economic Order.

Res. 3281 (XXIX) Dec. 12, 1974. Charter of Economic Rights and Duties of States. Declares that relations among States shall be governed by certain principles, which include "mutual and equitable benefit," "peaceful coexistence," "international co-operation for development," and "free access to and from the sea by landlocked countries within the framework of the above principles" (ch. I, clauses [e], [f], [n], [o]). "Every State has and shall freely exercise full permanent sovereignty, including possession, use and disposal, over all its wealth, natural resources and economic activities" (Art. 2[1]). "It is the duty of States to contribute to the development of international trade of goods particularly by means of arrangements and by the conclusion of long-term multilateral commodity agreements, where appropriate, and taking into account the interests of producers and consumers" (Art. 6. Compare Art. 5 as to organizations of primary commodity producers). "All States have the responsibility to co-operate in the economic, social, cultural, scientific and technological fields for the promotion of economic and social progress throughout the world, especially that of developing countries" (Art. 9). "Every State has the duty to co-operate in promoting a steady and increasing expansion and liberalization of world trade and improvement in the welfare and living standards of all peoples, in particular those of developing countries". (Art. 14). "All States have the duty to conduct their mutual economic relations in a manner which takes into account the interests of other countries. In particular, all States should avoid prejudicing the interests of developing countries" (Art. 24). "All States have the duty to coexist in tolerance and live together in peace, irrespective of differences in political, economic, social and cultural systems, and to facilitate trade between States having different economic and social systems. International trade should be conducted without prejudice to generalized non-discrimination and non-reciprocal preferences in favour of developing countries, on the basis of mutual advantage, equitable benefits and the exchange of most-favoured-nation treatment" (Art. 26). "All States have the duty to co-operate in achieving adjustments in the prices of exports of developing countries in relation to prices of their imports so as to promote just and equitable terms of trade for them, in a manner which is remunerative for producers and equitable for produccers and consumers" (Art. 28). "No State may use or encourage the use of economic, political or any other type of measures to coerce another State in order to obtain from it the subordination of the exercise of its sovereign rights" (Art. 32).

Res. 3336 (XXIX) Dec. 17, 1974. Reaffirms "the right of the Arab States and peoples whose territories are under Israeli occupation to full and effective permanent sovereignty over all resources and wealth" (par. 1). "Declares that the above principles apply to all States, territories and peoples under foreign occupation, colonial rule, alien domination and apartheid, or subjected to foreign aggression" (par. 4).

Res. 31/7 Nov. 5, 1976. Pars. 1, 2.

Res. 31/38 Nov. 30, 1976. Par. 1.

Res. 31/92 Dec. 14, 1976. Par. 4.

Res. 31/186 Dec. 21, 1976. Sovereignty over resources of occupied territories.

Res. 32/35 Nov. 28, 1977. Pars. 1, 3, 16.

Res. 32/154 Dec. 19, 1977. Par. 5.

Res. 32/161 Dec. 19, 1977. Sovereignty over resources of occupied territories.

Res. 34/41 Nov. 21, 1979. Pars. 1, 3, 22.

Res. 34/68 Dec. 5, 1979. Commending Agreement Governing the Activities of States on the Moon and Other Celestial Bodies.

Res. 34/92B Dec. 12, 1979. Sovereignty over resources of Namibia.

Res. 34/100 Dec. 14, 1979. Pars. 3,4.

Res. 34/136 Dec. 14, 1979. Sovereignty over resources of occupied Arab territories.

[Through December 31, 1979]

Security Council

Res. 330 (1973) Mar. 21, 1973. Noting "coercive measures which affect the free exercise of permanent sovereignty over the national resources of Latin American Countries" (preamble).

[Through December 31, 1979]

APPENDIX 6

Excerpts from the United Nations Charter and Statute of the International Court of Justice

United Nations Charter

Article 1

The Purposes of the United Nations are:

1. To maintain international peace and security, and to that end: to take effective collective measures for the prevention and removal of threats to the peace, and for the suppression of acts of aggression or other breaches of the peace, and to bring about by peaceful means, and in conformity with the principles of justice and international law, adjustment or settlement of international disputes or situations which might lead to a breach of the peace;

2. To develop friendly relations among nations based on respect for the principle of equal rights and self-determination of peoples, and to take other appropriate measures to strengthen universal peace;

3. To achieve international cooperation in solving international problems of an economic, social, cultural, or humanitarian character, and in promoting and encouraging respect for human rights and for fundamental freedoms for all without distinction as to race, sex, language, or religion; and

4. To be a center for harmonizing the actions of nations in the attainment of these common ends.

Article 2

The Organization and its Members, in pursuit of the Purposes stated in Article 1, shall act in accordance with the following Principles.

1. The Organization is based on the principle of the sovereign equality of all its Members.

2. All Members, in order to ensure to all of them the rights and benefits resulting from membership, shall fulfil in good faith the obligations assumed by them in accordance with the present Charter.

3. All Members shall settle their international disputes by peaceful means in such a manner that international peace and security, and justice, are not endangered.

4. All Members shall refrain in their international relations from the threat or use of force against the territorial integrity or political independence of any state, or in any other manner inconsistent with the Purposes of the United Nations.

5. All Members shall give the United Nations every assistance in any action it takes in accordance with the present Charter, and shall refrain from giving assistance to any state against which the United Nations is taking preventive or enforcement action.

6. The Organization shall ensure that states which are not Members of the United Nations act in accordance with these Principles so far as may be necessary for the maintenance of international peace and security.

7. Nothing contained in the present Charter shall authorize the United Nations to intervene in matters which are essentially within the domestic jurisdiction of any state or shall require the Members to submit such matters to settlement under the present Charter; but this principle shall not prejudice the application of enforcement measures under Chapter VII.

Article 10

The General Assembly may discuss any questions or any matters within the scope of the present Charter or relating to the powers and functions of any organs provided for in the present Charter, and, except as provided in Article 12, may make recommendations to the Members of the United Nations or to the Security Council or to both on any such questions or matters.

Article 11

1. The General Assembly may consider the general principles of cooperation in the maintenance of international peace and security, including the principles governing disarmament and the regulation of armaments, and may make recommendations with regard to such principles to the Members or to the Security Council or to both.

2. The General Assembly may discuss any questions relating to the maintenance of international peace and security brought before it by any Member of the United Nations, or by the Security Council, or by a state which is not a Member of the United Nations in accordance with Article 35, paragraph 2, and, except as provided in Article 12, may make recommendations with regard to any such questions to the state or states concerned or to the Security Council or to both. Any such question on which action is necessary shall be referred to the Security Council by the General Assembly either before or after discussion.

3. The General Assembly may call the attention of the Security Council to situations which are likely to endanger international peace and security.

4. The powers of the General Assembly set forth in this Article shall not limit the general scope of Article 10.

Article 14

Subject to the provisions of Article 12, the General Assembly may recommend measures for the peaceful adjustment of any situation, regardless of origin, which it deems likely to impair the general welfare or friendly relations among nations, including situations resulting from a violation of the provisions of the present Charter setting forth the Purposes and Principles of the United Nations.

ARTICLE 33

1. The parties to any dispute, the continuance of which is likely to endanger the maintenance of international peace and security, shall, first of all, seek a solution by negotiation, enquiry, mediation, conciliation, arbitration, judicial settlement, resort to regional agencies or arrangements, or other peaceful means of their own choice.

2. The Security Council shall, when it deems necessary, call upon the parties to settle their dispute by such means.

ARTICLE 36

1. The Security Council may, at any stage of a dispute of the nature referred to in Article 33 or of a situation of like nature, recommend appropriate procedures or methods of adjustment.

2. The Security Council should take into consideration any procedures for the settlement of the dispute which have already been adopted by the parties.

3. In making recommendations under this Article the Security Council should also take into consideration that legal disputes should as a general rule be referred by the parties to the International Court of Justice in accordance with the provisions of the Statute of the Court.

ARTICLE 37

1. Should the parties to a dispute of the nature referred to in Article 33 fail to settle it by the means indicated in that Article, they shall refer it to the Security Council.

2. If the Security Council deems that the continuance of the dispute is in fact likely to endanger the maintenance of international peace and security, it shall decide whether to take action under Article 36 or to recommend such terms of settlement as it may consider appropriate.

ARTICLE 38

Without prejudice to the provisions of Articles 33 to 37, the Security Council may, if all the parties to any dispute so request, make recommendations to the parties with a view to a pacific settlement of the dispute.

ARTICLE 39

The Security Council shall determine the existence of any threat to the peace, breach of the peace, or act of aggression and shall make recommendations, or decide what measures shall be taken in accordance with Articles 41 and 42, to maintain or restore international peace and security.

ARTICLE 43

1. All Members of the United Nations, in order to contribute to the maintenance of international peace and security, undertake to make available to the Security Council, on its call and in accordance with a special agreement or agreements, armed forces,

assistance, and facilities, including rights of passage, necessary for the purpose of maintaining international peace and security.

2. Such agreement or agreements shall govern the numbers and types of forces, their degree of readiness and general location, and the nature of the facilities and assistance to be provided.

3. The agreement or agreements shall be negotiated as soon as possible on the initiative of the Security Council. They shall be concluded between the Security Council and Members or between the Security Council and groups of Members and shall be subject to ratification by the signatory states in accordance with their respective constitutional processes.

Article 48

1. The action required to carry out the decisions of the Security Council for the maintenance of international peace and security shall be taken by all the Members of the United Nations or by some of them, as the Security Council may determine.

2. Such decisions shall be carried out by the Members of the United Nations directly and through their action in the appropriate international agencies of which they are members.

Article 51

Nothing in the present Charter shall impair the inherent right of individual or collective self-defense if an armed attack occurs against a Member of the United Nations, until the Security Council has taken the measures necessary to maintain international peace and security. Measures taken by Members in the exercise of this right of self-defense shall be immediately reported to the Security Council and shall not in any way affect the authority and responsibility of the Security Council under the present Charter to take at any time such action as it deems necessary in order to maintain or restore international peace and security.

Article 52

1. Nothing in the present Charter precludes the existence of regional arrangements or agencies for dealing with such matters relating to the maintenance of international peace and security as are appropriate for regional action, provided that such arrangements or agencies and their activities are consistent with the Purposes and Principles of the United Nations.

2. The Members of the United Nations entering into such arrangements or constituting such agencies shall make every effort to achieve pacific settlement of local disputes through such regional arrangements or by such regional agencies before referring them to the Security Council.

3. The Security Council shall encourage the development of pacific settlement of local disputes through such regional arrangements or by such regional agencies either on the initiative of the states concerned or by reference from the Security Council.

4. This Article in no way impairs the application of Articles 34 and 35.

Article 53

1. The Security Council shall, where appropriate, utilize such regional arrangements or agencies for enforcement action under its authority. But no enforcement

action shall be taken under regional arrangements or by regional agencies without the authorization of the Security Council, with the exception of measures against any enemy state, as defined in paragraph 2 of this Article, provided for pursuant to Article 107 or in regional arrangements directed against renewal of aggressive policy on the part of any such state, until such time as the Organization may, on request of the Governments concerned, be charged with the responsibility for preventing further aggression by such a state.

2. The term enemy state as used in paragraph 1 of this Article applies to any state which during the Second World War has been an enemy of any signatory of the present Charter.

ARTICLE 54

The Security Council shall at all times be kept fully informed of activities undertaken or in contemplation under regional arrangements or by regional agencies for the maintenance of international peace and security.

ARTICLE 55

With a view to the creation of conditions of stability and well-being which are necessary for peaceful and friendly relations among nations based on respect for the principle of equal rights and self-determination of peoples, the United Nations shall promote:

a. higher standards of living, full employment, and conditions of economic and social progress and development;

b. solutions of international economic, social, health, and related problems; and international cultural and educational cooperation; and

c. universal respect for, and observance of, human rights and fundamental freedoms for all without distinction as to race, sex, language, or religion.

ARTICLE 56

All Members pledge themselves to take joint and separate action in cooperation with the Organization for the achievement of the purposes set forth in Article 55.

ARTICLE 73

Members of the United Nations which have or assume responsibilities for the administration of territories whose peoples have not yet attained a full measure of self-government recognize the principle that the interests of the inhabitants of these territories are paramount, and accept as a sacred trust the obligation to promote to the utmost, within the system of international peace and security established by the present Charter, the well-being of the inhabitants of these territories, and, to this end:

a. to ensure, with due respect for the culture of the peoples concerned, their political, economic, social, and educational advancement, their just treatment, and their protection against abuses;

b. to develop self-government, to take due account of the political aspirations of the peoples, and to assist them in the progressive development of their free political institutions, according to the particular circumstances of each territory and its peoples and their varying stages of advancement. . . .

e. to transmit regularly to the Secretary-General for information purposes, subject to such limitation as security and constitutional considerations may require, statistical and other information of a technical nature relating to economic, social, and educational conditions in the territories for which they are respectively responsible other than those territories to which Chapters XII and XIII apply.

Article 76

The basic objectives of the trusteeship system, in accordance with the Purposes of the United Nations laid down in Article 1 of the present Charter, shall be:

a. to further international peace and security;

b. to promote the political, economic, social, and educational advancement of the inhabitants of the trust territories, and their progressive development towards self-government or independence as may be appropriate to the particular circumstances of each territory and its peoples and the freely expressed wishes of the peoples concerned, and as may be provided by the terms of each trusteeship agreement;

c. to encourage respect for human rights and for fundamental freedoms for all without distinction as to race, sex, language, or religion, and to encourage recognition of the interdependence of the peoples of the world; and

d. to ensure equal treatment in social, economic, and commercial matters for all Members of the United Nations and their nationals, and also equal treatment for the latter in the administration of justice, without prejudice to the attainment of the foregoing objectives and subject to the provisions of Article 80.

Article 82

There may be designated, in any trusteeship agreement, a strategic area or areas which may include part or all of the trust territory to which the agreement applies, without prejudice to any special agreement or agreements made under Article 43.

Article 83

1. All functions of the United Nations relating to strategic areas, including the approval of the terms of the trusteeship agreements and of their alteration or amendment, shall be exercised by the Security Council.

2. The basic objectives set forth in Article 76 shall be applicable to the people of each strategic area.

3. The Security Council shall, subject to the provisions of the trusteeship agreements and without prejudice to security considerations, avail itself of the assistance of the Trusteeship Council to perform those functions of the United Nations under the trustreship system relating to political, economic, social, and educational matters in the strategic areas.

Article 92

The International Court of Justice shall be the principal judicial organ of the United Nations. It shall function in accordance with the annexed Statute, which is based upon the Statute of the Permanent Court of International Justice and forms an integral part of the present Charter.

Article 96

1. The General Assembly or the Security Council may request the International Court of Justice to give an advisory opinion on any legal question.

2. Other organs of the United Nations and specialized agencies, which may at any time be so authorized by the General Assembly, may also request advisory opinions of the Court on legal questions arising within the scope of their activities.

ARTICLE 103

In the event of a conflict between the obligations of the Members of the United Nations under the present Charter and their obligations under any other international agreement, their obligations under the present Charter shall prevail.

ARTICLE 107

Nothing in the present Charter shall invalidate or preclude action, in relation to any state which during the Second World War has been an enemy of any signatory to the present Charter, taken or authorized as a result of that war by the Governments having responsibility for such action.

ARTICLE 108

Amendments to the present Charter shall come into force for all Members of the United Nations when they have been adopted by a vote of two thirds of the members of the General Assembly and ratified in accordance with their respective constitutional processes by two thirds of the Members of the United Nations, including all the permanent members of the Security Council.

ARTICLE 109

1. A General Conference of the Members of the United Nations for the purpose of reviewing the present Charter may be held at a date and place to be fixed by a two-thirds vote of the members of the General Assembly and by a vote of any seven members of the Security Council. Each Member of the United Nations shall have one vote in the conference.

2. Any alteration of the present Charter recommended by a two-thirds vote of the conference shall take effect when ratified in accordance with their respective consitutional processes by two-thirds of the Members of the United Nations including all the permanent members of the Security Council. . . .

STATUTE OF THE INTERNATIONAL COURT OF JUSTICE

ARTICLE 31

1. Judges of the nationality of each of the parties shall retain their right to sit in the case before the Court.

2. If the Court includes upon the Bench a judge of the nationality of one of the parties, any other party may choose a person to sit as judge. Such person shall be chosen preferably from among those persons who have been nominated as candidates as provided in Articles 4 and 5.

3. If the Court includes upon the Bench no judge of the nationality of the parties, each of these parties may proceed to choose a judge as provided in paragraph 2 of this Article.

4. The provisions of this Article shall apply to the case of Articles 26 and 29. In such cases, the President shall request one or, if necessary, two of the members of the Court forming the chamber to give place to the members of the Court of the

nationality of the parties concerned, and, failing such, or if they are unable to be present, to the judges specially chosen by the parties.

5. Should there be several parties in the same interest, they shall, for the purpose of the preceding provisions, be reckoned as one party only. Any doubt upon this point shall be settled by the decision of the Court.

6. Judges chosen as laid down in paragraphs 2, 3, and 4 of this Article shall fulfil the conditions required by Articles 2, 17 (paragraph 2), 20, and 24 of the present Statute. They shall take part in the decision on terms of complete equality with their colleagues.

ARTICLE 34

1. Only states may be parties in cases before the Court. . . .

ARTICLE 35

1. The Court shall be open to the states parties to the present Statute.

2. The conditions under which the Court shall be open to other states shall, subject to the special provisions contained in treaties in force, be laid down by the Security Council, but in no case shall such conditions place the parties in a position of inequality before the Court. . . .

ARTICLE 38

1. The Court, whose function is to decide in accordance with international law such disputes as are submitted to it, shall apply:

a. international conventions, whether general or paritcular, establishing rules expressly recognized by the contesting states;

b. international custom, as evidence of a general practice accepted as law;

c. the general principles of law recognized by civilized nations;

d. subject to the provisions of Article 59, judicial decisions and the teachings of the most highly qualified publicists of the various nations, as subsidiary means for the determination of rules of law.

2. This provision shall not prejudice the power of the Court to decide a case *ex aequo et bono,* if the parties agree thereto.

ARTICLE 41

1. The Court shall have the power to indicate, if it considers that circumstances so require, any provisional measures which ought to be taken to preserve the respective rights of either party.

2. Pending the final decision, notice of the measures suggested shall forthwith be given to the parties and to the Security Council.

ARTICLE 50

The Court may, at any time, entrust any individual, body, bureau, commission, or other organization that it may select, with the task of carrying out an enquiry or giving an expert opinion.

ARTICLE 65

1. The Court may give an advisory opinion on any legal question at the request of whatever body may be authorized by or in accordance with the Charter of the United Nations to make such a request. . . .

NOTES

Introduction

1. Kingman Brewster, "Reflections on Our National Purpose," *Foreign Affairs* 50 (1972):399, 404.

Chapter One

1. Samuel Puffendorf, *De Jure Naturae et Gentium Libri Octo* [On the law of nature and nations, eight books], trans. C. H. and W. A. Oldfather (Oxford, 1934), vol. 2, pp. 204–5; Arnold Brecht, *Political Theory: The Foundations of Twentieth Century Political Thought* (Princeton, 1959), pp. 395–98.

2. Elie Abel, *The Missiles of October,* (London, 1966), p. 83.

3. Oliver Wendell Holmes, *The Common Law* (Boston, 1881), p. 1.

4. For the benefit of those whose minds are attuned to philosophy of law issues, I wish to disclaim any intent to offer the three keys to the strategy of law for resolution of conflict as an independent philosophy of law. The analysis presupposes a common stake in peace and the reconcilability of the interests and aspirations of minkind. Rules that meet the tests of the strategy as indicated do in fact respond to man's sense of right. However, it is not my purpose to do more than identify those attributes of law that make it work as a strategy for the resolution of conflict.

Chapter Two

1. John Bassett Moore, *A Digest of International Law* (Washington, D.C., 1906), vol. 6, p. 402.

2. Ibid., p. 535.

3. Ibid., p. 546.

4. Ibid., pp. 548–49.

5. Ibid., p. 552.

6. Ibid., p. 563.

7. Ibid., p. 577–78.

8. Green Haywood Hackworth, *Digest of International Law* (Washington, D.C., 1943), vol. 5, p. 440. For the full text of the address, see Elihu Root. "The Real Monroe Doctrine," *American Journal of International Law* 8 (1914):427.

9. J. B. Moore, *A Digest of International Law,* vol. 6, pp. 594, 595; Hackworth, *A Digest of International Law,* vol. 5, p. 436.

10. J. B. Moore, vol. 6, p. 519.

11. *Papers Relating to the Foreign Relations of the United States,* 1906 (Washington, D.C., 1909), vol. 1, p. xlvii.

12. Charles Evans Hughes, "Observations on the Monroe Doctrine," *American Journal of International Law* 17 (1923):611, 619.

13. Ibid., pp. 620–26.

14. Dexter Perkins, *A History of the Monroe Doctinre,* (Boston, 1955), p. 343.

15. Hackworth, *A Digest of International Law,* vol. 5, pp. 454–55.

16. Ibid., p. 456.

17. Ibid., p. 442.

18. Ibid.

19. Ibid., p. 443.

20. Ibid., p. 456.

21. 49 Stat. 3097, Treaty Series No. 881.

22. Additional Protocol Relative to Nonintervention, Dec. 23, 1936, 51 Stat. 41, Treaty Series No. 923; Act of Chapultepec, March 6, 1945, Preamble, clause (b), 60 Stat. 1831, Treaties and Other International Acts Series No. 1543; Charter of the Organization of American States, April 30, 1948, Article 15, 2 U.S.T. (part 2) 2394, Treaties and Other International Acts Series No. 2361, 119 U.N.T.S. 48.

23. Elihu Root, *Addresses on International Subjects* (Cambridge, 1916), p. 120; Hackworth (excerpting Hughes), vol. 5, p. 452.

24. Root, *Addresses,* p. 120; Hackworth, vol. 5, p. 451.

25. See Marjorie M. Whiteman, *Digest of International Law* (Washington, D.C., 1971), vol. 12, pp. 723–24, for Secretary of State Dean Rusk's position as to reserve power.

26. 51 Stat. 15, Treaty Series No. 922.

27. Department of State, *Report of the Delegation of the United States of America to the Eighth International Conference of American States, Lima, Peru, December 9–27, 1938* (Washington, D.C., 1941), p. 189; Hackworth, vol. 5, pp. 463–64.

28. Department of State, *Report of the Delegate of the United States of America to the Meeting of the Foreign Ministers of the American Republics Held at Panama September 2—October 3, 1939,* (Washington, D.C., 1940) p. 62; *Department of State Bulletin* 1 (1939):331; Hackworth, vol. 5, pp. 464–65.

29. Havana Meeting of the Ministers of Foreign Affairs, Final Act and Convention, August 24, 1940, Article XV , (Reciprocal Assistance and Cooperation for the Defense of the Nations of the Americas), *Department of State Bulletin* 3 (1940):127, 136; Act of Havana, July 30, 1940, 54 Stat. 2491, Executive Agreement Series No. 199. See generally Hackworth, vol. 5, pp. 465–68.

30. Inter-American Treaty of Reciprocal Assistance, September 2, 1947, 62 Stat. 1681, Treaties and Other International Acts Series No. 1838, 21 U.N.T.S. 93.

31. "The Soviet Threat to the Americas," address by President Kennedy, *Department of State Bulletin* 47 (1962):715.

32. Elie Abel, *The Missiles of October,* p. 126.

33. Abram Chayes, *The Cuban Missile Crisis* (New York, 1974), appendix 1, p. 114.

34. Abel, pp. 173–74.

35. Robert F. Kennedy, *ThirteenDays* (New York: 1969), pp. 72–73.

36. Ibid., pp. 86–87.

37. Chayes, *The Cuban Missile Crisis,* p. 98.

38. Abel, p. 183.

39. For further comment on the Bay of Pigs see chapter 4, pp. 33–34.

40. See Arthur M. Schlesinger, Jr., *A Thousand Days* (Boston, 1965), pp. 234, 238, 249, 262.

41. Congressional Record, Sixty-Fifth Congress, First Session, vol. 55, part 1, p. 102; see also Ruhl J. Bartlett, ed., *The Record of American Diplomacy* (New York, 1947), p. 456.

42. *Papers Relating to the Foreign Relations of the United States,* 1901, appendix, p. 12; see also Bartlett, p. 413.

43. Nine-Power Treaty, February 6, 1922, Article I, 44 Stat. 2113, Treaty Series No. 723.

44. Bartlett, p. 88.

45. J. B. Moore, vol. 6, p. 402; Bartlett, p. 182.

46. *Papers Relating to the Foreign Relations of the United States,* 1917 (Washington, D.C., 1931), supplement 1, p. 24; Bartlett, p. 453; *The Messages and Papers of Woodrow Wilson, ed. Albert Shaw* (New York, 1918), vol. 1, p. 350.

47. Ibid.

48. See n. 18 above; Bartlett, p. 454.

49. Kellogg-Briand Peace Pact, August 27, 1928, 46 Stat. 2343, Treaty Series No. 796.

50. Henry L. Stimson, *The Far Eastern Crisis* (New York, 1936), p. 100.

51. *Papers Relating to the Foreign Relations of the United States,* 1932, vol. 3, p. 8; Stimson, The Far Eastern Crisis, p. 97.

52. Resolution Adopted by the Assembly of the League of Nations on March 11, 1932, League of Nations, Official Journal, Special Supplement No. 101 (Geneva, 1932), p. 87; Stimson, p. 178; *Papers Relating to the Foreign Relations of the United States, 1931–41* (Japan), vol. 1, p. 210.

53. Charter of the International Military Tribunal, Article 6(a), London Agreement, August 8, 1945, 59 Stat. 1544, Executive Agreement Series No. 472.

54. *Trial of the Major War Criminals before the International Military Tribunal, Nuremberg, 14 November 1945—1 October 1946,* vol. 1, p. 218.

55. Dean G. Acheson, *Present at the Creation* (New York, 1969), p. 217. That the guerillas were aided by and used the territory of Albania, Bulgaria, and Yugoslavia was subsequently found by the United Nations General Assembly. G.A. Res. 193 (III), November 27, 1948. See also G. A. Res. 109 (d)(II), October 21, 1947; G.A. Res. 193 A, B, (III), November 27, 1948; G.A. Res. 288 A, B, (IV), November 18, 1949; and G.A. Res. 382 A, B, (V), December 1, 1950.

56. Acheson, *Present at the Creation,* p. 219.

57. U.S. Code and Congressional Service, Eightieth Congress, First Session, p. 1813.

58. Neil Sheehan et al., *The Pentagon Papers* (New York, 1971), p. 151.

59. *Department of State Bulletin* 52 (1965):606, 607.

60. *Department of State Bulletin* 56 (1967):535.

61. For further comment on Vietnam see chapter 4, pp. 40–48.

62. U.S. Code and Congressional Service, Eightieth Congress, First Session, p. 1102.

63. See chapter 9.

64. See n. 62.

65. Eugene V. Rostow, "Eight Foreign Policies for the United States—Which is Yours?" *N.Y. Times Magazine,* April 23, 1972, p. 16. See also Rostow, *Peace in the Balance: The Future of American Foreign Policy* (New York, 1972), chapter 3.

Chapter Three

1. Gordon A. Craig, "*The United States and the European Balance,*" *Foreign Affairs* 55 (1976):187. See also Louis J. Halle, *American Foreign Policy: Theory and Reality* (London, 1960).

2. Treaty of Utrecht, July 13, 1713, (Great Britain-Spain), Clive Parry, ed., *Consolidated Treaty Series,* vol. 28, pp. 325–26.

3. *The Messages and Papers of Woodrow Wilson,* ed. Albert Shaw, vol. 1, p. 478.

4. Hedley Bull, *The Anarchical Society* (New York, 1977), pp. 101–2; Morton A. Kaplan and Nicholas deB. Katzenbach, *The Political Foundations of International Law* (New York, 1961), pp. 50–55.

5. Nicholas John Spykman, *America's Strategy in World Politics* (New York, 1942), p. 472.

6. Hans J. Morgenthau, *In Defense of the National Interest* (New York, 1963), p. 116.

7. Eugene V. Rostow, *Peace in the Balance: The Future of American Foreign Policy* (New York, 1972), p. 317.

8. Henry A. Kissinger, *American Foreign Policy: Three Essays* (New York, 1974), p. 92.

9. Bull, *The Anarchical Society,* p. 143; and see ibid., p. 108; see also Kaplan and Katzenbach, *The Political Formulations of International Law,* pp. 53–54.

10. Kaplan and Katzenbach, p. 102; see also ibid., p. 54.

11. *Department of State Bulletin* 73 (1975):692.

12. *Department of State Bulletin* 56 (1967):534.

13. *Department of State Bulletin* 66 (1972):319.

14. See, however, Arthur W. Rovine, "Contemporary Practice of the United States Relating to International Law," *American Journal of International Law* 69 (1975):382.

15. See n. 57 to chapter 2 above.

16. See n. 12 above.

17. Eugene V. Rostow, *Law, Power and the Pursuit of Peace* (Lincoln, Neb., 1968), p. 43.

18. Some may find surprising prescience in the words of Hugo Grotius in 1625 (*On the Law of War and Peace,* ed. of 1646, trans. by Francis W. Kelsey et al.)

> Quite untenable is the position, which has been maintained by some, that according to the law of nations it is right to take up arms in order to weaken a growing power which, if it becomes too great, may be a source of danger.
>
> That this consideration does enter into the deliberations regarding war, I admit, but only on grounds of expediency, not of justice. Thus if a war be

justifiable for other reasons, for this reason also it might be deemed far-sighted to undertake the war; that is the gist of the argument which the writers cited on this point present. But that the possibility of being attacked confers the right to attack is abhorrent to every principle of equity. Human life exists under such conditions that complete security is never guaranteed to us. For protection against uncertain fears we must rely on Divine Providence, and on a wariness free from reproach, not on force. (Classics of International Law, Carnegie Endowment for International Peace, 1925 at 184).

19. Louis Henkin, *How Nations Behave* (New York, 1968), p. 265.

Chapter Four

1. *The Complete Works of Abraham Lincoln,* ed. John G. Nicolay and John Hay (New York, 1920), vol. 1, p. 612 (Cooper Institute Speech, February 27, 1860).

2. Arthur M. Schlesinger, Jr., *A Thousand Days,* p. 262.

3. Ibid., pp. 290, 295.

4. Ibid., pp. 252–56.

5. Chayes, *The Cuban Missile Crisis,* chapter 3, and p. 14, n. 33.

6. Chayes doubts the threatened strikes would have been made. See Chayes, pp. 88–100.

7. John Norton Moore, "Law and National Security," *Foreign Affairs* 51 (1973):408, 417.

8. *Department of State Bulletin* 77 (1977):723.

9. Henry A. Kissinger, *The White House Years* (Boston, 1979), p. 516. In his address to the nation on April 30, 1970 announcing the Cambodia action, President Nixon stated that U.S. forces would withdraw from Cambodia "once enemy forces are driven out of these sanctuaries and once their military supplies are destroyed" (*Department of State Bulletin* 62 [1970]:629). Faced with the ensuing outcry, the president stated at a press conference on May 8, 1970: "The action actually is going faster than anticipated. The middle of next week the first units will come out. The end of next week the second group of American units will come out. The great majority of all American units will be out by the second week of June, and all Americans of all kinds, including advisers, will be out of Cambodia by the end of June" (*Department of State Bulletin* 62 [1970]:643).

10. For views opposing the right see Richard R. Baxter, *The Law of International Waterways* (Cambridge, 1964), chapter 7, and appendix, Draft Articles, article 7, p. 345; and Joseph A. Obieta, *The International Status of the Suez Canal* (The Hague, 1970), pp. 38–39.

11. [1923] P.C.I.J., ser. A, No. 1, p. 28.

12. Robert R. Bowie, *Suez 1956* (New York, 1974), p. 34. See also p. 106. For discussions of the Suez-Panama parallels and criticism of the attempted U.S. distinction of Panama, see Baxter, The Law of International Waterways, pp. 42–44, 47, 176–77, 307.

13. U.S. Department of State, *The Suez Canal Problem* (Washington, D.C., 1956), p. 45.

14. *Department of State Bulletin* 35 (1956):411.

15. United Nations, *Yearbook of the United Nations,* 1956, p. 23.

16. U.S. Department of State, *United States Policy in the Middle East, September 1956–June 1957* (Washington, D.C., 1957), pp. 127–30.

17. *Yearbook of the United Nations,* 1956, p. 24.

18. Baxter, p. 43.

19. Texts in Robert F. Randle, *Geneva 1954: The Settlement of the Indochinese War* (Princeton, 1969).

20. John Norton Moore, *Law and the Indo-China War* (Princeton, 1972), pp. 411–20.

21. See Randle, *Geneva 1954,* pp. 343–45, 428–30.

22. Ibid., p. 437.

23. It was generally accepted in the legal position later set forth by the legal adviser of the Department of State in a memorandum entitled "The Legality of United States Participation in the Defense of Viet-Nam," March 4, 1966, *Department of State Bulletin* 54 (1966):474, 483–84; *Yale Law Journal* 75 (1966):1085, 1099–1100.

24. Randle, pp. 429, 432–33.

25. Dwight D. Eisenhower, *The White House Years* (Garden City, 1963), vol. 1, p. 372.

26. I do not mean to be expressing here any opinion on the factual issue whether the charge that North Vietnam was guilty of aggression was or was not established by the evidence (see pp. 20–21). The offer to adjudicate advocated below in the text would have had to include an offer to adjudicate that issue. This would be so even in an adjudication of the limited issue of self-determination because the alleged aggression was part of the history bearing on South Vietnam's claimed right to a separate right of self-determination even after the 1954 Geneva Accords. But beyond this a reasonable offer of adjudication on the basis suggested in part three of this book would have had to cover all interlocking issues. It would have had to include the whole issue of the legitimacy of the U.S. action in Vietnam and the alleged aggression by North Vietnam upon which it was grounded. Without such an adjudication that factual issue is likely to remain a matter of controversy.

27. See memorandum, *Department of State Bulletin* 54 (1966):474. The essential point of law—that such armed attack may be across a provisional demarcation line, and by indirect aggression—have since been affirmed by the U.N. General Assembly, G.A. Res. 2625 (XXV), October 24, 1970 and 3314 (XXIX), December 14, 1974.

28. As will be developed further in chapter 8, where the determination of a "people" entitled to exercise a right of self-determination is really in dispute, some international process will always be necessary to make a determination.

Chapter Five

1. U.N.C.I.O., Summary Report of Twenty-Eighth Meeting of Committee I/2, June 17, 1945, Doc. 1086, I/2/77, U.N.C.I.O. Documents, vol. 7, pp. 262, 267. See also Leland M. Goodrich and Edvard Hambro, *Charter of the United Nations, Commentary and Documents,*-second and rev. ed. (London, 1949), pp. 143–44.

2. U.N. Doc. A/Conf. 39/27, May 23, 1969; *International Legal Materials,* 8 (1969):679.

3. U.N. General Assembly, Twenty-First Session, Official Records Supplement No. 9 (A/6309/Rev. 1) pp. 76, 88; *American Journal of International Law* 61 (1967):409–12, 437–38.

4. *Department of State Bulletin 61* (1969):127, 131; *American Journal of International Law* 64 (1970):165, 171.

5. S. Prakash Sinha, in the *Indian Journal of International Law* 14 (1974):332. Note that Sinha does not refer to G.A. Res. 2625 (XXV).

6. See Rupert Emerson, "Self-Determination," *American Journal of International Law* 65 (1971):459, 460–62. Note that most authorities cited by Emerson antedate the unanimous adoption of G.A. Res. 2625 (XXV) (October 24, 1970). See chapter 8.

7. Richard A. Falk, "On the Quasi-Legislative Competence of the General Assembly," *American Journal of International Law* 60 (1966):782, 783.

8. U.N. Charter, Articles 1(2), 55.

9. U.N. Doc. E/CN. 4/L. 610, April 2, 1962, entitled "Use of the Terms 'Declaration' and 'Recommendation,' Memorandum by the Office of Legal Affairs."

10. The S.S. *Lotus,* [1927] P.C.I.J. Ser. A, No. 10, p. 18.

11. *Asylum Case (Colombia v. Peru),* [1950] I.C.J. 216, 276–77; *Fisheries Case (United Kingdom v. Norway),* [1951] I.C.J. 116, 131. For discussion of the problem presented by the requirements of "general practice," see Sir Hersch Lauterpacht, *The Development of International Law by the International Court* (Oxford, 1933), pp. 186–99, 359–93, and C. Wilfred Jenks, *The Prospects of International Adjudication* (Dobbs Ferry, 1964), pp. 225–58.

12. The concept of a "peremptory norm," which international lawyers often refer to as *jus cogens,* is defined in Article 53 as "a norm accepted and recognized by the international community of States as a whole as a norm from which no derogation is permitted and which can be modified only by a subsequent norm of general international law having the same character." Article 66 provides for adjudication of any dispute as to the application or interpretation of Articles 53 or 64 by the International Court of Justice, unless the parties agree to submit it to arbitration. The language in Article 53 was prepared by the Drafting Committee after several sessions of debate in the Committee of the Whole at the 1968 session of the Vienna Conference on the Law of Treaties. The chairman of the Drafting Committee stated that the words "as a whole" had been included since "it appeared to have been the view of the Committee of the Whole that no individual State should have the right of veto." In response to a request for a further clarification the Chairman explained

> that by inserting the words "as a whole" in article [53] the Drafting Committee had wished to stress that there was no question of requiring a rule to be accepted and recognized as peremptory by all States. It would be enough if a large majority did so; that would mean that, if any State in isolation refused to accept the peremptory character of a rule, or if that State was supported by a very small number of States, the acceptance and recognition of the peremptory character of the rule by the international community as a whole would not be affected.

In view of the possibility of a different interpretation, Ghana moved for a separate vote on the phrase "as a whole," which was then approved by a vote of 57 to 3 with 27 abstentions. The full text of the article was then approved by a vote of 72 to 3 with 18 abstentions (U.N. Doc. A/CONF39/11 at 471-2). See generally R. D. Kearney and R. E. Dalton, "The Treaty on Treaties," *American Journal of International Law* 64 (1970):495, 537–38. The requirement of acceptance by "the international community of states as a whole" implies something more than a particular numbers count. While negating a requirement of unanimity it also implies a concept of consensus shared by nations standing in all traditions and all interests. Additionally, the concept of a "peremptory norm of general international law" implies that to qualify as a peremptory norm a rule must in any event qualify in character and legitimacy as a rule of general international law.

Chapter Six

1. Robert Rosenstock, "The Declaration of Principles of International Law Concerning Friendly Relations: A Survey," *American Journal of International Law* 65 (1971):713, 732.

2. Y. Z. Blum, "Reflections on the Changing Concept of Self-Determination," *Israel Law Review* 10 (1975):509.

3. See, for example, his position against U.S. covert intervention in Chile, in "Editorial Comments," *American Journal of International Law* 69 (1975):354.

4. Richard A. Falk, ed., *The International Law of Civil War* (Baltimore, 1971), p. 22. See also Morton A. Kaplan and Nicholas deB. Katzenbach, *The Political Foundations of International Law* (New York, 1961), pp. 53–55; and Hedley Bull, *The Anarchical Society* (New York, 1977), pp. 143–45, 216–25.

5. Falk, ed., *Civil War,* p. 14.

6. The right of counterintervention is supported in Michael B. Akehurst, *A Modern Introduction to International Law* (London, 1977), pp. 265–67; Ian Brownlie, *International Law and the Use of Force by States* (Oxford, 1963), p. 327, and John Norton Moore, ed., *Law and Civil War in the Modern World* (Baltimore, 1974), pp. 26–27. See also Quincy Wright, "United States Intervention in the Lebanon," *American Journal of International Law* 53 (1959):112, 123.

7. Kaplan and Katzenbach, *The Political Foundations of International Law,* pp. 53–55; Falk, ed., *Civil War,* pp. 19–20; Bull, *The Anarchical Society,* pp. 215–18.

8. Sir Hersch Lauterpacht, *The Function of Law in the International Community* (Oxford, 1933), pp. 110–11.

9. Falk, ed., *Civil War,* p. 18.

10. *United States v. Curtiss-Wright Corp.,* 299 U.S. 304, 318 (1936).

11. *Trial of the Major War Criminals before the International Military Tribunal, Nuremberg, 14 November 1945–1 October 1946* (Nuremberg, 1947), vol. 1, p. 223.

12. The issue as to limits on national sovereignty by international law is not the same issue as that contested by theorists between the so-called monist theory, under which international law seen as being the source of a nation's sovereignty is automatically applicable as municipal law, and the dualist theory, under which international and municipal law stand separately. See L. F. L. Oppenheim, *International Law* (ed. H. Lauterpacht), vol. 1, pp. 37–38; Ian Brownlie, *Principles of Public International Law* (Oxford, 1966), pp,. 280–81; Daniel P. O'Connell, *International Law* (New York, 1965), pp. 37–46.

13. *Nationality Decrees in Tunis and Morocco,* [1923] P.C.I.J., ser. B, No. 4, pp. 23–24; see also *Interhandel Case, (Switzerland v. United States),* Dissenting Opinion of Sir Hersch Lauterpacht, [1959] I.C.J. 95, 121–22, (Judge Lauterpacht concurring as to U.S. objection to jurisdiction 4[b]). See also U.N. Charter, Article 2(7), precluding intervention by the U.N. "in matters which are essentially within the domestic jurisdiction of any state." For reference to the so-called Connally Amendment, see note 4 to chapter 14.

14. Hague Convention, July 21, 1899, Article 9, 32 Stat. 1779, Treaty Series No. 392; Hague Convention, October 18, 1907, Article 9, 36 Stat. 2199, Treaty Series No. 536. See also James Brown Scott, *The Hague Conventions and Declarations of 1899 and 1907* (New York, 1915), pp. 45–46.

15. Hague Convention of 1889, Article 16; Hague Convention of 1907, Article 38.

16. See Lauterpacht, *The Function of Law,* pp. 27–31.

17. See generally ibid., pp. 26–45, 139–82.

Chapter Seven

1. Robert Rosenstock, "The Declaration of Principles of International Law Concerning Friendly Relations: A Survey," *American Journal of International Law* 65 (1971):713, 715.

2. See generally Leland M. Goodrich, Edvard Hambro, and Anne P. Simons, *Charter of the United Nations, Commentary and Documents* (New York, 1974), pp. 43–55; and Ian Brownlie, *International Law and the Use of Force by States,* pp. 268 and following. See also chapter 10, n.8.

3. U.N. General Assembly Official Records, Twenty-Fifth Session, Sixth Committee (1180th Meeting), 24 September 1970, U.N. Doc. A/C.6/SR. 1180, pp. 17, 19, par. 25.

4. Rosenstock, "The Declaration of Principles of International Law Concerning Friendly Relations," pp. 723–24.

5. U.N. Doc. A/9631, p.. 142; *American Journal of International Law* 69 (1975):480.

Chapter Eight

1. U.N.C.I.O. Summary Report of the Sixth Meeting of Committee I/1, May 15, 1945, Doc. 343, I/1/16, U.N.C.I.O. Documents, vol. 6, p. 296.

2. *U.N. Monthly Chronicle* 7 (Feb. 1970):36.

3. Articles 1(2) and 55. In defining the right of self-determination as one possessed by a "people," the 1970 Declaration follows not only the Charter, but also the proposed Covenants on Economic, Social, and Cultural Rights and on Civil and Political Rights adopted by G.A. Res. 2200 (XXI), December 16, 1966 and 1514 (XV), December 14, 1960.

4. See Article 45 of the Vienna Convention on the Law of Treaties.

5. Paragraph E7 of the 1970 Declaration itself covers the point, for the required compliance by the nation with "the principle of equal rights and self-determination of peoples as described above" must include the provision in paragraph E5 requiring a state to refrain from forcible action that deprives a people of the right to self-determination.

6. Its formulation seems unlikely, for example, to aid Welsh or Scottish nationalists, or the Quebecois, who may have to assert their rights, if any, under national law.

7. Harold S. Johnson, *Self-Determination Within the Community of Nations* (Leyden, 1967), p. 112. See also Wentworth Ofuatey-Kodjoe, *The Principle of Self-Determination in International Law* (New York, 1977), p. 65.

8. Julius Stone, "Hopes and Loopholes in the 1979 Definition of Aggression," *American Journal of International Law* 71 (1977):224, 235.

9. A policy of favoring larger units in areas of mixed population to assure viable national entities cannot be extended to deny the right of self-determination to which an identifiable people occupying a geographically and historically separate territory is entitled under the U.N. Charter. Thus many General Assembly resolutions listed in appendix 3, using almost identical terms, have stated with respect to the particular

nonself-governing territories involved that "the questions of territorial size, geographic isolation and limited resources should in no way delay the implementation of the Declaration on the Granting of Independence to Colonial Countries and Peoples with respect to these Territories" (quoted from G.A. Res. 2592 [XXIV] relating to American Samoa and other island territories). For a recent example see G.A. Res. 32/29 relating to Bermuda and other territories. The inadvisability of electing independence for some ministates is a problem that cannot be solved by denying a Charter right where the inhabitants qualify as a "people."

10. League of Nations, *Official Journal* (1921), no. 7, p. 699.

11. Treaty of Guarantee (U.K., Greece, Turkey—Cyprus), August 16, 1960, G.B.T.S. No. 5, (1961); 382 U.N.T.S. 3; Treaty concerning Establishment of the Republic of Cyprus, August 16, 1960, G.B.T.S. No. 4, (1961), 382 U.N.T.S. 8.

12. G.A. Res. 1013 (XI), February 26, 1957.

13. See n. 10 above. The vote was June 24, 1921.

14. In a number of cases the General Assembly has addressed the issue of units and directed or rejected separate units. See in appendix 3 the resolutions relating to Eritrea, Togoland, the Cameroons, Ruanda-Urundi, Ifni and Spanish or Western Sahara, Gibraltar, the Comoro Archipelago, and the South African bantustans, especially the following resolutions:

Eritrea 390(V)

Togoland under U.K. administration 944 (X)

Cameroons under U.K. administration 1350 (XIII), 1352 (XIV), 1473 (XIV), 1608 (XV)

Ruanda-Urundi 1743 (XVI), 1746 (XVI)

Gibraltar 2353 (XXII)

Ifni and Spanish Sahara 2354 (XXII), 2428 (XXIII), 2591 (XXIV)

Comoro Archipelago 3161 (XXVIII), 3291 (XXIX), 31/4, 32/7

South African bantustans 3411 D (XXX), 31/6A, 32/105 N, 34/93A

Unit determinations are also implicit in the General Assembly's many resolutions insisting on a unified Korea and (since the 1960 Accords) a unified Cyprus.

15. Some would contend that Article 107 of the U.N. Charter bars any application of the principle of self-determination to the two Germanys. Note, however, that paragraph A 10(a) of the 1970 Declaration excludes matters governed by Article 107 from the principle against the use of force, but no comparable saving clause applies to the principle of self-determination, other than the general provision in section 2ii.

16. G.A. Res. 2353 (XXII), December 19, 1967.

17. Moshen S. Esfandiary, "Comments," *Proceedings of the American Society of International Law* (1968):170, 174–75.

18. The S.S. *Wimbledon,* [1923] P.C.I.J., ser. A., No. 1, p. 25.

19. Arrangement, Leasing of Naval and Air Bases, September 2, 1940, (U.S.-U.K.), 54 Stat. 2405, Executive Agreement Series No. 181, 203 L.N.T.S. 201.

20. See Marjorie M. Whiteman, *Digest of International Law* (Washington, D.C., 1971), vol. 2, pp. 1221–22. The agreement with Spain was part of a defense agreement for an initial period of ten years. Defense Agreement, September 26, 1953, (U.S.—Spain), 4 U.S.T. 1895, Treaties and Other International Acts Series No. 2850, 207 U.N.T.S. 83.

21. Par. 12. For later resolutions, see for example G.A. Res. 2189 (XXI), par. 11, 2326 (XXII), par. 10; 2548 (XXIV), par. 8; 2708 (XXV), par. 9; 2878 (XXVI), par.

9; 2908 (XXVII), par. 10; 3163 (XXVIII), par. 9; also G.A. Res. 1949 (XVIII), par. 4 (Aden); 2066 (XX) (Mauritius); 2074 (XX), par. 7, (S.W. Africa); 2232 (XXI) par. 4; and 2238 (XXI), par. 6, (Oman).

22. Report of the Special Committee, Granting of Independence to Colonial Countries and Peoples, U.N. Document A/7200/Rev. 1, Chapter IV, Official Records of the General Assembly, Twenty-Third Session, Annexes, Addendum to agenda item 23 (1968).

23. Hugo Grotius, *De Jure Belli ac Pacis,* trans. Francis W. Kelsey et al., vol. 2, p. 261 (book 2, chapter 6, section 4). Commentary and practice to the contrary is collected in Whiteman, vol. 2, pp. 1088–1111.

24. U.N. Document A/7371, Official Records of the General Assembly, 23rd Session, Annexes, agenda item 23, p. 24. See also U.N. Document A/7200/Rev. 1 (n.22 above), Chapter XIV.

25. Note, however, that U.S. rights in Guantanamo Bay having no termination date were affirmed by treaty in 1934. Treaty of Relations, May 29, 1934 (U.S.—Cuba), 48 Stat. 1682, Treaty Series No. 866.

Chapter Nine

1. [1949] I.C.J. 4, 35.

2. Rosalyn Higgins, "Internal War and International Law" in C. E. Black and R. A. Falk, eds., *The Future of the International Legal Order,* vol. 2, pp. 81, 93–94.

3. See the criticisms, beginning at least as far back as 1924, in W. E. Hall, *A Treatise on International Law,* ed. Pearce Higgins (Oxford, 1924), chapter 8, and in the later writings referred to in the bibliography by Akehurst, Brownlie, Falk, Farer, Friedman, Higgins, J. N. Moore, Thomas and Thomas, and Wright.

4. Hall, *A Treatise on International Law,* pp. 346–47.

5. Eugene V. Rostow, "Remarks," *Proceedings of the American Society of International Law* (1973):263, 268.

6. It has been suggested that the best one can hope for in the actual behavior of nations is compliance with a rule that bans intervention by actions in excess of certain "maximum thresholds" of participation in the civil strife of another nation and accepts intervention by lesser means as tolerable. See Richard A. Falk, ed., *The International Law of Civil War* (Baltimore, 1971), introduction, pp. 22–29. See also the suggestion of T. J. Farer for acceptance of intervention by means short of tactical support. T. J. Farer, "Intervention in Civil Wars: A Modest Proposal," *Columbia Law Review* 67 (1967):266 and "Harnessing Rogue Elephants: A Short Discourse on Foreign Intervention in Civil Strife," *Harvard Law Review* 82 (1969):54. Such a rule would be contrary to the U.N. resolutions, which ban interference in the civil strife of another nation. See in appendix 1, paragraph C2 of G.A. Res. 2625. And it would be an unsound rule for reasons cited above in the text. Intervention by any means that may provide the decisive advantage to one side creates the risk of escalation. If some levels of foreign coercion of a people in the exercise of their right of self-determination is permitted, the principle of nonintervention is obfuscated and the distinction between intervention and counterintervention is obscured. It may be tempting in a supposed realism to accept a half-loaf version of a minimum public order goal in the control of intervention, but the realistic approach to the control of intervention lies instead in a clarity of principle around which to marshal the forces of restraint. A rule that

obscures this issue would only encourage nations to believe they can get away with what they will. The U.N. resolutions have wisely avoided this course.

7. This view should be compared with the attempt of Professor J. N. Moore to deal with the same problem. He would limit military assistance to the period before civil strife aimed at governmental structures reaches a status of insurgency and thereafter limit assistance to the preinsurgency level, defining insurgency in terms of a condition requiring use of most of the regular military forces, or defection of a substantial segment of the regular military forces, and loss of effective governmental authority on a significant percentage of the population. See John Norton Moore, ed., *Law and Civil War in the Modern World* (Baltimore, 1974), chapter 1, "Toward an Applied Theory for the Regulation of Intervention," p. 24. The element of truth in the proposed limitation of military assistance to the preinsurgency level is that an increase in assistance that merely enables a nation to devote a larger part of its own forces to suppressing the insurrection is in reality aid to the government against the insurgents. But (leaving aside Professor Moore's limited case of "insurgency" as he defines it) the occasion for increased military assistance need not be related to the existence or levels of local strife, and in such circumstances increased military assistance need not enter the scales of force in the local contest.

8. Some charge the United States with letting down a valued ally and undermining confidence in the United States as an ally. For some the forced departure of the shah demonstrates the defeatist consequences of a policy of nonintervention. But the crisis in Iran illustrates the realities that limit the application of power in international affairs. It would be folly to think that we could intervene with force in Iran without providing the pretext for exactly the kind of intervention by the U.S.S.R. it is the main aim of our policy to prevent. Nor could we expect to succeed in mounting effective pressure against Soviet intervention in other areas if we disowned the principle by our own conduct in Iran. How then can the United States best deal with crises like that in Iran where the outcome of local strife can affect the strategic balance? How can espousing the principle of nonintervention contribute to protecting the strategic balance? The answer lies in the potential for enhanced U.S. influence that can be built upon an explicit, credible, consistent commitment to law. There is a potential for influence that does not rest on power alone. It has to be carefully built and maintained. Nonintervention is not a gadget we can simply take down off the shelf when we get into trouble with a policy that has failed to nurture the potential of a commitment to law. As it is, we are perceived in Iran as having provided military assistance to support the shah, and this fact itself will work against our interests in the unfolding developments in Iran.

9. "A Few Words on Non-Intervention," reprinted from *Fraser's Magazine,* December 1859, in Mill, *Dissertations and Discussion: Political, Philosophical and Historical,* 4 vols. (London, 1875), vol. 3, p. 176.

10. Hall, p. 342.

11. Statements in support of a right of counterintervention, even under the limitations of the U.N. Charter, appear in the authorities cited in note 6 to chapter 6, above. It should be noted that counterintervention is usually stated in terms of aid to the established government when aid has been furnished by others to insurgents. But if the general nonintervention rule bars aid to either side, prohibited aid to the government should equally be able to be answered by counterinterventionary aid to the insurgents. Otherwise the rule is not neutral.

12. There is no intention here to rule out covert counterintervention in all circumstances. Undoubtedly, the intervention that has to be opposed is often covert. Perhaps the most dangerous form of intervention is the secret organization and equipping of cadres of terrorists and guerillas ready to capitalize on moments of confusion and crisis. Exposure of such intervention and countering it openly on an understandable and justifiable basis (without witch-hunts or violation of rights) will ordinarily be the most effective approach and must be the preferred form of counterintervention. Covert counterintervention presents obvious dangers of abuse as well as the very real risk that covert intervention and covert counterintervention will only serve to escalate each other. Nevertheless, the possibility the covert intervention must be met by covert counterintervention cannot be ruled out. But if and when it is ever justified, it is all the more necessary that the limitations on counterintervention be explicitly acknowledged to mimimize the dangers inherent in a course of covert counterintervention.

13. Efforts have been made by scholars criticizing the older rule to formulate new rules based on a multiple classification of civil strife situations. See Richard A. Falk, ed., *The International Law of Civil War,* introduction, pp. 18–19,, and John N. Moore, ed., *Law and Civil War in the Modern World,* chapter 1, pp. 21–23. The classification approach is useful as a tool of analysis, but it is not useful or necessary to formulate the rule of nonintervention as if it were six rules, each with its own conditions and qualifications. Formulated in this way it is likely only to produce the confusion that provides the cover for nations to disregard it. The U.N. rule can speak to the man in the street and has at least the potential to command the respect of peoples around the world. The text demonstrates that the simple U.N. rule and its counterpart right of counterintervention is all the classification needed for a sound formulation.

Chapter Ten

1. Department of State, *Report of the Delegation of the United States of America to the Eighth International Conference of American States, Lima, Peru, December 9–27, 1938* (Washington, D.C., 1941), p. 189; Green Haywood Hackworth, *Digest of International Law* (Washington, D.C., 1943), vol. 5, pp. 463–64.

2. Department of State, *Report of the Delegate of the United States of America to the Meeting of the Foreign Ministers of the American Republics Held at Panama September 2—October 3, 1939* (Washington, D.C., 1940), p. 62; Hackworth, vol. 5, pp. 464–65.

3. Act of Havana, July 30, 1940, 54 Stat. 2491, Executive Agreement Series No. 199; Hackworth, vol. 5, pp. 467–68.

4. Act of Chapultepec, March 6, 1945, 60 Stat. 1831, Treaties and Other International Acts Series No. 1543.

5. Inter-American Treaty of Reciprocal Assistance (Rio Pact), September 2, 1947, 62 Stat. 1681, Treaties and Other International Acts Series No. 1838, 21 U.N.T.S. 93; Charter of the Organization of American States, April 30, 1948, 2 U.S.T. 2394, Treaties and Other International Acts Series No. 2361, 119 U.N.T.S. 48.

6. Louis Henkin, *How Nations Behave,* 2nd ed. (New York, 1979), p. 296.

7. U.N.C.I.O., Summary Report of Fourth Meeting of Committee III/4, May 25, 1945, Doc. 576, III/4/9, U.N.C.I.O. Documents, vol. 12, pp. 679, 681. The specific reference to the Act of Chapultepec was in relation to the collective right of self-defense under what is now Article 51 of the Charter. However, the Act of Chapultepec was not limited to dealing with threats or acts of aggression against an American state and organizing the use of armed force "to prevent or repel aggression" (part II). It

also reaffirmed the Declaration of Lima in terms stating that in case the peace, security, or territorial integrity of any American republic is "threatened by acts of any nature that may impair them," the American states proclaim their determination to make effective their solidarity "using the measures which in each case the circumstances may make advisable" (preamble, clause [i]). 60 Stat. 1831, Treaties and Other International Acts Series No. 1543. The accompanying resolution further called for regular meetings of the ministers of foreign affairs and charged them with taking decisions on problems "with regard to situations and disputes of every kind which may disturb the peace of the American Republics" (par. 2). 60 Stat. 1847, Treaties and Other International Acts Series No. 1548.

8. The Report of Rapporteur of Committee 1 to Commission I at the San Francisco conference in 1945 states:

> The Committee wishes to state, in view of the Norwegian amendment to the same paragraph [Art. 2(4)], that the unilateral use of force or similar coercive measures is not authorized or admitted. The use of arms in legitimate self-defense remains admitted and unimpaired. The use of force, therefore, remains legitimate only to back up the decisions of the Organization at the start of a controversy or during its solution in the way that the Organization itself ordains. The intention of the Norwegian amendment is thus covered by the present text.

U.N.C.I.O., Doc. 944, I/1/34 (1), U.N.C.I.O. Documents, vol. 6, pp. 446, 459. Earlier the Report of Rapporteur of Subcommittee I/1/A to Committee I/1 had commented:

> The Norwegian Government proposed that no force should be used if *not approved* by the Security Council.
>
> The sense of approval was considered ambiguous, because it might mean approval before or after the use of force. It might thus curtail the right of states to use force in legitimate self-defense, while it was clear to the subcommittee that the right of self-defense against aggression should not be impaired or diminished.
>
> It was further clear that there will be no legitimate wars in any sense.

U.N.C.I.O. Doc. 739, I/1/A/19 (a), ibid., pp. 717, 721. These statements are susceptible of different readings in some respects, but at least they make clear (a) that the right of self-defense exists under the language of Article 2(4) itself and does not depend on the adoption of Article 51 and (b) that the language of Article 2(4) is not to be read as a prohibition against all use of force unless specifically permitted by some other provision of the Charter. Compare also Report of Rapporteur of Committee 1 to Commission I, Doc. 944, U.N.C.I.O. Documents, vol. 6, p. 451. It is reading too much into the San Francisco dcouments to conclude that Article 2(4) prohibits all use of force by member nations except individual or collective self-defense under Article 51 or force authorized by United Nations action. This is true, whether or not Article 51 is to be accepted as a Charter definition of the right of self-defense. For a general discussion of the San Francisco conference history see Brownlie, *International Law and the Use of Force by States* (Oxford, 1963), pp. 266 and following; also the arguments above at pages 70–72 and 96–97 upholding under Article 2(4) the use of necessary and proportionate force to counter the illegal use of force in other contexts and authorities cited in note 6 to chapter 6.

9. [1962] I.C.J. 151, 165.

10. See reference to Secretary of State Dean Rusk's position, note 25 to chapter 2 above.

11. The positions taken in the text are consistent with the positions taken in the Department of State Memorandum of October 23, 1962 on the legal basis for the quarantine of Cuba. It should be noted that the official U.S. position may have subsequently shifted on two points. Chayes states that the position shifted from reliance on the argument that the O.A.S. recommendatory action was not "enforcement action" under Article 53(1) to one that the disposition of the resolution of disapproval in the Security Council in which "by general consent it was not brought to a vote" amounted to an "authorization" under Article 53(1). See Abram Chayes, *The Cuban Missile Crisis* (New York, 1974), p. 61. The position of the official memorandum seems correct, however, and looking to the future is a necessary part of the legal position supporting a regional security zone.

The second point is the argument by Chayes distinguishing Arab League action against Israel on the ground that Cuba as a member of the O.A.S. had assented to the powers and procedures of the O.A.S. Charter. As he notes: "Implicit in this argument is the conclusion that vis-a-vis non-members the regional organization is limited to collective self-defense against armed attack within the meaning of Article 51 of the U.N. Charter" (p. 53). This argument, which was not made in the official memorandum, would make the result in the Cuba missile crisis wholly fortuitous, providing no security for the future. It is not necesary, and is rejected in the positions taken in the text here.

12. Leaving aside the issues raised by U.S. actions in Guatemala in 1954 and the Dominican Republic in 1965, the O.A.S. in the Caracas Declaration of 1954 walked a tightrope; the text would have been better stated in terms more clearly grounded in an emerging law capable of reciprocal application. The declaration that the "domination or control of the political institutions of an American state by the international Communist movement, extending to this Hemisphere the political system of an extra-continental power" would constitute a threat to the sovereignty and independence of American states, endangering the peace of America, was saved from ambiguity susceptible of damaging consequences only by the further explicit statement that this declaration "made by the American Republics in relation to dangers originating outside this Hemisphere is designed to protect and not to impair the inalienable right of each American state freely to choose its own form of government and economic system and to live its own social and cultural life." See Covey Oliver, *Working Paper in The Inter-American Security System and the Cuban Crisis* (Dobbs Ferry, 1964), pp. 62–63; and R. J. Vincent, *Nonintervention and International Order* (Princteton, 1974), pp. 197–98. The legitimate focus of the Declaration, which tended to be obscured by its wording, was on outside domination and control and not on the Communist policy or leaning of an American state.

13. See, for example, Morton A. Kaplan and Nicholas deB. Katzenbach, *The Political Foundations of International Law* (New York, 1961), pp. 50–55, Richard A. Falk, ed., *The International Law of Civil War* (Baltimore, 1971), pp. 14–15, 19–20; Hedley Bull, *The Anarchical Society* (New York, 1977), pp. 216–25.

14. In the joint communiqué of December 15, 1978 announcing U.S. recognition of the People's Republic of China, the two nations declared: "Neither should seek hegemony in the Asia-Pacific region or in any other region of the world and each is

opposed to efforts by any other country or group of countries to establish such hegemony" (*Department of State Bulletin* 79 (1979):25).

Chapter Eleven

1. [1949] I.C.J. 4, 28.

2. Draft Convention on the law of the Sea (Informal Text), cited herein as DC(IT) Article 34(2). A/CONF. 62/WP. 10/ Rev. 3 of August 27, 1980 and Corr. 1 August 29, 1980. *International Legal Materials* 19 (1980):1131.

3. DC(IT) Articles 38, 44. The 1958 Convention on the Territorial Sea and the Contiguous Zone (April 29, 1958, 15 U.S.T. 1606, Treaties and Other International Acts Series No. 5639, 516 U.N.T.S. 205), while retaining the regime of "innocent passage" for straits, had already attempted to correct one deficiency of the regime of innocent passage by providing that the right of a coastal state to suspend the right of passage in its territorial sea when essential for the protection of its security did not apply to passage of foreign ships through international straits (Article 16, par. 4).

4. DC(IT) Part XV.

5. "Freedom of Transit in International Law," *Grotius Society Transactions* 44 (1958–59):313, 319–20.

6. Ibid., p. 332.

7. Convention Regarding the Regime of Straits, July 20, 1936, G.B.T.S. No. 30 (1937), 173 L.N.T.S. 213. See Articles 10–21.

8. DC(IT) Article 35(c).

9. Richard R. Baxter, *The Law of International Waterways* (Cambridge, 1964), p. 217. See also review of practice, ibid., pp. 205–37; and Draft Convention, Article 5(1), ibid., appendix, p. 344.

10. Convention of Constantinople, December 22, 1888, *British Foreign and State Papers* 79 (1887–88):18; *Herslet's Commercial Treaties* 18:369; *Martens Nouveau Recueil,* 2nd series, 15:557; also appears as appendix B in Joseph A. Obieta, *The International Status of the Suez Canal* (The Hague: 1970). See Article I.

11. Ibid., Article X.

12. Article III, par. 1 and 2; 32 Stat. 1903, Treaty Series No. 401.

13. International Law Association, *Report of the Fifty-Second Conference, Helsinki, 1966* (London, 1967), pp. 477–533. See esp. Article XIII and comment. The proposed rules provide a right to a riparian state to permit navigation by vesels of a nonriparian state at the invitation of the riparian state. Article XX provides that rights are subject to derogation in time of war, etc. Even the high-water mark of efforts to secure rights in international rivers generally to nonriparian states, the Barcelona Convention and Statute on the Regime of Navigable Waterways of International Concern, April 20, 1921, G.B.T.S. No. 28 (1923), 7 L.N.T.S. 36, extended rights only to other contracting parties (Statute, Article 3), allowed the riparian states acting together to close the waterway (Statute, Article 10[6]), excluded vessels of war from its application (Statute, Article 17) and excluded rights and duties of belligerents and neutrals in time of war (Statute, Article 15).

14. League of Nations, *Official Journal* 7 (1921):699.

15. Aaland Islands Convention, October 20, 1921, G.B.T.S. No. 6 (1922), 9 L.N.T.S. 212.

16. Erik Bruël, *International Straits,* (London, 1947), vol. 1, p. 196.

17. Ibid.

18. See note 8 above.

19. Bruël, vol. 1, p. 250; vol. 2, pp. 155–56, 197–99.

20. Ibid., vol. 2, p. 199.

21. For early history, see Bruël, vol. 2, pp. 139 and following. See also Agreement, International Administration of Tangier, August 31, 1945, (U.K.—France), G.B.T.S. No. 24 (1946), 98 U.N.T.S. 249; Protocol of Modification, November 10, 1952, 3 U.S.T. 5501, Treaties and Other International Acts Series No. 2752, 214 U.N.T.S. 255; Tangier Zone Convention, November 10, 1952, 4 U.S.T. 2861, Treaties and Other International Acts Series No. 2893, 214 U.N.T.S. 265; Final Declaration of the International Conference of Tangier, October 29, 1956, 7 U.S.T. 3035, Treaties and Other International Acts Series No. 3680, 263 U.N.T.S. 165.

22. The principle of self-determination is expressly made applicable to strategic trusteeships by Article 83(2) of the Charter. See generally Leland M. Goodrich, Edvard Hambro, and Anne P. Simons, *Charter of the United Nations* (New York, 1974), pp. 506–12.

23. See Eleanor C. McDowell, "Contemporary Practice of the United States Relating to International Law," *American Journal of International Law* 70 (1976):557; Covenant to Establish a Commonwealth of the Northern Mariana Islands in Political Union with the United States, *International Legal Materials* 14 (1975):344.

24. See Baxter, *The Law of International Waterways,* pp. 147, 158.

25. Compare the "partial internationalization" alternative as visualized by Richard A. Falk in "Panama Treaty Trap," *Foreign Policy* 30 (1978):80.

Chapter Twelve

1. *Department of State Bulletin* 72 (1975):219, 220. See also President Ford's news conference of January 21, 1975 (*Department of State Bulletin* 72 [1975]:179); Secretary Kissinger's interviews for *Newsweek* magazine published January 13, 1975 (*Department of State Bulletin* 72 [1975]:97, 101); and Bill Moyers's Journal on January 15, 1975 (*Department of State Bulletin* 72 [1975]:165, 172).

2. Although beyond the subject of this chapter, there are also important developments in law relating to access to resources lying beyond the territorial jurisdiction of a nation. These developments do not impose limitations on territorial sovereignty, but they do evidence the interest of all nations in access to resources. Thus the pending Law of the Sea text declares the sea bed lying beyond the limits of national jurisdiction and its mineral resources to be "the common heritage of mankind" (DC(IT) Art. 136) and requires equitable sharing of benefits and access without discrimination (Arts. 140, 141). Closer to the territorial sovereignty issue is the problem of access to the natural resources of the 200-mile "exclusive economic zone," as to which provision is made for access by other nations to "the surplus of the allowable catch" (DC(IT) Art. 62[2]). Similarly, outer space and celestial bodies have been declared free for exploration and use by all nations and not subject to national appropriation (G.A. Res. 1721 [XVI] December 20, 1961; G.A. Res. 1962 [XVIII] December 13, 1963; Treaty on Principles Governing the Activities of States in the Exploration and Use of Outer Space, Including the Moon and Other Celestial Bodies, 1967, 61 A.J.I.L. 644 [1967]); Agreement Governing the Activities of States on the Moon and Other Cèlestial Bodies, *International Legal Materials* 18 (1979): 1434.

3. See appendix 1, paragraph C2. See also Preamble 9.

4. I. F. I. Shihata, "Arab Oil Policies and the New International Economic Order," *Virginia Journal of International Law* 16 (1975–76):261, 265, 267–68. See also his earlier articles, "Destination Embargo of Arab Oil: Its Legality under International Law." *American Journal of International Law* 68 (1974):591, especially pp. 616–19.

5. The Export Administration Act of 1969 declares it is the policy of the United States to use export controls "to the extent necessary to further significantly the foreign policy of the United States and to fulfill its international responsibilities" (50 U.S. Code Ann. App. §2402[2][B]).

6. Richard B. Lillich, "Economic Coercion and the International Legal Order," in Jordan J. Paust and Albert P. Blaustein, eds., *The Arab Oil Weapon* (Dobbs Ferry, 1977), pp. 151, 159–60.

7. 61 Stat. (5) and (6); Treaties and Other International Acts Series No. 1700, 55 U.N.T.S. 194; Part I.

8. Convention on the High Seas, April 29, 1958, 13 U.S.T. 2312, Treaties and other International Acts Series No. 5200, 450 U.N.T.S. 82; Article 3.

9. Richard R. Baxter, *The Law of International Waterways* (Cambridge, 1964), p. 158.

10. DC(IT) Article 125 (1).

11. Elihu Lauterpacht, "Freedom of Transit in International Law," *Grotius Society Transactions* 44 (1958–59):313, 351–52.

12. Shihata, "Arab Oil Policies," *Virginia Journal of International Law* 16 (1975–76):265.

13. E. Lauterpacht, "Freedom of Transit," pp. 337–38, 347–50.

Chapter Thirteen

1. The Arab-Israeli conflict illuminates the role of law in a number of ways. First, the only basis for any lasting peace is one that (a) recognizes the right of Israel to exist and enjoy the rights of an equal sovereign nation in the area, (b) returns to Arab nations areas seized by Israel in the 1967 war and (c) implements on some proper basis the rights of Palestinians on the West Bank. Israel can never be expected to accept less than (a), and the Arab nations can never be expected to accept less than (b) and (c). A peace that violates these principles can be in fact no more than a truce. Second, only a sense of the applicability of legal principle and of the tenacity that people derive from their sense of law—the determination of Arab nations, sooner or later, to secure their rights because they are rights, and the inevitable support of the Arabs in this by other governments once the Arab nations accord Israel its secure and rightful place as a nation—only this confrontation with the long-term inexorability of legal principle and judgment could possibly induce Israel to give up lands that mean so much to its own growth, power, and pride. Third, a resolution grounded in law minimizes the ability of the P.L.O. and other irreconcilables to block or disrupt a peace that accords Israel its place. It also minimizes the opportunity for Soviet Russia to exploit the tensions of the area for its own strategic ends. Fourth, we can bring a greater influence to bear toward a settlement when our efforts are for a resolution grounded in law, for if our commitment to law is genuine, we can perhaps use our influence effectively to bring about a settlement instead of having to hold back for fear of being perceived as taking sides. These are the ingredients that, however haltingly applied, produced the Camp David accords. And if Camp David leads to peace, they are the components of the dynamic that will carry this process to a consummation.

2. Free Zones of Upper Savoy, [1929] P.C.I.J. Ser. A., No. 22, p. 13.

3. See the arguments against conferring general legislative authority on adjudicatory tribunals in Sir Hersch Lauterpacht, *The Function of Law in the International Community* (Oxford, 1933), pp. 372–74; also id., *The Development of Law by the International Court of Justice* (London, 1958), pp. 319–29; and Charles de Visscher, *Theory and Reality in Public International Law,* trans. P. E. Corbett (Princeton, 1957), pp. 336–38.

4. See Article 9 of the Hague Conventions of 1899 and 1907 referred to on p. 64. The 1958 Model Rules on Arbitral Procedure commended by General Assembly Res. 1262 (XIII) November 14, 1958, provide in Article 10 for application of the same bases of decision as are provided for the International Court of Justice in Article 38 of the Statute of the Court.

Chapter Fourteen

1. The extent to which the president has the authority to act for the United States by executive agreement not submitted to the Senate as a treaty for its advice and consent is a much discussed issue. That such a power exists where the agreement is in the implementation of a power vested in the president has been upheld by the U.S. Supreme Court (*U.S. v. Belmont.* 301 U.S. 324, 330–31 [1937]; *U.S. v. Pink,* 315 U.S. 203, 229–30 [1942]). See A.L.I. Restatement of the Law Second, Foreign Relations Law of the United States, §§117–121. However, the agreement submitting a specific matter to a Voluntary Adjudication Tribunal—the compromis in an international arbitration—will in most important matters require either the advice and consent of the Senate as a treaty or authorization as a Congressional executive agreement. The legal adviser to the Department of State advised Senator Vandenburg in reference to consent to jurisdiction of the International Court of Justice under the U.N. Charter and the Statute of the Court that under the precedents concerning arbitrations the president would not act alone to agree to jurisdiction if "the complaint were against the United States, or even though the complaint were by the United States and the decision might result in an international obligation on the part of the United States" (memorandum, July 23, 1945, quoted in Marjorie M. Whiteman, *Digest of International Law* (Washington, D.C., 1971), vol. 12, pp. 1266, 1268. Of course, the submission of a particular matter could be made by the president acting alone where required or authorized by a general treaty provision or a general Congressional authorization.

2. No provision is suggested comparable to Article 31 of the Statute of the International Court of Justice permitting a nation which is a party before the court to choose a judge of its nationality to sit on the court for the case if there is none on the court. If it is desirable that an ad hoc tribunal should include judges who are nationals of the nations involved, the court can give effect to this consideration in appointing the members of the tribunal. Even in such a case a provision that can seem to make certain judges representatives of particular parties is likely to weaken rather than strengthen the perceived impartiality of the adjudicative process.

3. An absolute rule, like Article 34(1) of the Statute of the International Court of Justice, according to which only states may be parties, would be inappropriate. In self-determination controversies, for example, it would be a usual case for one group claiming a right of self-determination not to be currently recognized as an independent nation. A rule holding that only states may be parties would exclude many, perhaps most, self-determination controversies. It is not the intention here, however, to provide generally for any bypass of national courts by individuals, groups or corporations. The adjudication option should not be permitted to result indirectly in a nullification of

appropriate regulation by a nation of jurisdiction and process in claims against it by parties which are not other independent nations.

4. This statement of a domestic jurisdiction reservation does not adopt the so-called Connally amendment language in the U.S. acceptance of the jurisdiction of the International Court of Justice, reserving to the United States the right to determine for itself what is a matter of domestic jurisdiction and is therefore excluded from the court's jurisdiction. Aside from criticism that the Connally amendment approach is wrong in principle and contrary to the best interest of the United States, it is unnecessary and would be out of place here. Point 5 of the proposed Declaration makes clear that it is a statement of policy only, and point E of the proposed Charter makes clear that that policy does not include international adjudication of matters within the domestic jurisdiction of the United States. The question whether a particular dispute should or should not be excluded from adjudication on that ground, or whether its adjudicability should itself be determined by a tribunal, does not have to be decided in advance. The United States Senate in 1974 adopted Senate Resolutions 74, 75, 76, 77, and 78 containing policy statements favoring reference of legal disputes by the United States to the International Court of Justice. None of the resolutions contained any Connally amendment reservation language. The Senate Committee on Foreign Relations noted that U.S. rights were sufficiently protected, stating that "in no way do any of the resolutions repeal the so-called Connally amendment by which the United States reserves to itself the right to determine for itself what it considers to be a matter of domestic jurisdiction and therefore not within the purview of the Court" (*Digest of United States Practice in International Law 1974,* Department of State, Washington, D.C., p. 665). The wisest course in the proposed Declaration and Charter is to leave the Connally amendment problem open. This is the course taken in the language as proposed. In effect, the stated policy does not include international adjudication of matters within the domestic jurisdiction of the United States. The question whether a matter is within the domestic jurisdiction may in concrete cases be clearly seen to involve issues of international law to which international adjudication should be applicable. But if, for example, it should be claimed on spurious international law grounds that Alaska or Mississippi has a right to secede from the United States, we could insist the matter was one of domestic jurisdiction to which international adjudication is not applicable.

5. Giving effect to the principle of self-determination may involve revision or even termination of a treaty made in the past. But concern that revision of treaties to conform to the mandate of emerging law opens up all treaties on demand need not follow at all. The rule of law cannot be built upon a denial of the obligation of treaties. The Vienna Convention strikes a balance, as discussed in chapter 5, requiring treaties to bow only to so-called peremptory norms of general international law. The same solution is adopted here, applying the concept of emerging law to principles emerging as peremptory norms. The International Law Commission in its commentary on its draft of the proposed convention noted that some members had mentioned the principle of self-determination as a possible example of a peremptory norm that a treaty may not violate. See *American Journal of International Law* 61 (1967):255, 410–11. Under point G this position would be expressly established.

6. [1930] P.C.I.J., Ser. A, No. 24, p. 15. See also opinion of Kellogg, J., pp. 39–40.

7. See, for example, the 1958 Model Rules on Arbitral Procedure, Article 3, G.A. Res. 1262 (XIII), November 14, 1958.

8. The International Court of Justice has refused to adjudicate, even as between the parties, upon the international responsibility of a third state that was not a party and had not consented to the court's jurisdiction. See *Monetary Gold Case,* [1954] I.C.J. 19, 32–33. A similar rule applies even to exercising its advisory jurisdiction, where the advice is in effect sought on the merits of a dispute for the purpose of instructing the parties as to the dispute. See P. C. Szasz, "Enhancing the Advisory Competence of the World Court," in Leo Gross, ed., *the Future of the International Court of Justice,* vol. 2, pp. 499, 505–6 (Dobbs Ferry, 1976).

9. I assume that some kind of "standing" would be required for a party to invoke the voluntary adjudication process. There is no occasion for a nation to submit to an adjudication at the demand of a party having no legitimate stake in the issue, especially where nations that do have such a stake are not pressing that course. Those that do have a stake may justifiably believe, for example, that continuing negotiation can be fruitful and moving to adjudication would be premature and harmful to the negotiations. But assuming that the concept of standing has a place, it would have to be given a broad meaning. Many kinds of issues have an impact on balance of power and security considerations in which the whole world has a legitimate stake.

Chapter Fifteen

1. George F. Kennan, *American Diplomacy 1900–1950* (Chicago, 1951), p. 94.

2. Ibid., p. 97.

3. Ibid., p. 98.

4.. Ibid.

5. Ibid., p. 100.

6. Ibid., p. 101.

7. For further discussion of Kennan's argument, see Louis Henkin, *How Nations Behave* (New York, 1968), pp. 254–61.

8. "Remarks," *Proceedings of the American Society of International Law,* Fifty-Seventh Meeting (1963), pp. 13, 14.

9. Ibid.

10. Acheson's argument was also unrealistic, for law was a part of the reality against which the decisions to deal with the crisis had to be taken. We found, as noted above in chapter 2, that the legal principle of reciprocal application had enough practical force to lead us to give assurance to Russia that our Jupiter missiles would be removed from our bases in Turkey.

Appendix 1

1. The numbers and letters in brackets are not a part of the resolution as adopted. They have been inserted for convenience of reference. Thus, for example, the fifth paragraph under the principle of equal rights and self-determination of peoples in Section 1 may be referred to as paragraph E5 of the declaration.

Appendix 2

1. The numbers in brackets have been added for convenience of reference.

2. Explanatory notes on articles 3 and 5 are to be found in paragraph 20 of the report of the Special Committee on the Question of Defining Aggression (Official Records of the General Assembly, Twenty-ninth Session, Supplement No. 19 [A/9619 and Corr. 1]). Statements on the Definition are contained in paragraphs 9 and 10 of the report of the Sixth Committee (A/9890).

SELECTED BIBLIOGRAPHY

General

The Relation of Law, Power, and Policy

Acheson, Dean G. "Remarks by the Honorable Dean Acheson," *American Society of International Law, Proceedings* (1963):13–18.

Aron, Raymond, "The Quest for a Philosophy of Foreign Affairs." In *Contemporary Theory in International Relations,* edited by S. H. Hoffman. Englewood Cliffs: Prentice-Hall, 1960.

Bull, Hedley. *The Anarchical Society: A Study of Order in World Politics.* New York: Columbia University Press, 1977.

Dillard, Hardy C. "Some Aspects of Law and Diplomacy," *Académie de Droit International, Recueil des Cours* 91 (1957):447–552. See esp. pp. 499–516.

Falk, Richard A. "Law, Lawyers and the Conduct of American Foreign Relations." *Yale Law Journal* 78 (1969):919–34.

Fisher, Roger D. *Points of Choice.* New York: Oxford University Press, 1978.

Hoffman, Stanley H. "International Law and the Control of Force," In *The Relevance of International Law: Essays in Honor of Leo Gross,* edited by K. W. Deutsch and S. H. Hoffman. Cambridge: Schenkman, 1968.

Hoffman, Stanley H. "The Uses of American Power." *Foreign Affairs* 56 (1977):27–48.

Hoffman, Stanley H. "Weighing the Balance of Power." *Foreign Affairs* 50 (1972):618–43.

Kaplan, Morton A., and Katzenbach, Nicholas deB. *The Political Foundations of International Law.* New York: Wiley & Sons, 1961.

Kennan, George F. *American Diplomacy, 1900–1950.* Chicago: University of Chicago Press, 1951. See esp. chapter 6.

Kissinger, Henry A. American Foreign Policy: The Nature of the National Dialogue. Expanded edition. New York: W. W. Norton, 1974. See esp. chapters 3, 5.

Kissinger, Henry A. *American Foreign Policy: Three Essays.* New York: W. W. Norton, 1969.

Levgold, Robert. "The Nature of Soviet Power." *Foreign Affairs* 56 (1977):49–71.

McDougal, Myres S. "Law and Power." *American Journal of International Law* 46 (1952):102–14.

Moore, John Norton. *Law and the Indo-China War.* Princeton: Princeton University Press, 1972. See esp. chapter 1.

Moore, John Norton. "Law and National Security." *Foreign Affairs* 51 (1973):408–21.

Morgenthau, Hans J. *In Defense of the National Interest: A Critical Examination of American Foreign Policy.* New York: Alfred A. Knopf, 1951. See esp. pp. 99–129.

Morgenthau, Hans J. *Politics Among Nations: The Struggle for Power and Peace.* Third edition. New York: Alfred A. Knopf, 1963

Oliver, Covey T. "Relation of International Law to International Relations." *American Society of International Law, Proceedings* (1954):108–113.

Reves, Emery. *The Anatomy of Peace.* New York: Harper, 1945.

Rostow, Eugene V. *Law, Power and the Pursuit of Peace.* Lincoln: University of Nebraska Press, 1968.

Rostow, Eugene V. *Peace in the Balance: The Future of American Foreign Policy.* New York: Simon and Schuster, 1972.

Shklar, Judith N. *Legalism: An Essay on Law, Morals, Politics.* Cambridge: Harvard University Press, 1964. See esp. pp. 123–43.

Sohn, Louis B., and Clark, Grenville. *World Peace Through World Law.* Second edition, revised. Cambridge: Harvard University Press, 1960.

Spykman, Nicholas J. *America's Strategy in World Politics: The United States and the Balance of Power.* New York: Harcourt, Brace, 1942.

Visscher, Charles de. *Theory and Reality in Public International Law.* Translated by P. E. Corbett. Princeton: Princeton University Press, 1957.

The Strategy of Law

Brecht, Arnold. *Political Theory: The Foundations of Twentieth Century Political Thought.* Princeton: Princeton University Press, 1959.

Dworkin, Ronald M. *Taking Rights Seriously.* Cambridge: Harvard University Press, 1977.

Fisher, Roger D. *International Conflict for Beginners.* New York: Harper & Row, 1969.

Fuller, Lon L. *The Morality of Law.* Revised edition. New Haven: Yale University Press, 1969.

Grotius, Hugo. *De Jure Belli ac Pacis* [On the Law of War and Peace]. Edition of 1646. Translated by Francis W. Kelsey et al. Classics of International Law, Carnegie Endowment for International Peace. Oxford: Oxford University Press, 1925.

Holmes, Oliver Wendell, Jr. *The Common Law.* Boston: Little Brown, 1881.

Locke, John. *Two Treatises of Government.* Edited by Peter Laslett. Cambridge: University Press, 1960. See esp. book 2.

Pufendorf, Samuel. *De Jure Naturae et Gentium Libri Octo* [On the Law of Nature and Nations: Eight Books]. Edition of 1688. Translated by C. H. and W. A. Oldfather. Classics of International Law, Carnegie Endowment for International Peace. Oxford: Oxford University Press, 1934. See esp. book 2.

Rawls, John. *A Theory of Justice.* Cambridge: Harvard University Press, 1972.

The Problem of Law-making

Dumbauld, Edward. "Independence under International Law." *American Journal of International Law* 70 (1976):425–31.

Falk, Richard A. "On the Quasi-Legislative Competence of the General Assembly." *American Journal of International Law* 60 (1966):782–91.

Fried, John H. E. "How Efficient is International Law?" In *The Relevance of International Law: Essays in Honor of Leo Gross,* edited by K. W. Deutsch and S. H. Hoffman. Cambridge: Schenkman, 1968.

Gross, Leo. "The International Court of Justice and the United Nations." *Académie de Droit International, Recueil des Cours* 120 (1967):313–440.

Gross, Leo. "The United Nations and the Role of.Law." *International Organization* 19 (1965):537–61.

Henkin, Louis. *How Nations Behave: Law and Foreign Policy.* New York: Praeger, 1968. See esp. chapters 27 and 28.

Higgins, Rosalyn. *The Development of International Law Through the Political Organs of the United Nations.* London: Oxford University Press, 1963.

Higgins, Rosalyn. "The United Nations and Lawmaking: The Political Organs." *American Society of International Law, Proceedings* (1980):37–48.

International Military Tribunal. *Trial of the Major War Criminals Before the International Military Tribunal, Nuremberg, 14 November 1945–1 October 1946.* Volume 1. Nuremberg: Secretariat of the International Military Tribunal, 1947. See esp. pp. 8–18, 171–367.

Johnson, David H. N. "The Effect of Resolutions of the General Assembly of the United Nations." *British Yearbook of International Law* 32 (1955):97–122.

Larson, Arthur, and Jenks, C. Wilfred. *Sovereignty Within the Law.* Dobbs Ferry: Oceana, 1965.

Lauterpacht, Sir Hersch. *The Function of Law in the International Community.* Oxford: Oxford University Press, 1933.

Lauterpacht, Sir Hersch. *The Development of International Law by the International Court.* London: Stevens & Sons, 1958.

Parry, Clive. *The Sources and Evidences of International Law.* Manchester: Manchester University Press, 1965.

Tammes, Arnold J. P. "Decisions of International Organs as a Source of International Law." *Académie de Droit International, Recueil des Cours* 94 (1958):264–343.

Law in Foreign Policy

Sources

Acheson, Dean G. *Present at the Creation.* New York: W. W. Norton, 1969.

Bartlett, Ruhl J., editor. *The Record of American Diplomacy.* New York: Alfred A. Knopf, 1947.

Davis, Nathaniel. "The Angola Decision of 1975: A Personal Memoir." *Foreign Affairs* 57 (1978):109–24.

Eisenhower, Dwight D. *The White House Years.* Volume 1. Garden City: Doubleday, 1963.

Gravel, Mike, editor. *The Pentagon Papers: The Defense Department History of United States Decisionmaking on Vietnam.* Boston: Beacon Press, 1971–72.

Hackworth, Green H. *Digest of International Law.* Volume 5. Washington: U.S. Government Printing Office, 1943.

International Military Tribunal. *Trial of the Major War Criminals Before the International Military Tribunal, Nuremberg, 14 Novemeber 1945–1 October 1946.* Volume 1. Nuremberg: Secretariat of the International Military Tribunal, 1947. See esp. pp. 8–18, 171–367.

Kennedy, Robert F. *Thirteen Days.* New York: W. W. Norton, 1969.

Moore, John Bassett. *A Digest of International Law.* Volumes 1 and 6. Washington: Government Priting Office, 1906.

Root, Elihu. *Addresses on International Subjects.* Cambridge: Harvard University Press, 1916.

Scott, James B., editor. *The Hague Conventions and Declarations of 1899 and 1907.* New York: Oxford University Press, 1915.

Seabury, Paul, editor. *The Balance of Power.* San Francisco: Chandler, 1965.

Sheehan, Neil et al., editors. *The Pentagon Papers: As Published by the New York Times.* New York: Bantam Books, 1971.

Stimson, Henry L. *The Far Eastern Crisis: Recollections and Observations.* New York: Harper, 1936.

United States Department of State. *The Suez Canal Problem: A Documentary Publication.* Washington: U.S. Government Printing Office, 1956.

United States Department of State, Office of the Legal Adviser. "The Legality of United States Participation in Defense of Viet Nam." *Yale Law Journal* 75 (1966):1085–108.

United States Senate, Committee on Foreign Relations. *Background Information Relating to Southeast Asia and Vietnam.* Sixth revised edition. Washington, U.S. Government Priting Office, 1970.

Whiteman, Marjorie M. *Digest of International Law.* Volume 12. Washington: U.S. Government Priting Office, 1971.

History and Commentary

Abel, Elie. *The Missiles of October.* London: McGibbon & Kee, 1966.

Alford, Neill H., Jr. "The Legality of American Military Involvement in Viet Nam: A Broader Perspective." *Yale Law Journal* 75 (1966):1109–121.

Bailey, Thomas A. *A Diplomatic History of the United States.* Fourth edition. New York: Appleton Century Crofts, 1950.

Bemis, Samuel F. "Washington's Farewell Address: A Foreign Policy of Independence." *American Historical Review* 39 (1934):250–68.

Bowie, Robert R. *Suez 1956.* New York: Oxford University Press, 1974.

Bruël, Erik. *International Straits: A Treatise on International Law.* London: Sweet & Maxwell, 1947.

Chayes, Abram. *The Cuban Misile Crisis.* New York: Oxford University Press, 1974.

Craig, Gordon A. "The United States and the European Balance." *Foreign Affairs* 55 (1976):187–98.

Ehrlich, Thomas. *Cyprus 1958–1967.* New York: Oxford University Press, 1974.

Falk, Richard A. "International Law and the United States Role in the Viet Nam War." *Yale Law Journal* 75 (1966):1122–160.

Halle, Louis J. *American Foreign Policy: Theory and Reality.* London: Allen & Unwin, 1960.

Lawyers Committee on American Policy Toward Viet Nam. "American Policy Vis-a-vis Vietnam, In Light of Our Constitution, the United Nations Charter, the 1954 Geneva Accords and the Southeast Asia Collective Defense Treaty: Memorandum of Law." *Congressional Record,* Eighty-Ninth Cong., Second session, 9 February 1966, 112, part 2:2665–73.

Moore, John Norton, and Underwood, James L., in collaboration with McDougal, Myres S. "The Lawfulness of United States Assistance to the Republic of Vietnam." *Congressional Record,* Eighty-Ninth Cong., Second session, 13 July 1966, 112, part 12:15519–67.

Perkins, Dexter E. *A History of the Monroe Doctrine*. Boston: Little Brown, 1955.

Randle, Robert F. *Geneva 1954: The Settlement of the Indochinese War.* Princeton: Princeton University Press, 1969.

Rostow, Eugene V. "Eight Foreign Policies for the United States—Which is Yours?" *New York Times Magazine,* 23 April 1972, p. 16.

Scheinman, Lawrence, and Wilkinson, David, editors. *International Law and Political Crisis: An Analytic Casebook*. Boston: Little Brown, 1968.

Schlesinger, Arthur M., Jr. *A Thousand Days*. Boston: Houghton Mifflin, 1965.

Vagts, Alfred, and Vagts, Detlev F. "The Balance of Power in International Law: A History of an Idea." *American Journal of International Law* 73 (1980):555–80.

Young, George B. "Intervention Under the Monroe Doctrine: The Olney Corollary." *Political Science Quarterly* 57 (1942):247–80.

Emerging Law

General

Akehurst, Michael B. *A Modern Introduction to International Law.* Third edition. London: Allen & Unwin, 1977. See esp. pp. 214–18.

Briggs, Herbert W. "Reflections on the Codification of International Law by the International Law Commission and By Other Agencies." *Académie de Droit International, Recueil des Cours* 126 (1969):233–316.

Brownlie, Ian. *International Law and the Use of Force by States.* Oxford: Oxford University Press, 1963.

Brownlie, Ian. *Principles of Public International Law.* Oxford: Oxford University Press, 1966.

Ferencz, Benjamin B. *Defining International Aggression: The Search for World Peace; A Documentary History and Analysis.* Dobbs Ferry: Oceana, 1975.

Garvey, Jack I. "The U.N. Definition of Aggression: Law and Illusion in the Context of Collective Security." *Virginia Journal of International Law* 17 (1977):177–99.

Goodrich, Leland M., with Hambro, Edvard I. and Simons, Anne P. *Charter of the United Nations: Commentary and Documents.* Third revised edition. New York: Columbia University Press, 1974.

Hazard, John N. "New Personalities to Create New Law." *American Journal of International Law* 58 (1964):952–59.

Houben, Piet-Hein. "Principles of International Law Concerning Friendly Relations and Co-operation Among States." *American Journal of Internationl Law* 61 (1967):703–36.

Lee, Luke T. "The Mexico City Conference of the United Nations Special Committee on Principles of International Law Concerning Friendly Relations and Co-operation Among States." *International and Comparative Law Quarterly* 14 (1965):1296–313.

Rosenstock, Robert. "The Declaration of Principles of International Law Concerning Friendly Relations: A Survey." *American Journal of International Law* 65 (1971):713–35.

Russell, Harold S. "The Helsinki Declaration: Brobdingnag or Lilliput?" *American Journal of International Law* 70 (1976):242–72.

Sahovic, Milan. "Codification des Principes du Droit International des Relations Amicales et de la Coopération Entre les Etats." *Académie de Droit International, Recueil des Cours* 137 (1972):242–310.

Stone, Julius. *Aggression and World Order: A Critique of United Nations Theories of Aggression.* London: Stevens & Sons, 1958.

Stone, Julius. "Hopes and Loopholes in the 1974 Definition of Aggression." *American Journal of International Law* 71 (1977):224–46.

United Nations General Assembly. *Reports of the Special Committee on Principles of International Law Concerning Friendly Relations and Co-operation Among States.*

U.N. General Assembly Documents: Nineteenth Session (A/5746), 19 November 1964.

U.N. General Assembly Documents: Twenty-first Session (A/6320), 27 June 1966.

U.N. General Assembly Documents: Twenty-second Session (A/6799), 26 September 1967

U.N. General Assembly Documents: Twenty-third Session (A/7326), November 1968.

Official Records: Twenty-fourth Session, Supplement 19 (A/7619), October 1969.

Official Records: Twenty-fifth Session, Supplement 18 (A/8018), September 1970.

United Nations General Assembly. *Sixth Committee, Legal Questions, 1178 Meeting.* Official Records: Twenty-fifth Session, (A/C.6/SR. 1176–1244) 23 September 1970, pp. 5–54.

Self-determination

Blum, Yehuda Z. "Reflections on the Changing Concept of Self-Determination." *Israel Law Review* 10 (1975):509–14.

Buchheit, Lee C. *Secession: The Legitimacy of Self-Determination.* New Haven: Yale University Press, 1978.

Clark, Roger. "The Trust Territory of the Pacific Islands: Some Perspectives." *American Society of International Law, Proceedings* (1973):17–21.

Comras, Victor D. *Self-Determination and the Partition of States in International Law.* Unpublished Ll.M. thesis, Harvard University, 1975.

Emerson, Rupert. "Self-Determination." *American Journal of International Law* 65 (1971):459–75.

Esfandiary, Moshen S. "Comments by Moshen S. Esfandiary." *American Society of International Law, Proceedings* (1961): 170–79.

Johnson, C. Don. "Toward Self-Determination—A Reappraisal as Reflected in the Declaration on Friendly Relations." *Georgia Journal of International and Comparative Law* 3 (1973):145–63.

Johnson, Harold S. *Self-Determination Within the Community of Nations.* Leyden: Sijthoff, 1967.

Mattern, Johannes. *The Employment of the Plebiscite in the Determination of Sovereignty.* Baltimore: Johns Hopkins Press, 1920.

McDowell, Eleanor C. "Contemporary Practice of the United States Relating to International Law." *American Journal of International Law* 70 (1976):557–70.

Modeen, Tore. *The International Protection of National Minorities in Europe.* Turku: Åbo Akademi, 1969.

Nanda, Ved P. "Self-Determination in International Law: The Tragic Tale of Two Cities—Islamabad (West Pakistan) and Dacca (East Pakistan)." *American Journal of International Law* 66 (1972):321–36.

Nayar, M. G. Kaladharan. "Self-Determination Beyond the Colonial Context: Biafra in Retrospect." *Texas International Law Journal* 10 (1975):321–45.

Ofuatey-Kodjoe, Wentworth. *The Principles of Self-Determination in International Law.* New York: Nellen, 1977.

Pomerance, Michla. "The United States and Self-Determination: Perspectives on the Wilsonian Conception." *American Journal of International Law* 70 (1976):1–27.

Rivlin, Benjamin. "Self-Determination and Dependent Areas." *International Conciliation* 501 (1955):195–271.

Sinha, S. Prakash. "Is Self-Determination Passé?" *Columbia Journal of Transnational Law* 12 (1973):260–73.

Sinha, S. Prakash. "Has Self-Determination Become a Principle of International Law Today?" *Indian Journal of International Law* 14 (1974):332–61.

Umozurike, Umozurike O. *Self-Determination in International Law.* Hamden: Shoestring Press, 1972.

Wambaugh, Sarah. *Plebiscites Since the World War.* Washington: Carnegie Endowment for International Peace, 1933.

Wilson, James M., Jr. "The Applicability of Self-Determination to the Trust Territory of the Pacific Islands." *American Society of International Law, Proceedings* (1933):21–26.

Yale Law Journal. "Note: The United Nations, Self-Determination and the Namibia Opinions." *Yale Law Journal* 82 (1973):522–58.

Nonintervention

Barnet, Richard J. *Intervention and Revolution: The United States in the Third World.* New York: World, 1968.

Falk, Richard A., editor. *The International Law of Civil War.* Baltimore: Johns Hopkins Press, 1971.

Falk, Richard A. "President Gerald Ford, CIA Covert Operations, and the Status of International Law." *American Journal of International Law* 69 (1975):354–58.

Farer, Tom J. "Intervention in Civil War: A Modest Proposal." *Columbia Law Review* 67 (1966):266–79.

Farer, Tom J. "Harnessing Rogue Elephants: A Short Discourse on Foreign Intervention in Civil Stife." *Harvard Law Review* 82 (1969):511–41.

Fraleigh, Arnold. "The Algerian Revolution." In *The International Law of Civil War,* edited by Richard A. Falk. Baltimore: Johns Hopkins Press, 1971.

Franck, Thomas M., and Rodley, Nigel S. "After Bangladesh: The Law of Humanitarian Intervention by Military Force." *American Journal of International Law* 67 (1973):275–305.

Franck, Thomas M. "Who Killed Article 2(4)? Or: Changing Norms Governing the Use of Force by States." *American Journal of International Law* 64 (1970):809–37.

Franck, Thomas M., and Weisband, Edward. *Word Politics: Verbal Strategies Among the Superpowers.* New York: Oxford University Press, 1972.

Friedmann, Wolfgang. "Intervention, Civil War and the Role of International Law." *American Society of International Law, Proceedings* (1965):67–75.

Hall, William E. *A Treatise on International Law.* Eighth edition. Edited by A. Pearce Higgins. Oxford: Oxford University Press, 1924. See esp. chapter 8.

Higgins, Rosalyn. "Internal War and International Law." In *The Future of the International Legal Order,* edited by C. E. Black and Richard A. Falk. Volume 3. Princeton: Princeton University Press, 1971.

Moore, John Norton, editor. *Law and Civil War in the Modern World.* Baltimore: Johns Hopkins Press, 1974. See esp. chapter 1.

Moore, John Norton. *Law and the Indo-China War.* Princeton: Princeton University Press, 1972. See esp. chapter 4.

Oppenheim, Lassa F. L. *International Law.* Eighth edition. Edited by H. Lauterpacht. London: Longmans, Green, 1955.

Rostow, Eugene V. "Book Review: Law and the Indo-China War, by John Norton Moore." *Yale Law Journal* 82 (1973):829–55.

Rostow, Eugene V. "Remarks by Eugene V. Rostow." *American Society of International Law, Proceedings* (1973):263–71.

Rovine, Arthur W. "Contemporary Practice of the United States Relating to International Law." *American Journal of International Law* 69 (1975):382–405. (Contains discussion of memorandum of law issued by the office of the legal adviser concerning intervention.)

Thomas, Aaron J., and Thomas, Ann P. van Wynen. *Non-Intervention: The Law and its Impact in the Americas.* Dallas: Southern Methodist University Press, 1956.

Vincent, R. J. *Nonintervention and International Order.* Princeton: Princeton University Press, 1974.

Wright, Quincy. "United States Intervention in the Lebanon." *American Journal of International Law* 53 (1959):112–25.

Regional Security Zones

Campbell, James S. "The Cuban Crisis and the U.N. Charter: An Analysis of the United States Position." *Stanford Law Review* 16 (1963):160–76.

Chayes, Abram. *The Cuban Missile Crisis.* New York: Oxford University Press, 1974.

Chayes, Abram. "The Legal Case for U.S. Action on Cuba." *Department of State Bulletin* 47 (1962):763–65.

Chayes, Abram. "Law and the Quarantine of Cuba." *Foreign Affairs* 41 (1963):550–57.

Chayes, Abram. "Remarks by the Honorable Abram Chayes." *American Society of International Law, Proceedings* (1963):10–13.

Franck, Thomas M. and Rodley, Nigel S., "After Bangladesh: The Law of Humanitarian Intervention by Force." *American Journal of International Law* 67 (1973):275–305.

Franck, Thomas M. "Who Killed Article 2(4)? Or: Changing Norms Governing the Use of Force by States." *American Journal of International Law* 64 (1970):809–37.

Franck, Thomas M. and Weisband, Edward. *Word Politics: Verbal Strategies Among the Superpowers.* New York: Oxford University Press, 1972.

Henkin, Louis. *How Nations Behave: Law and Foreign Policy.* 2nd ed. New York: Columbia University Press, 1979. See esp. chapter 15.

Kahng, Tae Jin. *Law, Politics and the Security Council: An Inquiry into the Handling of Legal Questions Involved in International Disputes and Situations.* The Hague: Nijhoff, 1964.

McDougal, Myres S. "The Soviet-Cuban Quarantine and Self-Defense." *American Journal of International Law* 57 (1963):597–604.

Mecham, J. Lloyd. *The United States and Inter-American Security 1889–1960.* Austin: University of Texas Press, 1961.

Meeker, Leonard C. "Defensive Quarantine and the Law." *American Journal of International Law* 57 (1963):515–24.

Moore, John Norton. *Law and the Indo-China War.* Princeton: Princeton University Press, 1972. See esp. chapter 6.

Oliver, Covey T. "Working Paper." In *The Inter-American Security System and the Cuban Crisis: Background Paper and Proceedings of the Third Hammarskjold Forum Held November 19, 1962,* edited by L. M. Tondel. Dobbs Ferry: Oceana, 1964.

Partan, Daniel G. "The Cuban Quarantine: Some Implications for Self-Defense." *Duke Law Journal* (1963):696–721.

Tondel, Lyman M., editor. *The Inter-American Security System and the Cubban Crisis: Background Paper and Proceedings of the Third Hammarskjold Forum Held November 19, 1962.* Dobbs Ferry: Oceana, 1964.

Wright, Quincy. "The Cuban Quarantine." *American Journal of International Law* 57 (1963):546–65.

Wright, Quincy. "The Cuban Quarantine." *American Society of International Law, Proceedings* (1963):9–10.

International Rights in Strategic Areas

Baxter, Richard R. *The Law of International Waterways.* Cambridge: Harvard University Press, 1964.

Berber, Friedrich J. *Rivers in International Law.* Dobbs Ferry: Oceana, 1959.

Black, Cyril E., et al. *Neutralization and World Politics.* Princeton: Princeton University Press, 1968.

Bowie, Robert R. *Suez 1956.* New York: Oxford University Press, 1974.

Bruël, Erik, *International Straits: A Treatise on International Law.* London: Sweet & Maxwell, 1947.

Dean, Arthur H. "The Geneva Conference on the Law of the Sea: What Was Accomplished." *American Journal of International Law* 52 (1958):607–28.

Falk, Richard A. "Panama Treaty Trap." *Foreign Policy* 30 (1978):68–82.

Glass, G. E. *International Rivers: A Policy Oriented Perspective.* Singapore: University of Malaya Press, 1961.

Glassner, Martin I. *Access to the Sea for Developing Land-Locked States.* The Hague: Nijhoff, 1970.

International Law Association. *Helsinki Rules on the Uses of the Waters of International Rivers: Adopted by the International Law Association, August 20, 1966.* London: International Law Association, 1967.

Lauterpacht, Elihu. "Freedom of Transit in International Law." *Transactions of the Grotius Society* 44 (1958):313–56.

Moore, John Norton. "The Regime of Straits and the Third United Nations Conference on the Law of the Sea." *American Journal of International Law* 74 (1980):77–121.

Obieta, Joseph A. *The International Status of the Suez Canal.* The Hague: Nijhoff, 1970.

Oxman, Bernard H. "The Third United Nations Conference on the Law of the Sea: The 1976 New York Session." *American Journal of International Law* 71 (1977):247–69.

Oxman, Bernard H. "The Third United Nations Conference on the Law of the Sea: The 1977 New York Session." *American Journal of International Law* 72 (1978):57–83.

Oxman, Bernard H. "The Third United Nations Conference on the Law of the Sea: The Seventh Session (1978)." *American Journal of International Law* 73 (1979):1–41.

Oxman, Bernard H. "The Third United Nations Conference on the Law of the Sea: The Eighth Session (1979)." *American Journal of International Law* 74 (1980):1–47.

Smit, Hans. "The Panama Canal: A National or International Waterway?" *Columbia Law Review* 76 (1976):969–88.

Stevenson, John R., and Oxman, Bernard H. "The Preparations for the Law of the Sea Conference." *American Journal of International Law* 68 (1974):1–32.

Stevenson, John R., and Oxman, Bernard H. "The United Nations Conference on the Law of the Sea: The 1974 Caracas Session." *American Journal of International Law* 69 (1975):1–30.

Stevenson, John R., and Oxman, Bernard H. "The United Nations Conference on the Law of the Sea: The 1975 Geneva Session." *American Journal of International Law* 69 (1975):763–97.

United Nations, Third Conference on the Law of the Sea. Draft Convention on the Law of the Sea (Informal Text), (A/CONF. 62/WP. 10/Rev. 3) August 27, 1980 and Corr. 1 August 29, 1980. Reproduced in *International Legal Materials* 19 (1980):1131–1295.

United States Department of State. "President Carter and General Torrijos Sign Panama Canal Treaties." *Department of State Bulletin* 77 (1977):481–505. (Contains texts of the treaties, remarks by President Carter and General Torrijos, the Declaration of Washington and a fact sheet on the treaties.)

International Rights of Access to Resources

Bowett, Derek W. "Economic Coercion and Reprisals by States." *Virginia Journal of International Law* 13 (1972):1–12.

Brownlie, Ian. "Legal Status of National Resources in International Law (Some Aspects)." *Académie de Droit International, Recueil des Cours* 162 (1979):245–317.

Conference on Transnational Economic Boycotts and Coercion, University of Texas Law School, February 19–20, 1976. Papers by H. Askari, R. B. Bilder, Y. Z. Blum, R. B. Lillich, A. F. Lowenfeld, C. Parry and W. F. Schwartz. *Texas International Law Journal* 12 (1977):1–60.,

Lillich, Richard B., editor. *Economic Coercion and the New International Order.* Charlottesville: Michie, 1976.

Paust, Jordan J. and Blaustein, Albert P. "The Arab Oil Weapon—A Threat to International Peace." *American Journal of International Law* 68 (1974):410–39.

Paust, Jordan J. and Blaustein, Albert P., editors. *The Arab Oil Weapon.* Dobbs Ferry: Oceana, 1977.

Rajan, Mannaraswamighala S. *Sovereignty Over Natural Resources.* Atlantic Highlands: Humanities Press, 1978.

Shihata, Ibrahim F. I. "Destination Embargo of Arab Oil: Its Legality under International Law." *American Journal of International Law* 68 (1974):591–627.

Symposium on the New International Economic Order. Articles by D. W. Bowett, F. G. Dawson, R. B. Lillich, A. Rozental, I. F. I. Shihata and G. White. *Virginia Journal of International Law* 16 (1976):233–353.

Adjudication

Franck, Thomas M. *The Structure of Impartiality: Examining the Riddle of One Law in a Fragmented World.* New York: Macmillan, 1968.

Golsong, Heribert. "Role and Functioning of the International Court of Justice: Proposals Recently Made on the Subject." Zeitschrift für Ausländisches Öffentliches Recht und Volkerrecht 31 (1971):673–96.

International Law Association. *Report of the 55th Conference.* New York: International Law Association, 1972. See esp. pp. 355, 357 for text of proposed Draft General Treaty for the Peaceful Settlement of International Disputes.

International Law Association, American Branch, Committee on United Nations Charter, Daniel G. Partan, Chairman. "Report on Steps That Might Have been Taken by the General Assembly to Enhance The Effectiveness of the International Court of Justice." *Proceedings and Committee Reports of the American Branch of the International Law Association* (1971–72):142–63.

Jenks, C. Wilfred. *The Prospects of International Adjudication.* Dobbs Ferry: Oceana, 1964.

Katz, Milton. *The Relevance of International Adjudication.* Cambridge: Harvard University Press, 1968.

Lachs, Manfred. "Some Reflections on the Settlement of International Disputes." *American Society of International Law, Proceedings* (1974):323–30.

Lauterpacht, Sir Hersch. *The Development of International Law by the International Court.* London: Stevens & Sons, 1958.

Rovine, Arthur W. "The National Interest and the World Court." In *The Future of the International Court of Justice,* edited by L. Gross. Volume 1. Dobbs Ferry: Oceana, 1976.

Shore, William I. *Fact Finding in the Maintenance of International Peace.* Dobbs Ferry: Oceana, 1970.

United Nations General Assembly. *Report of the International Law Commission: Covering the Work of Its Tenth Session, 28 April—4 July 1958.* Official Records: Thirteenth Session, Supplement 9 (A/3859), 1958. See pp. 5–8 for Model Rules on Arbitral Procedure.

United States Department of State. *Widening Access to the International Court of Justice: A Study of the Office of the Legal Adviser of the Department of State.* Mimeographed. Washington: Department of State, 1976.

Visscher, Charles de. *Theory and Reality in Public International Law.* Translated by P. E. Corbett. Princeton: Princeton University Press, 1957.

INDEX